# DON'T KILL IN OUR NAMES

# DON'T KILL IN OUR NAMES

*Families of Murder Victims
Speak Out Against the Death Penalty*

RACHEL KING

RUTGERS UNIVERSITY PRESS
NEW BRUNSWICK, NEW JERSEY AND LONDON

Library of Congress Cataloging-in-Publication Data

King, Rachel, 1963—

Don't kill in our names : families of murder victims speak out against the death penalty / Rachel King.

p.   cm.

Includes bibliographical references.

ISBN 0-8135-3182-9 (alk. paper)

1. Capital punishment.   2. Capital punishment—United States.   I. Title.

HV8698 .K556 2003

364.66'0973—dc21

2002070505


British Cataloging-in-Publication information is available from the British Library.


Second printing, 2005

Manufactured in the United States of America

*This book is dedicated to the memories of Susan Jaeger, Jerry Hines and Dennis Eaton, Deborah Ruth Carlson Thornton and Karla Faye Tucker Brown, Ruth Pelke, Nancy and Richard Langert, the Reverend Billy Bosler, Ruth and Morris Gauger, Vicki Zessin and Janet Mesner, Cathy O'Daniel, and Tariq Khamisa.*

# CONTENTS

# PREFACE

This project began in 1996 as the brainchild of Barbara Hood. Barbara and I had worked together on a campaign to oppose legislation to reinstate the death penalty in Alaska. During that campaign, we learned about Marietta Jaeger, who had opposed the death penalty for her daughter's killer. We invited Marietta to Alaska to share her experience.

Marietta spoke to many people during her Alaskan trip. Among them were several members of the legislature, many of whom later told us that her story convinced them to change their mind and vote against the death penalty bill. The bill never passed, and Alaska still does not have the death penalty.

Because Marietta's story was so compelling, Barbara had the idea to produce a booklet of stories of people like Marietta—people who had lost family members to murder and opposed the death penalty. She enlisted my help, and over the course of the next few years I interviewed and photographed more than fifty people who were willing to publicly state their opposition to the death penalty.

Not all the people who participated in the project had firsthand experience with the death penalty. In some cases, the killer was never found. In others, the case was not prosecuted as a capital case, or the killer was not sentenced to death. However, all these people's firsthand experience with homicide convinced them that the death penalty was not the solution to the problem of violence in our society, nor did it help them personally to heal.

Barbara edited and self-published the stories in a publication called *Not in Our Name*. *Not in Our Name* has now gone through several editions and was turned into a traveling photo-text exhibit, which has been displayed at various venues across the country. Although I was proud of our final product, I felt that the stories needed to be told to a much wider audience; hence the idea for a "real" book. Barbara and I talked about writing a book together, but eventually she decided against it. Still, it was her idea and creativity that first gave the project life.

Throughout the process of writing this book, I experimented with different ways to present the information. Finally, I decided that the most powerful format was simply telling the story of what happened to each person. As much as possible, I try to use their words.

I think it is important to disclose to the reader that I am very much opposed to the death penalty. I have spent a large part of my legal career, and a lot of my spare time, working to end it. At the start of this project, I wanted to use the voices of the surviving family members to make the most compelling argument against the death penalty. However, as the project has evolved, it has turned into something much more than a book about the death penalty. The people in this book are models of how to live. These inspiring stories of family members reconciling with their loved one's killer demonstrate the power of forgiveness and compassion in helping a person heal from tragedy. By rejecting the death penalty, they have rejected the values of retribution and vengeance in exchange for a belief in the power of redemption and change—both for the victim and for the offender. Ultimately, this is a book about hope.

# ACKNOWLEDGMENTS

Many people helped on this project during the past five years. However, there are a few who deserve special mention: Renny Cushing and all the staff and members of Murder Victims' Families for Reconciliation; Barbara Hood, who first had the idea of photographing and interviewing victims' family members; the Washington Office of the American Civil Liberties Union, for material and emotional support, with special thanks to Laura Murphy, Eric Ham, Sharon Kissel, and interns Johanna Cohen and Philip Duloy; my agent, Carol Mann, for her faith in a first-time writer; Richard McAlee and Christine Kennedy, for typing and editing assistance; and my friend Laurie Loisel and my editor, David Myers, who told me I was a good writer when I needed to hear it the most.

# DON'T KILL IN OUR NAMES

# Introduction

The people in this book belong to an exclusive organization. However, it is not one you would want to join. It is called Murder Victims' Families for Reconciliation, or MVFR, and its membership requirements are that someone in your family was murdered and that you oppose the death penalty. Families of murder victims are often ardent supporters of the death penalty, but not so the people who are members of MVFR. Due to their own personal reasons—political, moral, ethical, social, religious—they reject the death penalty. Surviving the murder of their loved one has led them to understand that the death penalty does not serve their needs, and often offends their value system and that of the person they lost. While the term "reconciliation" in the title of the organization refers to a reconciling to the fact of the murder, rather than the murderer, for some members their journey has taken them on a path of forgiveness leading them to reach out to the killer. Others within the organization do not feel a need to have any contact with the killer, but still oppose executing him or her, and the death penalty system.

One of the most difficult aspects of writing this book was deciding which stories to tell. Every one of the dozens of people I interviewed had extraordinary experiences to share. In the end, I picked stories with the goal of making the most persuasive case against the death penalty. In that regard, the reader should be aware that this is not a random sampling of murder cases, because most of the stories related here involve murder by a stranger. In reality, murderers overwhelmingly kill people they know. According to Department of Justice statistics, between 1976 and 1999, only 14 percent of homicides were stranger homicides.[1]

Often, the family member's decision to oppose the death penalty has come at great personal cost. It seems that an understanding of the humanity of the killer, and his or her family, as well as an understanding of the human flaws that contribute to a biased and broken death penalty system, threatens to disrupt the order of the adversarial system and the social paradigm of retribution and vengeance. Many families have shunned, or even disowned, members for publicly opposing the execution of the person who murdered their loved one. This happened to Maria Hines and Ron Carlson.

Sometimes the justice system shuns them: prosecutors, parole boards, and judges have silenced people who have tried to speak against the death penalty. SueZann Bosler was nearly thrown into jail for contempt of court when she tried to tell the jury she didn't want her father's killer to be executed. Gus and Audrey Lamm were forbidden to speak before the Nebraska Pardons Board because they opposed the execution of the man who killed their wife and mother. Maria Hines and Ron Carlson were ignored by corrections officials at the same time that their family members who supported the death penalty were embraced.

The stories in this book highlight both the fallibility and inequality of the criminal justice system. Gary Gauger tells about his experience of being wrongfully convicted and sentenced to death for killing his parents after a police investigation and trial that can only be described as a sham. Jennifer Bishop and her family endured months of humiliating investigation into their private lives when the FBI focused its investigation on Jennifer's sister Jeanne, making the bizarre assumption that Jennifer and Jeanne's sister and brother-in-law were killed when the Irish Republican Army retaliated against Jeanne. Fortunately, the true killer was ultimately found and convicted.

Of course, not all police investigations are corrupt or misguided. Some investigators are brilliant, talented, and compassionate people, as in the cases of Marietta Jaeger, SueZann Bosler, and Linda White.

One universal conclusion that all MVFR members have reached is that the death penalty will not help them heal. For some, it actually impedes healing. The last two chapters in the book tell the stories of Azim Khamisa and Linda White, who are both actively involved in the restorative justice movement because they believe that the criminal justice system does little to help heal and restore crime victims.

Our society has been struggling with the question of the death penalty for several decades. The issue came to prominence most recently in January of 2000, when Illinois governor George Ryan declared a moratorium on executions after nearly presiding over the execution of Anthony Porter, an innocent man.[2] His innocence was brought to light not because of fancy legal maneuvers by sophisticated lawyers but because of the enterprising work of journalism students at Northwestern University who tracked down the real killer and obtained a videotaped confession from him.

Anthony Porter became the thirteenth innocent person to be exonerated in Illinois since reinstatement of the death penalty in 1976. That surpassed the total number of people executed in the state since 1976, twelve. These numbers were very troubling, even for ardent death penalty supporters—troubling enough, in fact, to make a pro–death penalty governor put a halt to executions.

Unfortunately, the situation in Illinois is not unique. As of January 2002, ninety-nine innocent people have been released from death rows nationwide, and the one hundredth exoneration is imminent.[3] Some death penalty supporters cite the exoneration cases as proof that our justice system works. However, others are not so convinced. As of February 2000, 94 percent of Americans believed that an innocent person had been executed within the past five years.[4]

The story in Illinois sparked national debate, and the media started to cover the issue of the death penalty in more depth. The next month, Professor James Liebman and two colleagues at Columbia University issued a report documenting that two-thirds of all death penalty convictions or sentences since reinstatement of the death penalty had been overturned because of serious errors in the trial or sentencing of the case. The Liebman report, like the innocence cases, emphasized serious problems with the administration of justice in our country.[5] The general public began questioning the wisdom of state-sanctioned killing, and by May 2001 public support had fallen to its lowest level in nearly two decades, 65 percent.[6]

Death penalty abolitionists rejoiced at this turn of events. Finally, the general public was learning what we already knew: the death penalty is an imperfect, inhumane punishment doled out not to those who commit the most serious offenses but to the most vulnerable in our society—the young, the mentally impaired, and the poor. There is a saying: "Capital punishment means those without the capital get the punishment." You don't find rich people on America's death rows.

While there are many reasons to oppose the death penalty, there are few to support it. The idea that the death penalty is a deterrent has been utterly discredited by criminologists. In 2000, the *New York Times* examined murder rates in the twelve states without the death penalty and the thirty-six states that reintroduced it before 1983. It found that murder rates had not declined any more in the states with capital punishment than in those without it. Ten of the twelve non–death penalty states had murder rates below the national average, while half the states with the death penalty had rates above the average. Most striking, during the past twenty years, the murder rate in states with the death penalty was 48 percent to 101 percent higher than in the states without it.[7]

Another assertion commonly cited to support the death penalty is that it saves money because killing people is cheaper than housing them in prison. This belief has been debunked in study after study. The following facts illustrate the financial costs to some of the states where the murders featured in this book took place.[8]

- The death penalty costs California (chapter 10) $90 million annually beyond the ordinary costs of the justice system; $78 million of that total is incurred at the trial level. Elimination of the death penalty would result in a net saving to the state of at least several tens of millions of dollars annually, and a net saving to local governments in the millions to tens of millions of dollars.
- Florida (chapter 6) spent an estimated $57 million on the death penalty from 1973 to 1988 to perform eighteen executions at an average of $3.2 million per execution. Enforcing the death penalty costs Florida $51 million a year above and beyond what it would cost to punish all first-degree murderers with life in prison without parole.
- In Texas (chapters 3 and 9), an average death penalty case costs $2.3 million, about three times the cost of imprisoning someone in a single cell at the highest security level for forty years.
- In Indiana (chapter 4), three recent capital cases cost taxpayers a total of over $2 million, just for defense costs.
- A report from the Nebraska (chapter 8) Judiciary Committee determined that any savings from executing an inmate were outweighed by the legal costs, concluding that the current death penalty law does not serve the best interests of Nebraskans.

Although the death penalty debate in the aftermath of the Illinois moratorium appears to be new, in fact Americans have been ambivalent about the death penalty for decades. In 1965, more Americans opposed the death penalty (47 percent) than supported it (38 percent). Support for the death penalty was right around 50 percent in 1970, shortly before the Supreme Court struck it down in the case of *Furman v. Georgia,* ruling that administration of the death penalty was so inconsistent that it violated the Eighth Amendment's prohibition against cruel and unusual punishment.[9]

But even the Court couldn't seem to make up its mind about the issue. Four years later, it reversed its decision, upholding a newly crafted Georgia statute in the case of *Gregg v. Georgia*.[10] By the time of the *Gregg* decision in 1976, support for the death penalty had returned to 66 percent, and over the next two decades it steadily rose, reaching an all-time high of 80 percent in September 1994.

Although trends in public support rise and fall, one factor remains constant: our criminal justice system has still not figured out a way to impose death sentences fairly. The same vagaries that existed at the time of *Furman* plague the system today—economic and racial bias, ineffective assistance of counsel, and wrongful convictions.

The stories in this book highlight these problems. They exemplify what researcher Craig Haney calls the "profile" of capital defendants. Over the course of twenty years, Haney compiled the histories of people on death row. He concluded: "The nexus between poverty, childhood abuse and neglect, social and emotional dysfunction, alcohol and drug abuse, and crime is so tight in the lives of many capital defendants as to form a kind of social historical 'profile.'"[11] Among the defendants in the following chapters, Paula Cooper, James Bernard Campbell, Dennis Eaton, Karla Faye Tucker, and Gary Brown all came from broken homes with little chance of leading successful lives. Richard McCarthy (name changed to protect family's privacy) suffered from serious mental illness; James Bernard Campbell, from mental retardation. Many did not receive adequate legal representation.

Haney's research also illustrates how our society, through the media, dehumanizes people on death row in order to justify killing them. By systematically analyzing information disseminated by television crime drama, Haney found that "television criminals were depicted uniformly without context, life connections, social relationships, basic human needs, wants, or hardships. They were, in short, non-people." Haney concluded that this lack of social context leaves the viewer with the impression that the only thing that led the killers to commit their dastardly deeds was their own personal evil.[12] The truly amazing thing about the people whose stories you are about to read is that they were able to look beyond the evil done by the killer to find his or her humanity.

Ultimately, the question of whether to have a death penalty is a moral one. Do we think the government has the right to kill its citizens? And if the only redeeming value of the death penalty is retribution, we need to ask ourselves whether we want our criminal justice system to encourage vengeance and retribution or healing and restoration. MVFR members have experienced the ugliness of violence firsthand. But instead of adding to the violence with another execution, they have chosen love and forgiveness. By renouncing violence and retribution, they have set themselves free and brought a small measure of peace to our troubled world.

# FORGIVENESS

orgiveness is the common thread that weaves together the people who are the subject of this book. All have forgiven their loved one's killer. Many have sought reconciliation with the killer, and some have even advocated for his or her release from death row.

It is sometimes difficult for people who have not been through the murder of a loved one to imagine how a person could ever get to the point of forgiving the killer. MVFR members are often treated as either saints or lunatics, but the truth is that they are neither. They are ordinary people who responded to extraordinary circumstances with tremendous courage and faith.

While we tend to think of forgiveness as something that a person does for someone else, it is actually a choice people make for themselves. Forgiveness is not for the weak of heart. It requires hard work and a willingness to delve deeply into intense pain and grief. Through much effort and perseverance, a person can redeem an incredibly horrible experience, thereby transcending it and going on to lead a full life.

People who have experienced a tremendous loss are sometimes led to believe that they will achieve a kind of "closure" where they will have healed their wounds and returned to "normal." But people who have lost someone to murder attest to the fact that there is no "closure." The best they can hope for is to turn their personal tragedy into positive action that gives them the strength to go on living and sometimes even gives life new meaning.

The irony of forgiveness is that while it appears to be a self-less act, it is really a very selfish one. People who are unable to forgive cling to their bitterness and rage and are therefore doubly wounded by the killer, who has taken away not only their loved one but also any chance of enjoying their own life. As Bill Pelke (chapter 4) says of the girl who killed his grand-mother, "Forgiving Paula Cooper did a lot more for me than it did for Paula Cooper."

The first three chapters tell the stories of Marietta Jaeger, Maria Hines, and Ron Carlson. While all the stories in the book focus to some degree on forgiveness, these three are particularly poignant because each person developed a relationship with the loved one's killer.

# CHAPTER 1

# The Lost Child

Marietta Jaeger stood on the riverbank at the Missouri River State Monument Campground breathing in the slightly chilly air on June 24, 1973. Just three days after the summer solstice, the sun was only just beginning its descent, casting shadows over the river valley. Waters from the Madison, Jefferson, and Gallatin rivers joined together, carving out a canyon surrounded on all sides by snow-peaked mountains. To the north were the Horseshoe Hills, to the south lay Gallatin Mountain, and to the east and west loomed Bridger and Tobacco peaks.

Marietta was happy to be vacationing in Montana, a state she loved. The Jaegers, in fact, were considering leaving the city and relocating there, although this was still a dream. She thought about the past week. The family had traveled two thousand miles from their home in the Detroit suburb of Farmington Hills, planning to drive around Montana soaking up its rugged beauty. Marietta's husband, Bill, had taken a month's vacation from his job as a die designer in the automobile industry. Now that their youngest child was old enough to enjoy a lengthy car trip, they were taking their first real family vacation. Marietta's parents, Marie and Bill Liptak, had driven from Arizona to accompany them for the month.

This day had started at the Catholic church in Three Forks, where the family attended mass. They spent the rest of the day at the Lewis and Clark Caverns a few miles from the campground. The children loved exploring the caves. Thirteen-year-old Heidi and fourteen-year-old Frank played tricks on nine-year-old Joey and seven-year-old Susie. Four feet tall with a medium build, Susie weighed fifty-five pounds and had light brown hair, a fair complexion, and lovely hazel eyes. Mostly good-natured and shy, she had a mischievous side that helped her hold her own as the youngest of five children. Too old for childish games, sixteen-year-old Dan hung around his father and grandfather.

*Marietta Jaeger Lane. Photograph by Barbara Hood.*

After spending the weekend in Three Forks, the family was going to pull down camp the next day. They had not settled on their next destination. The luxury of a long vacation allowed them the spontaneity to travel wherever they wanted without needing to plan out each stop.

Marietta left her musings with the setting sun and walked back to the campsite, where she found her family getting ready for bed.

MARIETTA:  Our sleeping arrangements involved several vehicles and a large tent. My oldest son, Dan, was sleeping in the back of our van, my husband and I were sleeping in the back of my parent's truck, and my parents were in a travel trailer. All three vehicles were circled around a two-room tent where the other children slept.

I went inside the tent to say good night to the children. They were side by side in their individual sleeping bags, still fully dressed to stay warm in the cold night air. I knelt down by their feet to kiss each one good night. Susie was the hardest to reach because she was the shortest and I had to hang over Heidi to reach her. My lips skimmed over her cheek. She didn't think my kiss satisfactory, so she got out of her sleeping bag and knelt in front of me and gave me a big kiss and said, "There, Momma, that's the way it should be." She insisted that we do it right. She was always loving and demonstrative with me. She could never walk through a room that I was in without stopping to run over and hug me or kiss me. It was important for her to make that connection with me.

Marietta crawled into her own sleeping bag and quickly fell into a sound sleep. Hours later, Heidi shook her. "Wake up, Susie's gone."

MARIETTA: It was about four o'clock in the morning when Heidi woke Bill and me out of a sound sleep. We grabbed our flashlight and ran to the tent. Heidi said she had spoken with Susie at around two o'clock, but now she couldn't find her. Susie would not have wandered off by herself. I assumed she'd snuggled down on the other side of the tent and Heidi couldn't see her in the dark.

When we got to the tent, Bill shone the light on it, and what I saw made my heart stop—someone had cut a large hole in the side of the tent next to where Susie had been sleeping. Lying on the ground next to the hole were the stuffed lambs that Susie always slept with. We started running all over the site yelling her name, waking up the other campers.

Bill Jaeger and Bill Liptak jumped into the van and drove into the nearest town, Three Forks, a community of some 1,100 people located just off Interstate 90 in south-central Montana. They doubted they'd find help at four A.M., but driving through they spotted a light on at the small town office. They rushed inside to speak with Tony Lutke, the town marshal. He told the men to return to the campsite and said he'd follow as soon as he made some calls.

•   •   •   •

Four years earlier, someone had attempted to abduct another child from the same campsite at the same campground, only feet away from where Susie Jaeger slept. During a Boy Scout outing, the intruder had cut into a tent and tried to kidnap twelve-year-old Michael Rainey, who yelled for help. Authorities assumed that Michael knew the kidnapper, who stabbed and struck the child to avoid being identified. Michael died two days later in the hospital. The autopsy ruled the cause of death to be a severe blow to the head. Scoutmaster Edgar Miller said he had been awakened early in the morning and thought he heard a child yell "help" three times. He checked inside the tents and saw nothing unusual, so he returned to sleep. The case remained unsolved.

Unfortunately, Michael Rainey's murder was not the only unsolved homicide in the Three Forks area. In March 1967, someone shot thirteen-year-old Bernard Poelman while he played on a railroad bridge twelve miles down the road from Three Forks. Bernard's body was found in the river with a bullet in his heart.

The community had severely criticized law enforcement for failing to solve the other crimes. This time, Tony Lutke intended to call in as much help as possible from the very beginning. He called the sheriff and, even though it was not yet within their jurisdiction, the Federal Bureau of Investigation.

By the time Tony reached the campground, almost all the campers were searching for Susie. Not willing to leave any stone unturned, he systematically questioned every person there. No one had seen or heard anything, not even the family of seven camping in the site adjacent to the Jaegers', who had slept outside in the open air.

By first light, police, sheriff's deputies, and dozens of volunteers fanned out in a "foot-by-foot" search looking for any clues to Susie's disappearance. The searchers used machetes to cut through the tall brush and grass. Temperatures reached ninety degrees under the sweltering summer sun. The search party included a number of vacationers from various parts of the country attending a travel-trailer owners' convention in Bozeman, twenty-file miles away; among them were half a dozen young men from Michigan, the Jaegers' home state. In spite of everything, tourists continued to visit the site to take in the spectacular vistas.

Meanwhile, back at the campsite, the family kept vigil, waiting for word from the kidnapper or some news of Susie's whereabouts. At least one law enforcement officer stayed with the family at all times.

MARIETTA: The people from the community were very helpful and loving. People came to the campground every day bringing food. They took my kids to their farms and ranches and on trips up into the mountains, trying to keep them busy and occupied. We felt safe and secure because of the presence of the FBI and deputies who were at the campground all the time. There were television crews, local people, and lots of conversations that helped keep us occupied.

The first twenty-four hours of a kidnapping investigation are crucial. With each passing hour, the chances of the victim returning home alive diminish. Susie had been missing three days before a man called from Colorado claiming to have her. He said that he would return Susie in exchange for fifty thousand dollars, to be placed in a locker in a bus station in Denver. Marietta's spirits rose. The fact that the kidnapper had made contact indicated Susie was likely still alive, and the phone call established interstate jurisdiction, which gave the FBI the authority to officially take over the investigation.

The FBI assigned Special Agent Pete Dunbar to lead the investigation. Tall and handsome with blond hair, Pete walked with a long stride and used western mannerisms that reminded Marietta of John Wayne. Agent Dunbar put Marietta at ease. She trusted him and believed that if anyone could find Susie, he could.

Pete, who worked from an office in Bozeman but had grown up in Three Forks and knew all the locals, believed that the same person who killed Michael Rainey had kidnapped Susie Jaeger. He also thought it likely that the kidnapper lived in the area. Given that everyone in Three Forks knew each other, he assumed that the kidnapper participated in the search party in order to avoid drawing attention to himself by his absence.

On June 29, a woman called, reporting that she had seen a child matching Susie's description in the company of three men driving a light blue Volkswagen sedan at an eastbound rest area on Interstate 90 west of Butte. The FBI put out an all points bulletin for the vehicle.

On July 2, the kidnapper called Mrs. Ronald Brown, the wife of a sheriff's deputy. This time he identified Susie by her thickened, rounded index fingernails, a birth defect that had not been disclosed to the media and that only someone who had seen Susie would know about. He repeated his ransom demand for fifty thousand dollars and said that he'd call again when he had a plan worked out to exchange the money.

When another week passed with no further word from the kidnapper, the police organized a media appeal. Marietta made an impassioned plea to the kidnapper, begging him to return Susie. National media advertised a phone number for people to call with information.

After two weeks with no further leads, Marietta experienced an emotional breakdown. By nature a cheerful and optimistic person, she felt unequipped to deal with the intensity of her emotions.

MARIETTA: For two weeks I had focused entirely on Susie and my worry and concern and fear for her. I had not allowed myself to experience or acknowledge my own anger. I was very adept at repressing anger, and I wasn't allowing myself to feel and own my anger. But finally the day came when feelings of revenge roiled and screamed inside me.

That day, all day long, small planes flew overhead, pilots scanning from their vantage point for any signs of Susie. The noise of the engines was a constant reminder of the horrible event that had violated the peace and beauty of this place. At the same time the planes flew overhead, a boat dragged the river. That was a real horrifying experience. Each time the boat stopped and they reeled in the net, my heart stopped, terrified that Susie's body would be in the catch.

The buildup of the previous two weeks and those particular activities made my anger come rushing to the fore. I felt intense rage I had never let myself experience before. I knew that if the kidnapper returned Susie unharmed at that minute I would strangle him with my bare hands because of the anguish he had caused my family. I knew I hated him and wanted to kill him.

But I also immediately recognized that I could not live filled with such intense hatred. For my own mental health I would have to move past the hatred and revenge.

I had a well-developed conscience and a strong religious faith, which called me to forgive. I knew that there was no way I could possibly forgive this man on my own. I prayed to God and asked to have my heart changed from rage to forgiveness. It did not happen that night, but almost immediately I had a sense of relief, like a burden had been lifted from me. It became clear to me that my own survival depended on my willingness and ability to forgive, because if I stayed in the rage it would tear me apart. I knew that was the direction I had to work towards, and I was willing to give myself whatever time I needed to get there.

Five weeks after the kidnapping, Pete Dunbar advised the Jaegers to return to Michigan. What started as a dream vacation ended in a nightmare beyond anything they could have imagined. Reluctantly, the family headed home. Instead of returning to Arizona, Bill and Marie Liptak accompanied the Jaegers to Michigan.

MARIETTA: It was very difficult for me to leave Montana. I felt like I was abandoning Susie. I couldn't bear to think of her with a stranger, wondering if she would ever see us again. But Bill had to return to work, and I knew that we had done all that we could do and now we needed to leave the investigation in the competent hands of the FBI. There was a very good chance that Susie wasn't even in Montana, so staying behind did not make any sense. The television and print media agreed to publish our telephone number in Michigan so the kidnapper would know how to contact us.

As best they could, the family tried to resume their lives. Marietta and Bill provided a calm and stable presence for their other children, trying to maintain some semblance of normalcy. Marietta shopped, cooked, cleaned, and helped the kids with their homework. The children attended school and sports and other activities, and Bill worked every day.

However, other than doing routine chores, Marietta rarely left home. Life became a waiting game. This being before the advent of answering machines, cell phones, and pagers, Marietta became a slave to the telephone, staying as close to home as possible on the chance the kidnapper might call.

MARIETTA: Bill and I had very different ways of dealing with Susie's kidnapping. Bill was a stoic, self-contained man who did not like to give in to his emotions. This is not a criticism of Bill. However, I needed desperately to talk and share my feelings. Fortunately my family and my very good friend Karen Zorney, Susie's godmother, provided the outlet I needed. But both Bill and I feared that if we really let ourselves feel the intensity of our pain we would go crazy, and we had to hold ourselves together for the sake of our other children, and ourselves.

Not knowing whether Susie was alive was the hardest. I continued to hope. I dreamed of her. I prayed for her. I begged God to give me information, some sign so that I might know how she was. The pain was, at times, unbearable. It came and went. Kind of like grief does, but I wasn't really grieving, because I held out hope that Susie was alive.

I also prayed for the kidnapper. That helped me a lot. I prayed for him even when I didn't want to. Even when I felt rage, I prayed. I knew that the rage had the power to consume me, and I knew that no matter what happened I did not want to live my life under the constant torment of rage. It helped to think about the kidnapper. I wondered what forces could possibly lead a person to take a small child from her family. It might sound strange, but I knew that he must be suffering, too. I imagined what I would say to him if he called. I had conversations with him in my head. I asked God to help me understand and forgive him.

I also thought about what would happen if Susie was dead and they arrested her killer. I knew that Montana had the death penalty. I had never really thought that much about the death penalty. Michigan doesn't have one and hasn't for over a century and a half.

To my way of thinking, support for the death penalty was based on revenge. I understood the desire for revenge because I had felt it myself. But I knew that revenge could easily consume me, too, like the rage. I decided that the death penalty would only increase my desire for revenge and would not help me. In fact, I believed it would hurt me. I decided that if it ever became an issue in this case, I would ask that it not be sought.

· · · ·

Back in Montana, Pete Dunbar pursued every possible lead with a passion born of desperation. He was determined to find the kidnapper, who, he suspected, was also involved in at least one murder. Each day the man roamed the streets put the community at risk. A month after Susie's kidnapping, two young girls disappeared from near Kalispell, their bicycles left along the highway.

Agent Dunbar considered almost every man of a certain age in Three Forks a potential suspect. He questioned them all and requested that they submit to lie detector tests. He obtained alibis and followed up on every one, unwilling to rule out anyone without hard proof.

The frustration at failing to solve the crime only intensified when nineteen-year-old Sandra Smallegan disappeared after attending a basketball game in Manhattan, Montana, on February 9, 1974. Although they feared she was dead, authorities were unable to find any evidence to substantiate that belief. Finally, after searching for three weeks, sheriff's deputies found her car in an outbuilding of an abandoned ranch, covered with a tarp, hay, and farm implements.

The area immediately became the focus of a thorough search. Ronald Green of the Bozeman–Gallatin County Investigative Team was examining ashes found near the house when he discovered a piece of bone. Eventually over 1,200 bone fragments turned up, none larger than two inches; authorities believed the bone had been chopped up or subjected to intense heat to create such small pieces. Sandra was identified from dental records and an undergarment found at the site.

· · · ·

In spite of the enormous resources spent working the case, the anniversary of Susie's disappearance approached without a solid suspect. The Montana media wanted to interview Marietta about the past year—what it had been like not knowing where or how her daughter was. Marietta told reporters, "I would do anything if I could just talk to him." The Jaeger phone number was published widely on television and in print media.

A year to the day after the kidnapping, at the exact hour of Susie's abduction, the Jaegers' phone rang. Marietta picked up the phone to hear a man say, "You wanted to talk to me. Well, here I am. I have Susie."

**MARIETTA:** As soon as I heard his voice, we turned on the tape recorder, and I said a quick prayer asking God to give me the right words to convince this man to return my Susie. Bill used another phone to contact the FBI, then listened to the conversation.

It was clear the kidnapper called me up to taunt me. I knew that for the FBI to place a trace on the call I needed to keep him on the line, so I started by asking him nonthreatening questions. I asked him how Susie was doing. I asked him what clothes she was wearing and how her hair was done. I asked if she had been eating well. This had the effect of relaxing him and getting him to talk. He told me that during the past year he had traveled around Montana working at different jobs. He said that Susie went with him and had a good time being with him. We spoke at length, and he gave a lot of details about the places he had been and the kind of work he did. I heard some loud noises in the background. At one point I thought I heard a train, and I thought that might help the investigators identify the location of the call.

I was surprised at how calm I felt. Instead of feeling rage at him, I felt genuine compassion. My courage grew, and I asked for information about Susie. I asked him if she was alive. He said that she was. I asked him if she was okay. I begged him to return her to me. I could sense that he was becoming more uncomfortable. I was terrified that he'd hang up the phone. Without really knowing where the words came from, I asked him, "How are you? You must be very burdened by what you have done." I honestly felt concern for him, and he could tell this from my voice. I heard him gasp and then cry. He replied, "I wish this terrible burden could be lifted," and then the line went dead.

The agent immediately requested a trace on the call, but it failed. As it turned out, they didn't need a trace to identify the caller. The kidnapper had described enough about his life that Pete Dunbar was sure he knew who it was. From the background noises Pete could identify where the call was made—a field near the train tracks, not far from where Susie was abducted. He sent an agent to the location and found that someone familiar with telephone technology had cut into the telephone cable in a field on the outskirts of Three Forks in the middle of the night, at the time the cargo train passed through town. Tapping into the phone line meant the call could not be traced to any telephone. Pete also realized how the kidnapper had been able to abduct Susie without anyone knowing: he waited until the moment the train passed by the campground, so any noise he made would be obscured by its heavy drone.

Pete knew of one local man who knew how to access the phone line—a man who had been seen with Sandra Smallegan the night she disappeared. Now the FBI was faced with the daunting challenge of gathering enough evidence to put all the pieces together and prove its case in court.

•   •   •   •

Twenty-five-year old handyman Richard McCarthy (the name has been changed to protect his family's privacy) grew up in the area near the campground. Five feet, six inches tall, weighing 160 pounds, Richard had light brown hair. People in the community described him as a hardworking man but a private person. One of Pete Dunbar's original suspects, Richard cooperated completely in the investigation, including taking and passing a lie detector test. Richard did not have a solid alibi for June 24. He told Pete that he had spent the evening at home, but since he lived alone no one could confirm or refute his claim. As Pete had suspected, Richard took part in the search party.

In spite of some problems as a teenager, Richard graduated high school and went on to become a Marine with an excellent record. He held down steady employment and took part in community activities. He was also intensely loyal and devoted to his mother.

At the time of Susie's kidnapping, the FBI had recently begun experimenting with psychological profiling. Pete made a visit to the behavioral sciences unit at Quantico, where the entire case was reviewed from beginning to end. A profile of a killer emerged that described Richard exactly. However, in spite of his strong suspicions, Pete did not have enough information to obtain a conviction against Richard for kidnapping. He might have been able to convince a judge to issue an arrest warrant, but U.S. Attorney Thomas Olson, the

prosecutor working the case, did not want to arrest Richard until he was certain they could convict him. He feared that once they arrested Richard, it
would be much more difficult to get him to confess or develop more evidence
against him. Arresting him might also make it more difficult to find Susie.
They still did not even know if she was dead or alive.

Instead, they placed Richard under round-the-clock surveillance, hoping
that by following him they would find Susie and obtain enough information
to convict him of the kidnapping. However, this strategy had risks. If Susie
was still alive, delaying Richard's arrest placed her in danger. There was the
additional concern that Richard might hurt another person.

Pete Dunbar decided to try to provoke Richard into confessing. He accused
him of kidnapping Susie. Richard denied the allegations, but Pete's accusation
put him on notice that he was under investigation, which Pete hoped would
lessen the likelihood that Richard would harm someone else.

Claiming to be innocent, Richard retained Douglas Dassinger to represent
him. He advised Richard to cooperate fully with the investigation. At Pete's
request, Richard agreed to take another polygraph test and a truth serum test.
Douglas arranged for Richard to take the tests in Bozeman.

On the same evening that Richard took the tests, a group of Girl Scouts
held a weekend outing at a campground outside Bozeman. In the middle of
the night, a man entered a tent and attempted to abduct a child. The other
girls woke up and screamed, scaring him off. They gave the police a description that matched Richard.

The attempted abduction intensified the pressure to arrest Richard, but
Pete still lacked the evidence to convict him of kidnapping Susie. After trail-
ing Richard for several weeks, there was no sign that he was caring for a small
child. Pete believed it highly unlikely that Susie was still alive. He also suspected that Richard might have kidnapped and murdered Sandra Smallegan,
but he did not have any evidence to arrest Richard for that crime or to connect the two crimes to each other.

Pete believed that Marietta could help solve the case. Because of the rapport she had established with Richard during the anniversary phone call, he
hoped that if Richard met Marietta he would break down and confess to her.
Pete asked Marietta to assist in the investigation. She readily agreed.

Pete wanted Marietta to identify Richard's voice before meeting him so that
her identification would be more trustworthy if she later became a witness at
trial. Before they flew to Montana, he arranged for the Jaegers to listen to a
telephonic voice lineup. Richard agreed to participate, and Pete selected four

other men to take part in the lineup, including a relative of Richard's who had a similar voice. On August 28, from their home in Michigan, Marietta and Bill listened to four different men read a few lines from the transcript of the anniversary call. Without hesitating, both Marietta and Bill identified Richard as the caller.

MARIETTA: I relished the opportunity to be part of the investigation. I felt so helpless waiting in Michigan for something to happen. I wanted to help find Susie—to know the truth about what happened to her. Bill was concerned that Richard would harm me, but I didn't believe that. I felt that something had happened between us during the call. I truly felt that Richard and I had made a genuine human connection. I believe that God was loving him through me. I was a medium for that love and was not afraid. Richard knew that I genuinely cared about him, and he desperately needed the love and compassion I felt for him.

•   •   •   •

On September 18, 1974, fifteen months after Susie's abduction, Bill and Marietta returned to Montana. Marietta still hoped Susie was alive but knew that was unlikely. Meanwhile, investigators had continued searching the ranch where they had found Sandra Smallegan's remains, and the day before the Jaegers arrived they found what appeared to be a child's bone in an outhouse pit. They sent the bone to the Smithsonian Institution for identification and were waiting for the results.

Pete introduced Marietta to prosecutor Thomas Olson, a tall, handsome man with a kind demeanor. Marietta liked him right away.

MARIETTA: I felt a close rapport with Thomas as soon as I met him. At this point, we still didn't know if Susie was dead, but it seemed almost certain that she was. I told Thomas that if he arrested the kidnapper and it turned out that Susie was dead, I did not want the killer to get the death penalty. I told him that I was Catholic—he was, too—and that I just did not see how the death penalty would help me. I said I had been working hard on forgiving the kidnapper and I thought the death penalty would stimulate all the feelings of rage and revenge that I was trying to be free of.

I also told him that I knew it was his decision whether to seek the death penalty and that I would respect any decision he made. Thomas reassured me that he agreed with me. He didn't make a big deal about it. He acted as though he had known all along that I would not want it. By this point I had gotten to be quite close to Pete Dunbar and the other agents, and they knew without me having to say so that I would not want the death penalty.

But apart from wanting to respect my personal desires, I also sensed that Thomas and the other agents did not really want the death penalty either. They were not vindictive. They were very professional and caring.

Thomas told me that he thought that seeking the death penalty in this case might actually hurt their investigation. Like Pete, Thomas thought they might be able to get Richard to confess to the crime. He believed that Richard would be more likely to confess if the government agreed not to seek the death penalty.

I felt very relieved after this conversation. The issue had been weighing heavily on my mind. I didn't want to play a role in an investigation where in the end a person might be killed.

On Saturday, September 21, Marietta and Bill entered the law office of Douglas Dassinger. Pete Dunbar had arranged the room to intimidate Richard. He placed two chairs at one end of an eight-foot-long table—a large desk chair for Marietta and a small chair for Richard, enabling Marietta to tower over him. Pete moved Douglas's chair to the opposite end of the table, as far away from his client as possible. He stationed FBI agents in an adjoining office so they could immediately intervene at any sign of danger to Marietta. Bill stayed in the room with the agents.

MARIETTA: Richard showed no signs of recognition as he entered the room. I stood up and walked towards him to shake his hand. As I shook his hand, I thought how he was the last person to touch Susie. The most striking thing I noticed about Richard was his eyes. His pupils were completely dilated, making his eyes appear black. I later learned that dilated pupils are a symptom of schizophrenia.

Richard was a short man, stocky but not fat. He had the body of a man who made his living doing manual labor. He wore blue jeans and a western-style flannel shirt.

We took our assigned seats, and I was no more than three feet from him. He was very polite. He told me how very sorry he was about what had happened to my daughter. He told me that he would help me if he could but he didn't kidnap Susie and didn't know where she was. He said that he had been upset by news of the kidnapping and had taken part in the search party.

I steeled myself to stay in control. I was determined not to break down or become so emotional that Richard would not talk with me. I kept asking him for information. He continued to deny knowing anything. At one point, I reached over and touched him on the arm, hoping that human contact would move him, but it did not. This went on for about an hour, and then his lawyer ended the interview, claiming that his client had nothing further to say.

Before he left, I shook his hand again and looked firmly into his eyes, but he looked away from me. One of the hardest things I've ever done in my whole life was to let go of that hand. He was my only connection to Susie, and I was desperate to find her. I wanted to try to keep him from leaving, but I knew that would hurt the investigation. I could not afford the luxury of breaking down. I had a job to do for the FBI, for Susie, and I was not going to blow it by becoming hysterical.

After Richard left the office, Bill joined me. He felt the same desperation I did. Bill said to me, "I want to go after him. Should I?" I knew he was thinking that he wanted to kill Richard or at least beat him until he told us where Susie was. I told Bill to let him go.

We were all very disappointed by the meeting, but I still believed it was possible to break through to Richard. I thought he might feel less threatened talking to me on the phone instead of in person, so I called him at his home that same night. I felt relieved when he answered the phone. He said that he had just returned home from his weekly bowling game. He thought the conversation was being taped, so he would not talk to me at length, but he agreed to meet the next morning on the condition that I go alone. I agreed.

Neither Pete nor Bill wanted me to meet Richard alone, but I had made Richard a promise, and I knew that the only chance I had of getting him to talk to me was if I approached him alone.

It's hard for others to understand, but I was certain that Richard would not harm me. We had made a very genuine connection when he called on the night of Susie's anniversary. I felt real concern for his well-being. I knew that he knew that I cared about him. My concern for him had so disarmed him that he had opened up to me in a way that I don't think he had done with another person in a long time.

Although I did not fear for my physical safety, I was terribly worried that I would not be able to accomplish the goal of getting him to talk to me. I did not sleep at all the night before the meeting. My mind raced. I was filled with fear and anxiety. I believed that what I said would make the difference in whether we solved the case or not. I worried that I might never know what happened to Susie. I worried that Richard might kidnap another child. I also feared that I might learn that Susie was dead, even though I had very little hope that she was still alive. To conquer the fear, I prayed constantly throughout the night, asking God to give me the strength to face Richard and the words to convince him to talk to me.

The next morning, Bill dropped me off at the warehouse where we had arranged to meet. I was very nervous. Richard acted nervous, too. He talked quickly. He said some of the same things he had said the day before. He told me he was sorry about Susie. He told me he wished he could help me.

Then his tone changed, and he became more aggressive. He accused me of "being bugged." I was not, and I told him that. I begged him to tell me where Susie was. I kept reminding myself that I needed to be strong, but my voice was filled with desperation. He just kept saying over and over again that he didn't do it, he didn't know anything. I knew he was lying, and I knew I could not get him to tell me the truth.

Bill and I left Montana deeply disappointed that nothing had come from our trip. We tried to remain hopeful, but it was becoming more apparent that Susie was dead.

On September 24, less than a week after their trip to Montana, the Jaegers got another collect call from the kidnapper, who called himself "Mr. Jarvis."

MARIETTA: I could tell by his voice that it was Richard on the phone. He identified Susie by her unpublished birth defect. He said that the FBI was looking for the wrong man, that Richard was not the kidnapper, he was. He said that he was calling from Salt Lake City and that he had Susie. He asked if I wanted to talk with her. I said yes, then I heard a young girl say, "He's a nice man, Mommy, I'm sitting on his lap right now." I could tell by her voice and the way she spoke to me that the girl was not Susie. I decided not to play along with his ruse and began calling him by his name. At first he kept up the act, but then panicked as I continued to call him by his name and talked about things we had spoken about together. He eventually slipped up and mentioned things that Richard and I had talked about the week before in the presence of his attorney and that no one else would know except him. When he realized he had incriminated himself he yelled, "You'll never see your little girl again!" and slammed down the phone.

Richard had indeed managed to elude FBI surveillance and had driven to Salt Lake City, where he made the call, and back. The FBI arrested him three days later on Friday afternoon, September 27, while he was watching a Homecoming Day parade that he had worked on the organizing committee for.

The FBI now felt confident that it had sufficient evidence to prove its case against Richard. Besides the self-incriminating statements he had made to Marietta, there was now physical evidence connecting him to Susie. The Smithsonian test results confirmed that the bone found in the outhouse pit at the ranch was the sacrum (a vertebra that forms part of the pelvis) of a six- to eight-year-old child who was likely to be female. This was the first physical evidence to corroborate what they had all feared for months: Susie was dead.

Once Richard was in custody, agents grilled him for hours. He did not confess but did give the FBI permission to search his home, where they found evidence of multiple murders, including human remains, and evidence positively linking him to Susie's murder. Armed with this new evidence, agents returned to the jail and continued interrogating Richard. Thomas Olson promised Richard that if he confessed he would not face the death penalty for Susie's murder or any other crimes he had committed within that jurisdiction. The questioning continued throughout the night, and by four o'clock on Saturday morning Richard had confessed to kidnapping and killing Susie. He also confessed to three other murders: Michael Rainey, the boy killed at the same location four years earlier; Sandra Smallegan, the young woman abducted in February; and Bernard Poelman, the thirteen-year-old killed in 1967. Richard's confession closed the book on these unsolved cases. Authorities in other jurisdictions suspected he had committed at least two more murders, but because prosecutors in those counties insisted on pursuing the death penalty, Richard would not confess.

Pete Dunbar kept Marietta and Bill informed of each new development in the case. He told them that after listening to Richard's confession for hours, he believed that Richard suffered from paranoid schizophrenia.

After waiting nearly a year and a half, Marietta finally learned what had happened to Susie. In his confession, Richard said he had not intended to kill her and had only kidnapped her because he needed money. He took her to the ranch, where he held her hostage. Then he had "touched" her, and she became hysterical and fought him. He choked her to subdue her and killed her unintentionally. When Richard made the first phone call on June 28 requesting a ransom, Susie was still alive. By the time of the second call, she was dead.

**MARIETTA:** When Agent Dunbar told me that Richard had been arrested and confessed to Susie's murder, I felt tremendous relief but also sadness. I hoped that he would be able to get the treatment he so desperately needed. I made a bargain with God. I told God that I would accept Susie's death if I could see Richard's life restored to wholeness. I was hoping for a miracle.

That Sunday's edition of the *Billings Gazette* ran a story about the family's reaction to the news of Susie's death. Marietta said, "God has been very good to us. We depend upon God for everything in our daily lives. We obviously hoped [Susie] would be returned to us, but with God's grace we will accept this."[1]

•    •    •    •

Pete Dunbar had left the jail early Saturday morning, September 28, after spending most of the night questioning Richard. On the advice of his attorney, Richard had agreed to plead guilty in court on Monday. Pete believed that Richard was at risk for killing himself, so before leaving he alerted the deputy in charge of the jail to put Richard on suicide watch, which meant that he was to be under nearly constant supervision and that extra precautions should be taken to keep potentially dangerous items away from him.

The shift changed at eight o'clock Sunday morning. At the start of his shift, the new deputy took Richard his breakfast. Richard asked him for a towel to clean up with and was given one. When the deputy returned several minutes later to retrieve the breakfast tray, he found Richard hanging from his bunk, asphyxiated.

MARIETTA: I wasn't relieved when I learned of Richard's suicide. I grieved a lot. I grieved for what this meant for his mother. But in the end I had to accept his death like I had to accept Susie's.

·    ·    ·    ·

In October 1974, Marietta and Bill made their third trip to Montana—this time to bury Susie's remains, the sacrum and a skull the police had found. The FBI slipped the Jaegers quietly into Bozeman, where they stayed at Pete Dunbar's home. Pete arranged for his priest, Father Joseph Mauser, to perform the service, which he attended with Bill and Marietta.

MARIETTA: It was a beautiful, sunny fall day as we stood in the small cemetery in Three Forks. Emotions overwhelmed me. I grieved for my beautiful, sweet daughter who died a horrible death. But I also felt relief that our interminable wait was finally over. I thought about Richard's mother and what she must be feeling to lose her child after learning that he was a serial killer. I felt so much pity for her. She lived in a very small town where everyone knew each other. No matter what else he had done, Richard had been a devoted and loving son to her. I decided that before leaving Montana I would visit her and tell her that I did not harbor any hatred or bad feelings towards him or her.

Bill drove me to the antique store in Bozeman where Richard's mother worked. I entered her small, crowded store and was relieved that she was alone. I introduced myself, "I'm Marietta Jaeger, Susie's mother." I said, "I just want you to know that I don't feel badly towards you or Richard." She started crying and I started crying, and we hugged each other. She told me how sorry she was for my loss. I sensed the torment and anguish she felt knowing her son killed my daughter. I told her how sorry I was for her loss, too. When I left the store I felt lighter.

The Jaegers left Montana the next day. This time they knew where Susie was.

MARIETTA: Life continued, as it had to. In some ways, life went on as usual, except that I was going through a radical transformation. Bill and I had handled Susie's kidnapping and murder very differently. Bill did not like to speak about the situation, so I had to take on the role of being the family spokesperson.

It was such a high-profile case that many people called me asking for interviews. The interview requests increased after Richard's arrest and suicide. Soon after returning from Susie's funeral, I received an invitation to speak to a church women's group. I told the story of the kidnapping and how my faith had gotten me through the experience. I shared with them how forgiving Richard had enabled me to communicate with him in a way that led to solving the crime. I told them I believed that had my heart been filled with anger and hatred when he first called, he would have hung up immediately and we might never have solved the crime.

Within months a speaking ministry evolved. I received regular requests to speak in the area, and then requests came in from other parts of the country. What I saw happening was people looking at their own lives and finding places where they needed to forgive. I was profoundly moved to see their transformations. I believe it was God's way of redeeming Susie's death. I also wrote a book. Putting my experiences down on paper helped me to understand them better.

The president of the Society of Former Special Agents of the FBI mentioned Marietta's book in his president's message:

In this small, simple little book Marietta grieves the loss of someone so precious and innocent as her daughter Susan. She dwells on how she will miss all aspects of Susan's life as it would have unfolded had she not been killed. In viewing Susan's life she concludes that she has no choice but to forgive [Richard] for what he did, because to do otherwise would defile and lessen the life and memory of Susan. This was the ultimate example of forgiveness. A mother forgave the killer of her daughter, whom she will miss all her life. Many of us carry burdens in our hearts that would not be there if we opened our hearts and forgave others for the small things we perceive they have done to us. There are so many examples we see today in families; brothers, sisters, husbands, wives, children, neighbors, co-workers, etc., where hurt is allowed to live. A mother forgiving her child's killer makes all hurts pale in comparison.[2]

On October 22, 1982, eight years after they learned that Susie was dead, shortly after the publication of Marietta's book *The Lost Child*, Marietta and Bill divorced. By then their children were adults and living on their own. It was difficult for Marietta to leave Bill after all they had been through together, but their lives had evolved in different directions. For most of their marriage Marietta had been a wife and mother; now she was a sought-after public speaker and an author.

**MARIETTA:** When I tell my story, I talk about the death penalty and how I believe that it would have harmed the resolution of Susie's murder. If I had spent the year after her death feeding the anger and rage that I felt and hoping that Richard would be executed, I would not have achieved any ability to empathize with him as a person. Had I been in that frame of mind, I know that on the night of the anniversary call I would have lost my temper and he would have hung up the phone, and that might very well have been the last we ever heard from him.

When Richard called me on the anniversary of Susie's kidnapping, he wanted to get his kicks and hang up. He had no idea what had been going on inside of me. The last thing in the world he would have imagined is that I could express concern for him as a person. But because I had worked so hard on forgiving him, I was able to see him not just as a horrible kidnapper but as a child of God who was suffering. That connection to him made him stay on the phone and continue talking with me so that I was able to get enough information from him that the FBI could identify him.

Also, because Thomas Olson had agreed not to seek the death penalty, Richard confessed to Susie's murder. He also confessed to three other murders in that county. We will never know if he was responsible for murders in other jurisdictions, because he refused to confess to any crimes that happened in counties that were seeking the death penalty. Had I insisted that Thomas seek the death penalty, Richard would likely not have confessed to Susie's murder either. So you can't tell me that the death penalty helps prevent or solve crime. That just wasn't true in my case.

Sometimes when I speak against the death penalty, people accuse me of not loving my little girl very much. It is difficult for people to understand what it takes to get past that initial response of wanting revenge, so they assume that my lack of feelings of revenge reflects a lack of love for Susie. All I can say to them is that I loved her very much and I hope they never have to go through what I did in order to be able to understand what I am talking about.

But the main reason I oppose the death penalty is because it dishonors Susie's life. She had a sweet and gentle spirit. I don't want that spirit dishonored by having her death avenged with more violence.

# CHAPTER 2

# Turning Grief into Love

On February 20, 1989, twenty-four-year-old Judy McDonald and thirty-two-year-old Dennis Eaton decided to run away to Mexico. Both had seen better days. Judy had been living in a trailer in Shenandoah County, Virginia, with her boyfriend, twenty-six-year-old Walter Custer Jr., also known as "Noonie." She worked as a domestic in a motel in nearby Harrisonburg. Noonie and Judy drank a lot and sometimes ended up fighting. Noonie had beaten Judy up more than once.

Judy confided in Dennis, an old high school friend, about her problems with Noonie. Dennis did not have steady employment or a place to live and was facing criminal charges of burglary and larceny. Judy asked Dennis to move in with her, thinking the presence of another man might save her from Noonie's blows. The three lived together for a few weeks. Dennis developed romantic feelings for Judy. He asked her to leave town with him, but Judy feared breaking off the relationship with Noonie, worrying that he might turn violent. The two decided to kill Noonie and run away together.

They chose the twentieth so that Dennis could avoid his court date. That afternoon when Noonie returned from work, Dennis lured him out of the trailer and into a wooded area near Dennis's mother's house, shot him, and disposed of his body in the thicket. He then went to his mother's house to take a shower.

Now that he had solved the problem of getting rid of Noonie, he needed a getaway car. A semiretired businessman, sixty-eight-year-old Ripley Elwood Marston, lived next door to Dennis's mother in a modest white frame house and owned a 1981 Ford Fairmont. After showering, Dennis knocked on his door and was invited inside. Dennis shot Ripley Marston dead, leaving his body face down in a pool of blood while he emptied the dead man's pockets and found a wallet and car keys. Dennis met Judy back at the trailer, and shortly before ten o'clock the two set off for Mexico in the Fairmont, Judy driving and Dennis riding shotgun. They had plenty of alcohol and drugs with them for the long drive.

The two didn't get very far down the highway before Virginia State Trooper Jerry Hines pulled them over on suspicion of drunk driving. He approached the driver's side and asked Judy to go with him to his patrol car. Judy and Dennis didn't know if anyone had yet reported the Fairmont stolen, but they knew that if the trooper ran a license and registration check he would learn the car didn't belong to them. In fact, according to dispatch records, it appears that he did not know he had pulled over fleeing felons.

Judy went with Jerry to his car but refused to cooperate with him further. He contacted radio dispatch and asked for a "signal twenty-five," which indicated that he needed backup. The dispatcher transmitted the message to all state troopers in the vicinity. Trooper Allen K. Golleher Jr. was just minutes away when he heard Jerry request assistance with a drunken driver.

Dennis, worried about being discovered, got out of the car and brought along the gun. What happened next is disputed. Charles W. Dees, an interstate truck driver heading south on Interstate 81 at the time, later reported that he saw a man and a woman and the trooper standing between the two vehicles, lit by the headlights of the trooper's car. The trooper, he said, was "really chewing out" the man. When Trooper Golleher arrived at the scene at 11:55 P.M., he found the police cruiser's engine running and the lights flashing. Jerry was lying just beyond the bumper face down in a pool of blood. The two shots, one to his neck and the other to his chest, killed him instantly. An all points bulletin was immediately transmitted stating that a trooper had been killed and giving a description of the car the killers were driving.

Like Bonnie and Clyde, Dennis and Judy took off down Highway 81, knowing that the odds of making it to Mexico were not good. They made a murder/suicide pact: if they were stopped by the police, Dennis would shoot Judy, then kill himself.

Fifty miles later, Salem, Virginia, police officer Michael Green spotted the Fairmont and followed it to a Hardee's restaurant, where he ordered Dennis and Judy out of the car. They refused. Dennis and Michael exchanged shots before the Fairmont sped away.

Michael followed, reaching speeds as fast as one hundred miles per hour before the Fairmont crashed into a utility pole at 1:40 A.M. True to their agreement, Dennis fired one shot into Judy's left temple, exchanged gunfire with Michael and other police officers who had arrived at the scene, and then

*Trooper Jerry Hines. Photograph produced by the National Law Enforcement Officers Memorial and provided with permission of the family.*

shot himself in the head. The car burst into flames, and the officers pulled Judy and Dennis from the burning vehicle. Judy was dead, but police took the unconscious Dennis to Roanoke Memorial Hospital, where he was treated for the gunshot wound. He lost his right eye but survived.

Killed at age forty-eight, Trooper Jerry Hines was two years shy of retirement. He was survived by his wife, Carol, and their three children—seventeen-year-old Justin, fifteen-year-old Jonathan, and thirteen-year-old Jennifer—as well as his mother and his older sister Maria, who was devastated by her little brother's death.

**MARIA:** Jerry's death was like a bombshell exploding in my life, with pain too deep to be felt, at least in the beginning. The funeral was very sad. Jerry's family was very distraught. We were all devastated. Our mother was eighty at the time and quite senile, so she didn't really understand everything that was happening. Thousands attended his funeral, including the governor, where Jerry was eulogized for his devotion to his work, his community, and his family.

The first months after Jerry's murder were really a blur to me. I immediately resumed working. I am a trained psychotherapist and was practicing at the time. I had spent two decades helping people heal from psychological trauma. I thought I knew everything there was to

*Maria Hines and Ray Schweri. Photograph by Christian Bright.*

know about healing. It would be a while before I realized how long grief lasts.

My husband of fourteen years, Ray, was a tremendous support to me, as was my faith. Before Ray and I married, I was a nun and he was a Carmelite seminarian. Our faith sustained me through the crisis.

While authorities sorted out the carnage of Dennis's killing spree, he was held in a locked ward at Central State Hospital in Petersburg, where he received emergency psychological counseling. Dennis was charged with four counts of murder and, once stabilized, found competent to face them. On November 21, 1989, he entered into a plea agreement in Shenandoah County, pleading guilty to the first-degree murder of Noonie Custer and the capital murder and robbery of Ripley Marston, and was sentenced to three consecutive life terms plus forty-four years. He subsequently entered a guilty plea in Rockbridge County to the murder of Judy McDonald in exchange for an agreement that the sentence would run concurrently, but he refused to plead guilty to killing Trooper Hines, claiming Judy had done it.

On November 29, 1989, Dennis went on trial for killing Jerry Hines. The state had a strong case that either Dennis or Judy, or both, killed Jerry, but its case against Dennis was by no means open-and-shut: Judy was the one giving Jerry trouble when he called for help, and an autopsy report showed that she had gunpowder residue on her hands.

One of the state's witnesses was a jailhouse snitch named Chadwick Holley, a twenty-two-year-old cocaine user who testified that Dennis had told him he had "shot the cop." Dennis denied the statement and testified in his own defense. He said that he initially got out of the car and tried to talk Jerry into letting them go, then returned to the car and shut the door. He heard two gunshots, got out of the car, and saw Jerry on the ground in front of the patrol car and Judy with her arm pointing to the ground with a gun in her hand. Of course, Dennis lacked credibility, given that he killed three other people that same day. On December 1, the jury convicted him of capital murder.

Less than two weeks later, the jury met again to decide whether to impose the death penalty. On the morning of December 11, they heard testimony on Dennis's character. At 2:30 P.M. they began deliberations, and at 8:15 they returned with a verdict—death.

•   •   •   •

Maria followed these events from a distance. She lived in Louisville, Kentucky, and going to northern Virginia for Dennis's trial would have taken her away from her clients and her husband. No one involved in the proceedings had ever contacted her, not the prosecutor or the defense attorney. No one asked her what she wanted for her brother's murderer.

MARIA: I didn't really follow what happened in the criminal case. Every once in a while Carol would tell me, but I couldn't really focus on it that much. I couldn't take the time off from work to go to Virginia for the trial. I just spent my energy trying to resume my life. I focused a lot on my clients. Friends sent me articles about the case. The articles always mentioned Jerry's wife and kids but never mentioned me.

It didn't really bother me that reporters didn't ask me for my opinion about the case. I didn't want to be in the limelight because of my brother's murder. Besides, it would have been difficult for me to answer their questions. Most of the stories focused on the death penalty. I knew that I didn't really support the death penalty, but I thought my sister-in-law did, and I didn't want to publicly contradict her. Everyone who spoke about the case supported it, from the governor and the Fraternal Order of Police down to the man on the street. In Virginia, if you killed a cop, you got the death penalty.

On February 21, 1990, exactly one year after she learned of Jerry's murder, Maria was diagnosed with breast cancer.

**MARIA:** The diagnosis was a wake-up call to me. I believe the cancer was triggered by the stress of Jerry's murder and my inability to grieve. I knew that in order to survive the cancer, I needed help.

I wanted a support group—people who knew what it was like to lose someone to murder. I contacted the group Concerns of Police Survivors (COPS), an organization for family members of police officers killed in the line of duty. Each year, COPS organizes an event to honor all the officers who have been killed in the line of duty during the previous year. It is held in conjunction with activities for National Police Week. I decided to attend.

In April, Maria flew to Washington, D.C., where she met her sister-in-law, Carol, and niece, Jennifer, who were also attending the event. She spent the week going to seminars and meetings with other police survivors. The experience was very cathartic for Maria.

**MARIA:** The week really marked a turning point for me. It was amazing to be in the presence of nineteen hundred other people who had all experienced losses similar to mine. It finally felt safe to feel the grief I had been holding in the previous year.

However, I did not feel comfortable with all of the programs. I attended a luncheon where the director of the organization, Suzie Sawyer, gave an update on all the "cop-killer" cases. Although COPS does not take an official position on the death penalty, at this luncheon Suzie read through a roster of cases. Whenever she announced that a particular person got the death penalty, the audience burst into applause. I cringed, but I did not feel safe expressing my reservations about capital punishment.

The issue of the death penalty was putting more of a strain on my relationship with Carol. Out of respect for her beliefs, I did not state my opposition to the death penalty. It seemed Carol believed she would only find peace after Dennis was executed, and I just didn't feel that way.

The highlight of the week for me was the memorial service held in honor of the slain officers. On the final day of the conference, we were picked up by bus from our hotels and driven with a police escort to the lawn in front of the U.S. Capitol. An honor guard flanked the aisles as the families filed in to take our seats.

An announcer read the name of each slain officer. When they read Jerry's name, Carol, escorted by a Virginia state trooper, placed a red carnation in honor of Jerry into a large wire wreath. By the time all the names had been read the flowers were transformed into a giant memorial wreath.

After returning from Washington, Maria had no time or energy to worry about Dennis's fate. Between her career, her marriage, and her course of cancer treatment, she was fully occupied. In October, she attended a professional workshop on dealing with loss.

MARIA: One presenter asked the participants to do a visualization exercise. I had read Bernie Siegel's book *Love, Medicine, and Miracles.* In it, Siegel compares human loss to the losses that other creatures experience. For example, if a salamander loses its tail it will grow another one. Likewise with humans, if we experience a life-changing loss we may grow another part.

During the meditation, I saw a hole in my heart. I knew that hole was there because of losing Jerry. I had an insight that my body had needed to fill up that hole. I saw the cancer as my body's attempt to fill that hole. The cancer was located in my left breast right above my heart.

By 1994, Maria began regaining her strength. For the first time in five years, she had no major crisis to face. In the last five years she had dealt with her brother's murder, breast cancer, and the death of her mother. She was ready for a break.

MARIA: I was getting to the point in my life where I started thinking about retiring from my psychotherapy practice. I had always been interested in writing, so I signed up to take a writing class with Dianne Aprile, a popular columnist for the local newspaper.

I hadn't thought about it at the time, but the class turned out to be an excellent forum for me to process some of the feelings I had about Jerry's murder and about the death penalty. For one assignment, I wrote an essay called "The Place I Can't Forget."

Part of the essay said: "Within this place, there is a man whom I have never seen, never met—yet his influence on my life has been profound. I wish I could forget him, as well as the place, but the effect of his actions has changed my life forever.

"The place to which I refer is a prison, located in the southern part of the state where I was born. The man is the one who killed my brother more than seven years ago. Within that prison, he sits within a cell and the sign—not far from the place where he spends his days—says Death Row. Someday this man will die for his crime. I would like to live—free of the cloud that he has placed over my life. . . .

"Someday in the future, the governor of Virginia will issue an order for the man to be executed. When that will be, I don't know. It could be months, it could be years; but I've almost grown used to the unknowing. When the time comes, I will take a journey—a journey to the place I can't forget."

Without consciously intending to, Maria had articulated her need to go to death row.

•    •    •    •

Maria continued to maintain an uneasy balance between her silent opposition to the death penalty and her loyalty to Jerry's family until the summer of 1996. It was an unbearably hot Kentucky summer day, and Maria and Ray decided to seek relief from the humidity by going to the movies. They chose *Dead Man Walking*. Maria knew the film was about the death penalty, but she didn't expect it to affect her personally.

She watched the entire movie without a strong emotional reaction, until the execution scene.

MARIA: After watching the execution scene, I began sobbing uncontrollably. Watching the cold and methodical way the state prepared to kill another person convinced me that there was no difference between state-sanctioned murder and what Dennis had done to Jerry. I knew I could not stay on the sidelines any longer. The next day I called George Edwards, a retired Presbyterian minister. George and his wife, Jean, are longtime activists for a lot of different social justice issues. I knew that they would know who was active in opposing the death penalty. George told me that the Kentucky Coalition to Abolish the Death Penalty (KCADP) met at their house. A couple of weeks later, I attended my first meeting.

In November, KCADP held a statewide meeting. I called the chairperson, Father Pat Delahanty, and asked if I could speak at the meeting. He said I could.

I wanted people to know that not all victims' family members supported the death penalty, but I wasn't sure what to say. I decided to read the essay I had written for my class. Many people came up to me after the meeting and told me how glad they were that I had joined them. Pat asked me if I would speak at a rally, to be held the following month, commemorating the twentieth anniversary of the reinstatement of the death penalty. At first I was nervous. I was afraid that if I spoke publicly word would get back to Virginia and it would stir up a hornet's nest, but I eventually agreed. I felt like I had to speak out.

On December 10, 1996, a large group of KCADP members gathered in the rotunda of the capitol. I spoke for about five minutes. Afterwards, a couple of reporters asked me questions.

I figured my family was going to find out sooner or later, so I decided just to send all of them copies of the essay I wrote. I didn't hear anything back until the following summer, when Ray and I were on vacation and met my nephew Justin for lunch. We briefly talked about the death penalty. He said he understood my position but disagreed with it. The lunch was cordial, so I thought maybe I had overestimated what their reaction would be.

•   •   •   •

As her participation in the abolition movement increased, Maria's curiosity about Dennis grew. She felt a strong desire to see the place where her brother's killer lived. She contacted the Virginia Capital Case Clearinghouse and learned that Dennis was at the Mecklenburg Correctional Center. For their spring vacation, Maria and Ray decided to stay at a cottage on Smith Mountain Lake in Virginia and make a day trip to Mecklenburg. Knowing nothing about prisons, they were unsure what to expect.

MARIA: One morning we woke up and decided to find Mecklenburg. We drove a couple of hours until we found the facility. We saw a lot of cars in the parking lot, so we decided to park there. Ray hadn't even turned off the engine when a guard drove up and yelled at us. I jumped out of the car and went over to him. I told him who I was and that I wanted to see the place where my brother's murderer lived. He wanted to know who the person was. I told him Dennis Eaton, and he confirmed that Dennis was there. We talked for a few minutes more, then he told us that we could not stay. I asked him if I could at least take a picture of the prison before I left. He said no, but then he said that if he continued on his rounds and was on the other side of the building, he wouldn't know if I had taken a picture. I took a quick picture and we left.

From there, Maria and Ray drove another hour or so to the Greensville Correctional Center, where the State of Virginia kills its condemned prisoners. This time they knew not to drive onto prison grounds. They took a picture from a distance and started the trip back, arriving at the cottage tired from driving several hundred miles.

They prepared dinner and turned on the television to watch the evening news. To their utter astonishment, the screen showed pictures of Jerry and Dennis. The story explained that Dennis had had a hearing that day. Along with a description of the court proceeding, the reporter gave details of the original crime, using Jerry's photograph as a visual image.

MARIA: It made me sad to see the picture of Jerry, but it was such a bizarre coincidence that we turned on the TV to a story about that case—it felt like some kind of portent.

In the days following that vacation, Maria pondered the trip to the prisons and wondered about Dennis Eaton. She knew that if the day ever arrived when he was executed, she would attend. She tried to imagine what it was like to spend your day in a small cell waiting to be killed.

MARIA: I disliked living with the specter of Dennis's execution always in the back of my mind. Part of me just wanted the case to be over with. But every time I thought about the case being over with, I knew that meant another person would be dead, and that meant another family would be left grieving.

•    •    •    •

During the summer of 1997, several events increased Maria's commitment to abolition of the death penalty. On July 1, the State of Kentucky executed

Harold McQueen, the first Kentuckian to be executed since reinstatement of the death penalty in 1976. Maria and Ray attended a demonstration at the prison on the night he was killed.

Soon after the execution, Ray and Maria left for vacation in Georgia. They again made arrangements to meet Justin for lunch. This time the visit was not pleasant.

**MARIA:** I'm not sure why the second visit with Justin went so poorly, but from the time that we greeted each other I could feel the tension. It continued throughout the meal. We returned to the Savannah Visitors' Center, where we had met before lunch. Feeling that I could no longer take the discomfort of the situation, only a few minutes after arriving there, I said that Ray and I must leave. As brief good-byes were exchanged, I could sense Justin's relief. I wondered what had happened over the past year to change his attitude so drastically.

On August 27, after twenty years, Maria retired from practicing psychotherapy. In November, she attended a conference in Chevy Chase, Maryland, sponsored by a group called Religious Organizing Against the Death Penalty. The four-day event, bringing religious people from around the country together to talk about the church's role in ending the death penalty, attracted hundreds of participants and featured dozens of workshops.

During one session, Maria sat next to Chuck Culhane, a man who had spent more than a decade on death row for a crime he did not commit. She told him about her brother's murder and how her decision to oppose the death penalty had created conflict within her family. She also told him that she wanted to reach out to Dennis Eaton but wasn't sure if she should. Chuck told Maria how much it had meant to him to receive letters when he was on death row, and he strongly encouraged her to contact Dennis.

Later in the conference, Maria met a professor named William Guymer who kept track of all of the prisoners on death row in Virginia. He gave Maria the name of Dennis's lawyer, Ross Haine.

The conference helped Maria to feel less alone. For the first time she was surrounded by people who opposed the death penalty, many of whom had experienced the loss of someone to murder. She felt she had found a community. Among the many people she met was Sister Helen Prejean, who had written the book *Dead Man Walking*, which was made into the movie that had inspired Maria to speak against the death penalty. She returned home with renewed energy and commitment. One of the first things she did was call Ross who gave her Dennis's address and urged her to contact him.

Maria wrote to Dennis, doubting that he would respond. She did not even know if he knew that Jerry Hines had a sister, since few of the newspaper articles reporting the murder mentioned her. Although she hoped to hear from him, she decided it did not matter whether he replied or not. Writing the letter was something she needed to do for herself.

Once she got started, the words flowed freely. "It is difficult to forgive someone who has hurt you so deeply but I believe that, for me, forgiveness is the only way. I grew up as a Catholic and, from my earliest years, learned the teachings of Jesus—the main one being that my life must be governed by love and forgiveness. Hell has been defined as the absence of love. With hatred instead of love in my heart, my life would be a living hell. So forgiving you is not only for you but also for me—for what it would do to my soul if I refused to forgive."

Maria heard nothing for many weeks and had given up on hearing back when a letter from Dennis arrived dated February 3, 1998. "I was very, very glad to hear from you," he began. "Please forgive me for my delay in answering your letter. I have had a lot of things on my mind. I didn't know that Jerry had a sister until Ross told me."

Dennis praised Maria for her courage in speaking out against the death penalty and complimented her on her career of public service. Then he told her about himself.

My parents' first child was still born, after their first still born, my parents had 10 other children, five girls and five boys, and I am the youngest. Father died when I was 17. My oldest brother was killed in an auto accident. My mother died in 1991 when I was here on death row. I have one brother and five sisters living. I was born on June 4, 1956. I have lived in Virginia all my life. I lived in a small town, Mt. Jackson, Virginia. I dropped out of high school after the 8th grade and started working in an orchard. I really regret dropping out of high school, I wish I would have stayed in school and finished high school. I worked in the orchard for 17 years. We grew apples, peaches and nectarines. I liked it outside. I like the outdoors. I like to write letters and I like to get letters. I like to draw. I make a lot of my own cards that I send to people. I am involved in a Church. I would like very much to continue to write to you if it is all right with you. I will tell you more about myself as I write to you. If there is anything I can do to help you in any way, please let me know. Thank you so very, very much for your prayers. Thank you again very, very much for writing to me. I pray and hope you will write back to me. You are in my thoughts and prayers. Take care and God bless.

Yours Truly,
Dennis.

Maria responded to Dennis's letter on March 12 by sending a St. Patrick's Day card. The card struck a chord with Maria because she sensed from Dennis's letter that he had experienced a genuine religious conversion—that he had had the snakes driven from his soul, so to speak, just as St. Patrick drove the snakes out of Ireland, symbolizing the conversion of the pagans to Christianity.

Around this time, Maria received another letter—this one from Jerry's children, accusing her of caring more for the man who murdered their father than for her own family. They told her they did not want to have any contact with her. She suspected that the children's mother, Carol, might have encouraged them to write it. The letter hurt her deeply; Maria did not have children of her own, and when Jerry was alive she had been close to her niece and nephews. She hoped that someday she could be close to them again. Maria decided that for now it was better not to answer the letter, thinking that a response would only aggravate the situation.

Dennis wrote a second letter, dated April 19. To her surprise, he asked Maria if she would consider visiting him in prison. He also asked her if she would witness the execution on his behalf.

MARIA: As soon as I read the letter, I knew that I would honor both his requests. I knew that I needed to do everything I could to support him. I wanted to. I looked upon it as an opportunity. I don't know if, at that point in time, I was also looking at it as a chance to make a statement about the death penalty, but I had already decided that I would attend the execution, and I felt better doing it on his behalf.

Things started to move quickly. In late April, Ross called Maria to tell her that the State of Virginia had set a date for Dennis's execution—June 18. On May 6, Maria wrote to Dennis telling him that she would visit him and attend his execution. Ross helped Maria get approval for a visit, and she and Ray made plans to travel to Virginia over Memorial Day weekend.

An enterprising reporter from the *Richmond Times Dispatch*, Frank Green, had learned of Maria's plans to visit her brother's killer. He contacted her and asked for an interview. Maria agreed. Although it was very painful that Jerry's children didn't want contact with her, at least she'd been freed from the constant worry that her public statements would alienate them. At the moment she felt a more pressing concern—trying to save Dennis's life. Maria didn't know if anything she said or did would make any difference, but she knew she had to try. She could not live with herself if she did not.

• • • •

Saturday, May 23, was a typical early summer day, hot and humid. Maria sweated nervously as she walked to the entrance of the Mecklenburg prison. She entered through a metal detector, then a guard patted her down. The officer told her she could not take anything inside with her. She asked permission to take her glasses, in case her contact lenses bothered her during the visit. The guard said no. He did allow her to carry a lightweight jacket to wear if she got chilled from the air-conditioning.

She said good-bye to Ray and Frank, who stayed behind in the waiting room. An armed guard escorted her to death row. He led her into a small room the size of a telephone booth with a thick Plexiglas window and a telephone.

Dennis had sent Maria a picture of himself, so she knew what he looked like. She watched as the guard escorted him in. He weighed about 250 pounds and was missing an eye. Dressed in blue prison-issue cotton pants and long-sleeved shirt, he had long brown hair pulled back in a ponytail, and a day's growth of whiskers darkened his face. He gave her a warm smile, picked up the receiver, and told her how happy he was to see her.

> **MARIA:** Any nervousness I felt soon left me. He was easy to talk to. Early in our visit, we started talking about religion.
>
> Dennis told me that right after his arrest, he had an experience that affected him deeply. He had been placed on suicide watch in the county jail with another man who was also charged with murder for killing his wife. The two of them talked about baptism and afterlife. They wrote letters to different ministers wanting to know whether a person who had been baptized would go to heaven if he killed himself. One minister wrote back, "Once a child of God, always a child of God." After getting the letter, Dennis's cellmate hanged himself. I was moved that he shared such a personal story with me.

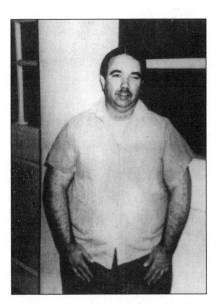

*Dennis Eaton being baptized in prison. Photograph provided by Maria Hines. Used with permission of Marilyn Kerstin, executor of his estate.*

I felt connected to him, even though we came from very different backgrounds. Dennis grew up in a poor family, the youngest of ten children who had very little attention growing up. I came from a middle-class family. Both of my parents were professionals. They expected me to go to college and then to graduate school. Dennis dropped out of high school in his first year. But still I felt like we had been close friends for a long time.

Dennis kept telling me how much it meant to him that I visited him. It made me feel very special. We talked for four hours. By the end of our visit, my ear hurt from holding the phone next to it for so long.

After the visit, Frank, the reporter, was filled with questions. I answered them as honestly as I could. I knew he was writing a big story about the execution, and I wanted to do everything I could to try to help Dennis. I hoped the story would help humanize him in the eyes of the public and increase his chances for clemency.

I had so many emotions to process from the visit, I needed time to contemplate all that had happened. I woke up really early the next morning and wrote down everything that we had talked about in my journal. This is part of that passage:

"It's five A.M. on Sunday, May 24, 1998. I woke up an hour or so ago. I was lying in bed, thinking about Dennis and our conversation when I visited him on death row for the first time yesterday. I was thinking, especially, about the fact that there was this instant rapport between us. I asked myself, 'How could this be? What is the common thread between us?' There is, of course, Jerry and his death, the event that caused our lives to intersect, but this didn't seem to be the answer.

". . . It is, I believe, what I would call spirituality—a spirituality based on the concept that love is the guiding force in our lives. I say spirituality because it couldn't be religion, since we are of different religious traditions—I, a Catholic, and Dennis, a born-again Christian—but we both value our spiritual lives.

"I realized the importance of his spiritual life to him when Dennis was telling me that, for a time after his conversion in prison, he found himself becoming filled with self-pity and that he was on the verge of becoming bitter. He realized, he said, that if he continued in this frame of mind he would 'lose his spiritual life.' He spoke often of love, saying more than once that he loves everyone, and this is reflected in his presence, although I don't mean his actual physical presence. He looks like a roly-poly teddy bear, his front teeth are missing, and he has only one eye, but there is a sense of peace and serenity about him that comes from within.

"He is to me a living example of redemption and the subsequent transformation that it brings into our lives. Many of us who are Christians take our redemption for granted because we have always been Christians and, thus, we aren't as aware of its effects. But in Dennis it is so evident."

I arrived early Sunday morning for the second visit. We only had two hours. As I knew it would, the issue of Jerry's murder finally came up. I knew that he had claimed at his trial that he did not kill Jerry. I told him that even if he hadn't killed Jerry, I still considered him to be responsible since he had been part of the circumstances that led up to Jerry being killed.

He told me he was very sorry. He said he wished that he could erase the past. I believed him. I knew he was a changed man. He was not the same person who took part in killing my brother.

He told me how he tried to spend his time in jail productively. He wrote letters to youths in detention centers urging them to change their lives. He made cards to send to family and friends. He remembered birthdays and anniversaries. He wanted to contribute something positive to the world, even though he was limited in what he could do.

Shortly after returning to Louisville, Maria received another letter from Dennis, dated May 24, 1998. In the four-page letter Dennis expressed his feelings about their visit:

I think a lot about the wonderful visits we had this weekend. I have so very, very many loving wonderful, beautiful memories of our wonderful visits this weekend. I am so glad and so very, very thankful that you came to visit me. We shared smiles, laughter, tears and so many other things with each other. As we both said, it is as if we have known each other all our lives. There is a very, very special place in my heart and in my life for you and there always will be. If you need to talk about anything, please feel free to talk to me. I am here for you and I will do everything I can to help you. If there is anything I can do for you, please let me know. I am so very, very glad you had a good time when you came to visit me. Thank you again so very, very much for the very, very wonderful visit this weekend.

Dennis also included a letter for Ray, thanking him for driving Maria to visit him and asking him to take care of her.

Please watch over her and protect her and take care of her so that no one or anything ever hurts her again. I thank you so very, very much for this and everything else that you do for her. Maria is one of the most loving, caring, courageous people that I have the honor of meeting and knowing. Thank you so very, very much for all the help and support that you give Maria. Please take care of yourself and Maria. You and Maria are in my thoughts and prayers. Take care and God Bless.

Love,
Dennis.

    •    •    •    •

Resolved to do all that she could for Dennis, Maria called Ross Haine and asked to attend Dennis's clemency hearing. She wanted to let the parole board officials know that not every member of Jerry's family wanted to see him killed. Maria also asked Ross if he could help her get permission to serve as a spiritual advisor for Dennis. In that capacity, she would be permitted to spend the day of the execution with him right up until the very end.

Larry Traylor, spokesperson for the Department of Corrections, refused both requests. The clemency hearing, he said, was "for lawyers only"; Maria wondered if he would have given her the same answer if she had supported, instead of opposing, Dennis's execution. He denied Maria's request to be Dennis's spiritual advisor on the grounds that he already had two, even though Virginia law permitted a condemned person to have as many as seven. The Department of Corrections was not there to "support" people, he said; the State of Virginia had an execution to carry out and could not allow any disruptions. Clearly, Maria was perceived as a "disruption."

The irony of the situation was that the law allowed Maria to witness the execution as a family member of the victim. However, as such she would be required to watch from the "family witness room," and this would have been very uncomfortable because Carol and Justin were planning to be there. It would be hard for Maria to be in the room with them knowing that they supported the execution.

Another concern for Maria was that the family witness room had a one-way glass window, so the person being killed could not see the witnesses. As Dennis's spiritual advisor, Maria would have watched the execution from the condemned person's room, which had two-way glass. Under the circumstances, Maria decided not to witness.

Two weeks later, Maria and Ray made the long drive to Virginia again. The execution was scheduled for June 18, but Maria wanted to go a few days early to visit Dennis and take part in some opposition events. On Tuesday, June 16, she attended a press conference in Richmond organized by Virginians for Alternatives to the Death Penalty where she met a woman named Leigh Eason whose uncle, also a police officer, had been killed in the line of duty. Like Maria, Leigh opposed the death penalty.

By the time of the press conference, the media knew about the rift within Maria's family around Dennis's execution. The story had a soap-opera quality to it—"family torn over whether to execute their loved one's killer." It seemed to Maria that reporters only wanted to write about the family tension and were not particularly interested in why she believed Dennis should not be executed.

MARIA: Throughout the press conference, reporters kept asking me one question after another about my family. Was it true that we disagreed?

Was it true that we were not on speaking terms? I just kept repeating, "I am not going to talk about that issue. That is a private family matter." However, at one point a reporter really egged me on. He asked me if it was true what my nephew Justin said, that he guessed that next I would be a guest on the Oprah Winfrey show and get a book deal. I had to answer that question because nothing could have been further from the truth. When I first decided to speak against the death penalty I realized that position might give me the opportunity to speak publicly, which also might bring with it the opportunity for remuneration. I vowed that I would never accept any financial gain from my brother's murder. If someone or some organization paid me honoraria, I donated the money to charity.

That question really shook me up because it made me see the lengths Jerry's family was willing to go to discredit me. I managed to make it through the press conference, but I was deeply shaken.

With the press conference behind her, Maria's main focus was to give Dennis as much emotional support as possible to help him face his death. Although the prison officials had denied her request to be Dennis's spiritual advisor, they did agree to let her visit Dennis with the two women who were serving in that capacity, Marilyn Kerstin and Liz Fiene. They had become close friends to Dennis during his time in prison.

MARIA: Although I felt that I had to be in Virginia to support Dennis and to protest his execution, I dreaded the next few days. In all my years as a nun and a therapist, I had never counseled a man facing execution. I had been praying that his life would be spared, but I didn't think that would happen. Mostly I just asked God for the strength to help me support Dennis and face whatever else was to come.

On the morning of June 17, Maria, Marilyn, and Liz boarded a van to go to the death house, where Virginia's condemned prisoners spend the final days before the lethal poisons are injected into their veins. (Because of security concerns, Virginia, like many other states, built its death chambers in a location separate from its regular prison facilities.) During the last forty-eight hours, prisoners are placed under suicide watch and held in a small room adjacent to the room where the execution will take place.

The visiting booth at the death house was similar to the other one Maria had been in, two small rooms separated by a thick Plexiglas wall. It had two telephones on the visitor side, so the three women took turns talking to Dennis.

Liz and Maria spoke with Dennis first, and Marilyn sat in a waiting area. A phone rang on the wall nearby. Unsure what to do, Marilyn answered it. The person on the other end said that she was calling from the Bon Marche department store to tell her about a sale. Between gasps of laughter Marilyn said, "I don't know how you got this number, ma'am, but you're calling the death house at the Greensville Correctional Facility. I don't think we'll be buying anything today." When the others heard the story, they all had a good laugh.

Before she left the prison, Dennis told Maria that he would call her the next day. Although they knew it was unlikely, both held out hope for a stay of his execution. Maria spent most of the next twenty-four hours talking to reporters. Many wanted to arrange for interviews with her after the execution. When she found the time, she prayed.

At four o'clock the next afternoon, Dennis called Maria at her hotel room. They still hadn't heard whether the governor had granted clemency, but both thought it would be their last conversation.

MARIA: It was strange talking to someone knowing that it would be the last time you ever spoke with him. In spite of the fact that he was facing his own execution in a few hours, Dennis spent the conversation counseling me instead of the other way around. He thanked me for making the effort to get to know him and for trying to help save his life. He asked me to thank Ray for driving me to Virginia to visit him. He told me to keep fighting for what I believe in. Then he said something that really struck me: "This started in tragedy and is ending in tragedy, but I'm glad I got to know you."

I thanked him and told him that even though I wouldn't be witnessing his execution, I would be with him in spirit. He said, "And I'll always be with you in spirit whenever you give death penalty talks." Before he hung up he told me that he loved me, and I said, "I love you, too, Dennis." Two hours after this conversation, I learned that the governor had denied his last appeal.

Ray and I drove to the prison. A small group of protesters had organized a vigil, and we wanted to be there for it and to be available to speak to the press. I knew that Carol and Justin were going to be watching the execution. When we got to the prison I wondered if they were already inside. I really hoped that I would not run into them.

While Maria stood outside the prison, Carol and Justin arrived, escorted by a Virginia state trooper, in an official state vehicle. The two were taken into the prison, where they were introduced to members of the governor's staff, prison officials, and state police officials. The prison provided food and drinks for the guests while they waited. When the appointed hour arrived, prison guards escorted them into the witness room.

A small group began gathering in the field next to the prison. Most of the participants attended every execution and were actively involved in opposing the death penalty in Virginia. Henry Heller from Virginians for Alternatives to the Death Penalty organized the event. Mary Allen, whom Maria had met at the religious organizing conference in Chevy Chase, came to support her.

Reporters surrounded the group recording Maria, the sister who fought to save the life of her brother's murderer. The group tried not to let the media divert their attention, but the flashing cameras and hovering reporters affected the atmosphere. Maria thought about asking the reporters to leave but decided that the benefits of media coverage outweighed the disruption to their vigil.

The group learned that Dennis had died at 9:09 and that his body would soon be removed from the prison and taken to a nearby funeral home. People spread out on both sides of the road waiting for the undertaker's large black station wagon to drive by.

MARIA: When the hearse drove by I thought about Dennis. I said a prayer for him and also for Jerry, Carol, and the kids. I hoped that the execution brought them peace.

The next day Ray and Maria drove to Lynchburg, Virginia, to attend a memorial service for Dennis. Marilyn had organized the service, held at a small United Church of Christ church with which she was affiliated.

MARIA: We arrived early, and while we were waiting for the service to begin, a young man and an elderly woman arrived together. Marilyn told us that the man was David, Dennis's twenty-three-year-old nephew, and the woman was a family friend who had known Dennis. We approached

David and told him we were sorry for his loss. He thanked us and said the same to me.

It was a special time for me, made even more so by the fact that I was able to express personally my sympathy to the Eaton family. In doing so, I felt that forgiveness and reconciliation had come full circle.

The short service lasted only about thirty minutes. Marilyn and Maria made a few remarks, and Ray read a poem he had written. Afterwards, the small group shared refreshments.

Maria and Ray headed to Bristol, Virginia, the next day to attend Maria's fiftieth high school reunion weekend. The festivities had begun on Friday; Maria and Ray missed the first night because of the memorial service but arrived in time to attend the main event, the Saturday night banquet. There, they met up with Maria's best friend and her husband.

MARIA: As soon as I arrived, I felt uncomfortable. People at the table didn't smile or act excited to see me. My friend was nice, but I sensed something was wrong.

After dinner, I called my aunt who lived in Bristol. I mentioned to her that people were acting really coldly towards me. She said, "Oh honey, I am so sorry." I asked her what she meant. She said, "You mean you didn't see the article?" She told me that the Bristol paper printed a front-page story, "Family Divided over Execution." The article had quotes from a number of my family members. One cousin was quoted as saying, "The family isn't really divided. It is forty to one. Maria is the only person who opposed the execution." The last sentence of the story was a quote from Justin, "We don't consider her as part of our family anymore." I realized why everyone was treating me like a pariah. As soon as I got back to the table I told Ray, and we left immediately.

• • • •

A week later, back in Louisville, a large manila envelope with a return address from Mecklenburg prison arrived in the mail. The package contained several items, including a homemade anniversary card from Dennis. He had drawn two large hearts intertwined with a padlock; one said MARIA, the other said RAY. On the back of the undated card Dennis had written:

Dear Maria and Ray,

I send all my love to you as always. I hope you have a very, very wonderful loving Happy Anniversary that is filled with love, joy, happiness, beautiful memories and everything else wonderful and beautiful. There are so very, very many loving wonderful beautiful Happy Anniversary Wishes in this card for you. Happy Anniversary to a wonderful couple. I am thinking of you with love. Take care and God Bless. Happy Anniversary.

Love,<br>Dennis.

The package also contained a picture of Dennis as a baby and a picture of his grandmother.

**MARIA:** I couldn't believe that Dennis had remembered that Ray and I were celebrating our wedding anniversary. He went to all the trouble of making the card and arranging for it to be mailed after his death so we would get it in time. Most of our friends didn't even remember our anniversary, but here was Dennis, in his last days, making us a card. I felt sad to think about what the world lost when we killed him. By the time of his death, Dennis was a changed man who had a lot of love to give.

•    •    •    •

In February 1999, nearly ten years after Jerry's death, and nine months after Dennis's execution, Maria spoke at a training session in Louisville organized by COPS. The annual event brought together members of COPS to speak to police officers in training about what it is like to lose a family member. Maria reluctantly accepted the invitation to speak.

**MARIA:** Normally I welcome any opportunity to tell my story, but part of my story is my opposition to the death penalty. I did not feel that I could tell my story without speaking against the death penalty.

I had attended a number of COPS events over the years and never felt comfortable speaking against the death penalty at them. When I got the invitation to speak at the event, I asked Pat Delahanty, and he told me I should do it. Another reason why I accepted was that Sharon Story was the scheduled moderator, not Suzie Sawyer. Sharon was the past president of COPS, and she lived in Virginia, so I figured she must have read or heard the coverage of Dennis's execution and therefore knew that I opposed the death penalty. If Sharon knew I opposed the death penalty and had invited me to speak, then it must be okay for me to talk about the death penalty.

On February 1, I walked into the conference room at the Executive Inn in Louisville, and my heart stopped when I saw Suzie Sawyer. I panicked and thought to myself that I could leave before anyone saw me. But then I thought that Sharon must have talked to Suzie about Dennis's case, so Suzie must also know that I had been speaking publicly against the death penalty.

When I walked into the room, Suzie was talking with the other panelists: the first lady of Kentucky, Judi Patton; a retired judge, Armand Angelucci; and the judge's wife, Joyce. When she saw me, Suzie walked over to say hello.

In the interest of full disclosure I wanted to make absolutely sure that Suzie knew where I was coming from. I said, "I think you already know this, but I just wanted to make sure that you knew that I oppose the death penalty and asked Governor Gilmore to grant clemency to Dennis Eaton."

She looked at me with complete surprise and said, "No, I certainly did not know that," and the tone in her voice implied that if she *had* known, she never would have invited me to speak. I thought about offering to step down from the panel but then thought that if she wanted me to do that she could ask me herself. I thought she might ask me not to talk about the death penalty, but there was a pause, and I waited, and she said, "You know these are cops and they will be very upset with you." I said that I understood. Then she said, "I am really afraid of what their reaction will be." Again I nodded that I understood. I think she kept hoping I'd offer not to speak, but I didn't, so she said, "Well, I wouldn't say too much about the death penalty." I nodded.

As it turned out, I was the third panelist, so I had some time to prepare my thoughts before speaking. I decided that I would just start my remarks with a general disclaimer. I said that my opinions did not reflect the opinions of COPS. I then told my story, which took about ten minutes. When I was finished, the audience applauded politely.

Judge Angelucci, who was a former prosecutor, spoke next. His son, a Kentucky state trooper, had been killed in the line of duty. He began by saying that as far as he was concerned the cop killers could die. The audience burst into applause. Some people even stood up to clap.

The last speaker was the judge's wife. She told the story of her son's murder from a more personal perspective than her husband. I felt very moved when she said that she still visits her son's grave daily, even though he died the same year as Jerry.

Suzie opened the panel up for questions from the audience. Two people asked the judge questions. The next question came from a dark-haired woman, one of the people who had earlier given the judge a standing ovation. She said, "Ms. Hines, I admire your forgiveness. I'm a Christian, but I'm just not where you are yet." I thought that this would be a time to really get into issues of forgiveness, but before I even had a chance to say anything, Suzie interrupted me and said, "It's been a long day. Why don't we close now?" It was only four-thirty, and the panel had been scheduled until five o'clock.

As the group broke up, several people in the audience approached me. A police chaplain quietly told me that he, too, opposed the death penalty. Another person said, "I admire your courage." I sought out the dark-haired lady and asked her if I could give her a hug. I said, "It's okay to be where you are."

The next day, Maria flew to Cincinnati. Ohio was getting ready to conduct its first execution since 1976, and she had been invited to speak at a demonstration opposing it. To prepare herself for the execution, she attended mass.

MARIA:  I was still thinking a lot about the COPS talk and feeling uncomfortable about it. During the sermon, the priest told the story about Jesus telling the apostles and disciples that if you go into a village to preach and you are not accepted, "shake the dust from your feet" and move on. That story resonated with me. I thought, "If COPS doesn't want to hear my story, I'll move on and tell it to those who do."

·    ·    ·    ·

In March 2000, the clothing company Benetton ran a controversial ad campaign featuring men on death row from around the country. An Italian businessman and abolitionist known for his in-your-face advertising, Benetton bought space in several major national publications. The ads were large black-

and-white photographs of people on death row with brief captions describing them. The pictures both glamorized and humanized the inmates and many found this offensive. Because Kentucky prisons give relatively easy access to death row, six of the ads used men from there; one of them had murdered a police officer.

Several victims' organizations encouraged members to boycott Benetton products. Suzie Sawyer wrote an article in the COPS newsletter in support of the boycott, saying: "Regardless of one's view about the death penalty, Concerns of Police Survivors feels sure everyone will find this campaign to be despicably insensitive for victims and their surviving families."

Reading the article, Maria thought that perhaps Suzie now understood what it felt like when society disregarded your feelings. She seized the moment and wrote a letter to Suzie:

I have told you in the past all that COPS has meant to me and how I feel that the organization literally helped save my life after I was diagnosed with cancer a year after Jerry's death. It was at my first COPS Police Week activities in 1990 that my physical and emotional healing began, and for this I will be eternally grateful.

My involvement with COPS always had its conflicted side, however. When I would hear announcements regarding cop-killer trials at meetings—announcements that gave the clear message that the policy of COPS is that "Cop-killers must fry"—I would cringe inside. It was conflicting because, with much soul-searching, I had come to a place where my conscience told me that any killing is wrong. I felt at times like walking away from COPS but, at the same time, desperately needed it, so I sat there and suffered in silence as I listened.

I am saying all of this now because of my personal knowledge of other individuals who have not become involved with COPS for this very reason. COPS, as I have indicated, has much to offer those of us in law enforcement families—more than I could ever adequately express—but its policy on the death penalty is as offensive to some of us as the Benetton ad was to many other murder victims' family members. I believe that COPS' position on the death penalty is, in the words of the COPS article, "despicably insensitive" to some law enforcement families. I want to thank you for all you have done in the past for me and many others. In closing, I only ask that, in the future, you "tread softly" on the feelings of those who may disagree with your point of view.

• • • •

Maria continues her abolition work in Kentucky. She has come a long way from the timid woman in 1990 who was afraid to tell anyone she opposed the death penalty. She now testifies in front of the Kentucky legislature in favor of repeal bills that have been introduced during the last several sessions. In her testimony, she explains the relationship between forgiveness and the death penalty:

> I want to comment on the relationship, as I see it, between forgiveness and the death penalty, because I believe that, before the death penalty can be abolished in this country, we must become a nation of forgiveness. Instead we are to a great extent a nation of vengeance, with so many of us having the need for revenge. In a word, if someone wrongs us, we want to do the same thing back.
>
> I have observed other murder victims' family members who seem to be filled with vengeance. They say that when the person who did this to their loved one is killed, they will feel better and will find closure. To say, however, that vengeance and closure can exist together is a contradiction in terms because the other side of the coin of vengeance is anger, and as long as we hold on to our anger, our grieving isn't over. It's over only when we come to the stage of acceptance and understanding, which may, in turn, lead to forgiveness. It is only then that we can find the peace we are seeking. For when we have forgiven, we truly have no need to kill.

The healing and reconciliation Maria achieved with Dennis have so far eluded her with her family. She still has no contact with Carol and Jerry's children. She recently attended the funeral of a distant cousin with whom she had been close, but most family members ignored her.

During a trip to Ohio, Maria stayed with Marilyn, one of Dennis's spiritual advisors and the executor of his "estate." He had had his ashes sent to her, and she had scattered them in her backyard and made a small garden and memorial to him there. Maria spent time meditating in the garden, reflecting upon all that had transpired with Dennis.

MARIA: It is strange to me that it is harder for me to find forgiveness within my own family than with the man who killed my beloved brother. But miracles do occur. Although nothing can compensate for losing Jerry, I have gained much also. Perhaps the greatest gift is the sense of my own integrity for having stood up for what I believed in, but I also count among my blessings the many people whom I would never have met had this not happened. In life, there are always things lost and things gained. For those lost in my life, I console myself with these words: "Grief is the price we pay for love."

# CHAPTER 3

# The Last Party

The summer sun scorched Houston on Sunday, June 12, 1983. To escape the heat, Debbie Thornton attended a pool party at her apartment complex. Outgoing and attractive, Debbie normally liked to go to parties, but this day she was upset, having argued with her husband, Richard, earlier. When she left for the party, Richard angrily told Debbie not to come home that night. She made arrangements for a friend to take care of her twelve-year-old son, Bucky, and her stepdaughter, Kate, then stuffed a green dress and large hair rollers into an overnight bag before leaving the house.

Debbie, a five-foot, nine-inch blonde who weighed 111 pounds, was accustomed to male attention. Besides being good-looking, she was kind and friendly and got along well with most people. So it was not surprising that she struck up a conversation with Jerry Lynn Dean at the party. At five-seven, Jerry weighed 142 pounds, sported a mustache, and had long blond hair. He invited Debbie to spend the night with him. Still upset from the fight with her husband, she agreed and followed Jerry to his home at the Windtree Apartments in the Oak Forest section of Houston. She was driving her blue pickup truck, which sported vanity plates with her name.

That same evening in a different part of town, another party was in full swing at the home of Karla Faye Tucker. Though the façade of the three-bedroom house looked ordinary enough, its occupants lived unconventional lives. Karla Faye shared one room of the house with her lover, Danny Garrett; Karla's sister, Kari Tucker Burrell, lived in a second room; and Kari's ex-husband, Ronnie Burrell, lived in a third. Jimmy Liebrant, although not an official occupant, spent most of his time there because he and Ronnie ran an illegal drug operation selling amphetamines out of the house.

Karla and Kari made their living as prostitutes, having learned the trade from their mother, Carolyn. Servicing a high-class clientele, Carolyn had made enough money to support her children, have a nice house, and wear fine clothes. Although she loved her daughters, Carolyn failed to provide them with a stable home environment. Karla first smoked pot at age eight and by eleven was addicted to heroin. She shot up any drug or ate any pill she could.

At age thirteen, Karla left home after attending an Allman Brothers concert with her mother and sister. With her mother's permission, she traveled the country as a roadie with the band, exchanging sex for drugs and other favors. She did not go to school regularly and dropped out after failing seventh grade three times. When she turned sixteen, she got married; it didn't last.

Partying was a way of life at 2205 McKean, but that weekend the occupants pushed beyond their normal limits. Kari's birthday was June 11, and the celebration began on the tenth and lasted through the weekend. A constant stream of people entered and left the house. Karla, Danny, and Kari drank tequila, shot crystal meth, and popped pills for three days. By Sunday night, Karla was hyper from lack of sleep and constant drug use. She was itching to get out of the house. She and Danny concocted a plan to break into Jerry Lynn Dean's house to steal motorcycle parts. Karla loved motorcycles and one of her goals was to have a Harley-Davidson. Jerry, also a motorcycle enthusiast, had a Harley.

Jerry was married to, but separated from, Shawn, Karla's best friend. Karla justified stealing from Jerry because the two had been feuding for several weeks after Karla and Shawn used Jerry's ATM card to go on a shopping spree. When Jerry found out, he threatened to bring charges against Shawn and to "get Karla" by burning her face with acid. Stealing from Jerry was Karla's way of getting back at him for his threat. Since she had keys to his house, it would be easy to get inside.

So Danny grabbed a .38-caliber pistol and a pair of gloves, and he, Karla, and Jimmy Liebrant drove in Danny's blue Ranchero to Jerry's apartment. Karla thought Jerry might not be at home. She and Danny agreed to go inside and scope things out while Jimmy cased the building from the outside.

Danny and Karla let themselves into the apartment with the keys and heard Jerry call out, half asleep, "Who's there?" They walked into Jerry's bedroom, where he lay naked on a mattress on the floor. A variety of tools that Jerry used for his job laying cable were scattered around the room: ladders, a hammer, assorted garden tools, and a pickax. The motorcycle and all its pieces occupied the living room.

By now it was early morning, somewhere between three and four A.M. Karla jumped on top of Jerry and sat on his chest. Recognizing her, Jerry said,

"Come on, Karla, we can work this out. I didn't press charges against Shawn."
Karla replied, "Don't move, motherfucker, or you're dead." Jerry grabbed
Karla's arms to defend himself, but Danny struck Jerry's head with so much
force that it disconnected from his neck. Danny then left the room in search
of motorcycle parts, leaving Jerry unconscious and lying face down on the
mattress, dying. He made loud gurgling noises as blood and other body flu-
ids filled his breathing passages.

Karla stayed behind in the bedroom, riveted to a spot on the mattress. She
couldn't stand listening to the sounds of Jerry dying. Murder had not been
part of the plan, but once set in motion, death continued inexorably toward
its natural conclusion. She stood up and turned on the overhead light and saw
a four-foot-long pickax with a two-foot-long iron head lying against the wall.
Karla grabbed the ax and struck Jerry in the back.

By this time, Jimmy had joined Karla and Danny inside the apartment. As
he walked into the bedroom to check on Karla, he saw her wiggling the ax
back and forth in an effort to dislodge it from Jerry's back. When she succeeded, she smiled at Jimmy, then brought the ax down with full force on
Jerry's head. Jimmy left the room, remarking that he "hadn't signed up for
this." Karla kept striking Jerry until the gurgling stopped for good. Jimmy
wanted nothing to do with murder, so he called Ronnie Burrell, who came
and picked him up.

After finishing with Jerry, Karla noticed another person huddled against
the wall under a sheet, shaking in terror. She struck at the body, burying the
ax in the unknown flesh. A terrified Debbie Thornton emerged from under
the covers and grabbed at the ax trying to wrestle it away from Karla. Danny
returned to the bedroom, separated the women, and took the ax from Karla,
who then left the bedroom. A few minutes later, Karla returned to find Danny
standing over the woman, who pleaded, "Oh God, if you are going to kill me,
please hurry up, it hurts." Danny kicked Debbie in the head and pulled the ax
out of her shoulder. As she lay on her back, exposed, he plunged it into her
heart. Danny and Karla left the bedroom, grabbed the Harley frame from the
living room, got in the Ranchero, and drove home just as the sun was starting
to rise.

· · · ·

On the afternoon of June 13, Debbie Thornton's brother, Ron Carlson, was at
home unwinding after work. His wife, also named Debbie, was in the kitchen

*Ron Carlson. Photograph by Rachel King.*

cooking. The phone rang, and Debbie answered it. It was Bill List, Ron's biological father. Debbie passed the phone to Ron and, without saying hello, Bill said, "Ronnie, you need to come out to the shop right now. The police contacted me, and they have reason to believe that your sister has been murdered." Bill hung up the phone, leaving Ron stunned.

**RON:** My first thought was *This is a sick joke.* Bill was always pressuring me to visit him, and I thought this might be another lie to get me to go by his shop. I told Debbie about the conversation, and she told me I had to call back and find out what was going on. I called back and said, "Bill, this is Ronnie, what the hell is going on?" Bill said the same thing again. "We have reason to believe that your sister has been murdered. You need to come to the shop right now. The Houston police department called me to tell me that a woman has been murdered who they think is Debbie, and they are bringing a picture over for me to identify."

Getting news like that over the phone is the most unnatural thing you can imagine. It was like somebody taking their fist and for no apparent reason just knocking you upside the head. I drove to Bill's shop. He had a business manufacturing gooseneck trailers, large rigs designed for hauling heavy loads. My sister and I had both worked for Bill at various times. I walked into his office, and he stood there holding a Canadian Club and Seven Up in one hand and sucking on a Pall Mall nonfiltered in the other. The ashtray was filled with cigarette butts, and he was obviously drunk.

I didn't like being around Bill under the best of circumstances, and these were not the best of circumstances. Bill and my mother divorced when I was three years old. My mother remarried, a very nice man named Homer Carlson. My mother died when I was young, and Homer raised us. I never even met Bill until I was eleven.

Bill is rich, and he used his wealth to exploit other people. He was notorious for picking up children and bringing them to his house to do chores for him, which sometimes included sexual favors. Plus, he was mean.

I was very close to my sister because in many ways she was like a mother to me. Debbie used to take care of me while Homer worked the second and third shifts to make enough money to support us. Losing Debbie felt like losing my mother again.

I felt uncomfortable waiting for the police to arrive. I still wasn't entirely sure I believed Bill. He often lied to get what he wanted. I fixed myself a drink and fixed Bill another drink and sat down in the chair I used to sit in when I worked for Bill. It was the same chair Debbie sat in when she worked for Bill. We didn't say a whole lot, just sat there for about twenty or thirty minutes, waiting for the police to arrive.

Finally an officer from the Houston police department arrived with a Polaroid snapshot in hand. He showed it to Bill, and Bill said, "Yes, that's her." I said, "I want to see it. I want to make sure it's my sister." Bill said, "No, Ron, you don't want to see it." The officer agreed with Bill and did not show me the photograph.

·   ·   ·   ·

The grotesque facts of what became known as the "pickax case" captured widespread media attention and dominated the news for weeks.

RON: Whenever there was a development in the case, the media always flashed a picture of the police removing Debbie's body from the crime scene. I know it hurt me, and it hurts other family members, too. I must have seen those bodies wheeled out of that apartment a thousand times. They kept showing it over and over, every day.

Given that Debbie and her husband, Richard, had quarreled the evening before Debbie was found murdered in bed with another man, the police considered Richard an obvious suspect, but further investigation quickly disproved that theory. The police also suspected that Bill List might have killed Debbie or arranged for her to be murdered because she had been subpoenaed by the IRS to testify against him at a tax evasion hearing.

At 2205 McLean Street, Danny and Karla resumed their lives, convinced the police would not catch them. Neither tried to hide their involvement in the murder; in fact, they bragged about it. Once, while watching the evening news, Karla saw a story about the murder and gleefully remarked that she was "spectacular." Karla's behavior disturbed Kari greatly. She confided in Danny's brother, Douglas, and the two decided to go to the police. Douglas called the Houston police and asked for Officer J. C. Mosier, a childhood friend. He told J. C. that a friend of his and his brother had information about the case. J. C. asked, "What kind of information?" Douglas said, "They did it."

J. C. arranged for Douglas to wear a microphone and try to record a conversation with Karla and Danny. On Sunday, July 20, five weeks after the murder, Douglas showed up at 2205 McKean. Karla and Danny were lying in bed together, resting before Danny left for his job as a bartender. Trying to act as natural as possible, Douglas told them that the police had been asking him questions. He said that he had dreamed of people coming after him with guns. He began to cry. Karla and Danny reassured Douglas that the police didn't have anything on them.

Douglas asked them if they had planned to kill Jerry when they went to his apartment. They said no, they just "freaked." He asked why they used the pickax. They answered, "Because it was there." Karla had previously bragged that she experienced an orgasm each time she struck the bodies with the ax. Douglas asked her if it was true that she "got a nut" from the killings, and Karla replied, "Well, hell, yes." Douglas got up to leave, and Karla walked him to his motorcycle and hugged him good-bye. Within the hour, the Houston police arrived with a warrant to arrest Karla and Danny. Both were charged with capital murder.

•　　•　　•　　•

Nine months later, April 11, 1984, the trial of the State of Texas versus Karla Faye Tucker began. The state's case against Karla was strong. Jimmy told the jury how he had seen Karla wielding the pickax and about the smile on her face as she delivered the final blow. Kari testified about helping Karla dispose of the evidence and about how Karla bragged about the killings and threatened to kill again. She quoted Karla telling her what she had said to Jerry, "Don't move, motherfucker, or you're dead."

In fact, the evidence against Karla was so strong that her own attorney, Mack Arnold, told the jury in his closing argument, "The evidence is overwhelming that my client is guilty of capital murder, and I think it would be an injustice for you to arrive at any other verdict." He knew his client would be convicted; he could only try to convince the jury to spare her life. He hoped that his brutal honesty during his closing argument would help his credibility with the jury for the penalty phase of the trial. It took the jury only seventy minutes to deliver its guilty verdict, which was still longer than most people thought it would take.

At the sentencing trial, Mack called three witnesses—a psychiatrist and Karla's grandparents. The psychiatrist testified that Karla had good prospects for rehabilitation, but on cross-examination she could not offer compelling reasons why the jury should not sentence Karla to death. Karla's grandmother, through tears, told the jury that she wanted to help her granddaughter lead a better life. Karla's grandfather asked the jury to spare his granddaughter's life, but even he admitted that he would be "asking for justice" if his offspring were the victim.

The witnesses did not provide the jury with much reason to spare Karla's life. Mack Arnold decided his only hope was Karla herself. He called her to the stand.

Karla had changed significantly during her time in prison. For the first time since she was a young girl, she was clean and sober. She had started attending Bible classes, educating herself, and making crafts for friends and fellow inmates. Gone was the bravado of the young woman who bragged about killing two people.

Karla gave heart-wrenching testimony about her life—drug use as a child, prostitution, traveling with the band, and marrying in her teens. She admitted her guilt in the crime and accepted responsibility for her actions. She summed up her testimony by saying she did not deserve mercy and didn't know what she could possibly do to make up for what she had done. On cross-examination, prosecutor Joe Magliolo asked her if she deserved the death penalty. Karla answered, "I don't know."

In his closing arguments, the prosecutor posed the same question to the jury. Did Karla deserve the death penalty? In answer, he pressed a button on a tape recorder and played the tape Douglas had secretly recorded. The jury heard Karla saying in a drunken, slurred voice, "Well, hell, yes." It took the jury three hours to sentence her to death.

After her conviction, prosecutors asked Karla to testify against Danny, even though they offered her nothing in return. The state's case against Danny was not as strong as it was against Karla. Karla agreed to testify, saying that "it was the right thing to do" because the jury deserved to know "the truth about what happened." Karla's testimony helped convict Danny, who was also sentenced to death.

Ron did not attend the trials; he could not afford to take time off from his job at Samco Enterprises, where he worked as a lead man in charge of a crew manufacturing compressor valve parts. His wife, Debbie, attended nearly every day and kept him abreast of the progress. What she saw bothered her greatly. She told Ron that Karla and Danny "were not nice people."

Ron managed to attend court the very last day of Danny's trial, the day the jury sentenced him to death. Someone from the prosecutor's office said to Ron, "We got the death penalty for the people who killed your sister. Is that what you wanted?" Ron replied, "I guess they got what they deserved."

RON: At that time I thought Karla and Danny deserved to die. I was in so much emotional pain that I could barely cope. I felt alone in the world. I was drinking and doing drugs. I felt an insurmountable mountain of grief. Then, to add to everything else, that October during Danny Garrett's trial, Bill was murdered. I was not really surprised that someone murdered Bill. He treated his customers like garbage. He drank like a fish. He fired people on the spot. To be quite honest, he was a sorry drunk, a slob. Anybody that knew him would agree with what I just said. He didn't know when to stop. He used everybody.

Bill hung out in the Montrose area of Houston and frequently picked up male prostitutes. He'd take them to his house and then treat them very badly. He would allow them to live with him for a short time in exchange for sexual favors. He also forced them to clean up after him, doing his cooking, washing dishes, washing his clothes and cleaning his house. At that time he had four young prostitutes living with him, ages fourteen through eighteen. The oldest was a kid named Elbert "Smiley" Homan. Smiley felt that Bill didn't deserve to live because of the way he treated his friends, so he shot and killed him.

Although I didn't really like Bill, his murder still shook me up. I couldn't believe that I'd lost both my sister and father. There was no one left in my family. Everyone was dead.

I was very angry. I didn't like the person I was becoming. I felt that if I had the opportunity and it was possible, I would kill those who had killed my family. I wanted to take that same pickax and leave it in the heart of Karla Faye Tucker, and I wanted to take that same shotgun and blow off Elbert Homan's head. I wanted revenge—I wanted to kill them with my own hands. Of course, I knew I didn't have the opportunity to kill them, so it was all just fantasy, but I also soon realized that I had lowered myself to their standards. I had become a person who would kill. I had gotten so mean and nasty I didn't care about anybody or anything. I gave my wife a very hard time. She stayed with me because she loves me, but at times I didn't know why.

My days were pretty much all the same. I'd get up in the morning and start my day with a joint. I'd go to work high and stay high. I'd drink and smoke pot during lunch, and as soon as I left work I was smoking another joint and drinking more beer. I basically never came down. As soon as I started to come down I'd get high again. I wasn't really living, just existing. Over all those years, I changed jobs, but I never got fired. I don't know how I ever managed to keep a job, but I always did. I must have had a guardian angel or something watching over me.

My life continued this way for years, and then toward the end of 1989 I got a call from Randy, my dealer, and he told me he had something for me. I thought he meant he had some good drugs, so I told him to come by. He got to my house and handed me a brown paper bag and said, "This belonged to your father. I think you should have it."

I opened the bag and saw a Bible and three audiotapes. I opened the Bible and looked in the front. It was signed, "Given to William Gerald List by Dr. Steven Harris," and next to the signature was a telephone number. There was also a list of certain books in the Bible to read. Randy, who also knew Bill, explained that after Bill's murder a lot of people had ransacked Bill's house looking for stuff to take. Randy took those things because he thought I'd want them.

I was having such a hard time that I was desperate enough to try anything, even religion. On New Year's Eve 1989, I got down on my knees and prayed the sinner's prayer. I said, "Lord Jesus, I believe in you and believe you died for my sins, and I'm asking you to come into my life and make me the kind of believer you want me to be. Would you please take this hatred and fill it with love and compassion for those who destroyed my family?"

I went to bed crying, but when I woke up the next morning I felt totally different. I still didn't like all the things that had happened in my life, but I had a different attitude about them. I was able to accept them and try to learn from them.

Ron had thought often over the years about contacting Karla. These feelings increased after his New Year's conversion to Christianity. He wanted to ask her questions so he could understand why she did what she did.

RON: I had thought for some time about contacting Karla Tucker. For some reason, I had not thought about contacting Danny Garrett. It didn't make sense, really, because Karla was convicted of killing Jerry Dean, not Debbie. I guess I focused on Karla because I heard her name the most. The media did not hype Danny the way they did Karla. Her name was always mentioned before his.

I found out that Karla was at Mountain View prison. I contacted the prison and talked to someone about visiting her. The person at the prison said that I couldn't just visit an inmate unless I was on their visiting list. I didn't want to get on her list. I just wanted to go there and confront her.

•  •  •  •  •

Like Ron, Karla was going through a personal transformation. She thrived in the structured environment of prison. Shortly after her arrest, on October 23, 1983, a prison ministry organization called StraightWay performed a puppet show at the Harris County Jail. Initially, Karla balked at the idea of attending a puppet show, but other inmates were going, and it gave her an excuse to leave her cell. After the show, the performers gave personal testimonials. A woman named Karen told of how she started shooting heroin at age twelve and ended up at the Harris County Jail, where she found the Lord.

After the performance, Karla took a Bible back to her cell. She spent the evening reading and praying. For the first time, she realized the extent of the harm she had caused others. She felt tremendous remorse. She asked God to help her change her life. She later told Karen that the Lord took all the bad things and pulled them right out of her. Karla felt born again, and like a curious child she yearned to explore the world.

A seventh-grade dropout, Karla grew up believing she was stupid. Now she wanted to learn. She set a goal of passing the high school equivalency test. She divided her days between reading, studying for the exam, and making quilts and dolls that she gave as gifts or to charities. She began walking at least an hour a day, pacing circles around the small walled-off piece of dirt that served as the "exercise yard."

By 1986, people who knew Karla Tucker believed that she had truly rehabilitated herself. She was not the same woman who only three years earlier had committed one of the most grisly murders in Texas history. U.S. Attorney Henry Oncken, the top law enforcement official in the Southern Judicial District, brought his wife and daughter to visit Karla on death row. She knitted him a sweater as a Christmas present. When asked his opinion of Karla, he told a *Houston Chronicle* reporter in 1986, "She is a caring person. That's hard for people to understand, given what she did. She genuinely cares about other people, is genuinely interested in improving the quality of her life at this point. She is someone I've developed a liking for, a fondness for. The person who is Karla Tucker today is not the same person who was Karla Tucker at that time." He concluded by saying that if Karla were executed, "It would be a tremendous loss to me personally."[1]

Joe Magliolo, the prosecutor who tried Karla, and Rusty Hardin, who had assisted him, both softened toward her. The *Chronicle* story quoted Joe as saying that he believed the jury's verdict of death was appropriate at the time and should be respected. But he added, "If she is executed, I'll be a little sad but really sad for society almost more than for Karla. We allowed Karla to get into the predicament that she was in. She was a child when she started going down the [wrong] path. Somebody should have noticed that and cared enough about her to help her."[2]

Rusty Hardin, with a long track record of sending many defendants to death row, said of Karla, "It is such a horrible crime. It goes beyond the pale of the ordinary crime. And yet I've gotten to know her enough that I personally see, if I'm any judge, a person who has changed. I like her and I hope she doesn't die."[3]

Karla developed friendships with the people from the StraightWay ministry. When Karen married, Karla and the other women on death row arranged a surprise party for her. As Karen and her husband had children,

Karla knit each of them blankets and booties. Karen named her fourth child after Karla.

Karla participated in prison ministry programs whenever they were offered. At one program she met an earnest, handsome prison minister named Dana Brown, a car salesman from a suburb of Houston. He visited Karla regularly and the two fell and love and got married in the prison.

• • • •

In 1990, about a year after Ron had first made inquiries about visiting Karla Tucker, he learned that she was back in Houston at the Harris County Courthouse for an evidentiary hearing on a postconviction motion her lawyer had filed.

RON: When I found out she was in Houston, I called over to the courthouse to find out if I could visit her in the holding cell. The person who answered the phone told me that I could request a visit and if Karla accepted, then I could see her. I requested a visit, and Karla agreed.

I hadn't attended the trial, so I had never seen her in person before. I had seen her picture on television many times, and the pictures were not pretty. Karla walked up to the glass, and I was surprised to see an attractive, slender brunette dressed in an orange Harris County Jail uniform. My first thought when I saw her was *I can't believe she is a murderer.* She sure did not look like the monster the media painted her to be.

There were other inmates in the holding cell and other visits going on. It was loud and hard to hear. She said, "Who are you?" kind of defiantly, and I said, "I'm the brother of Deborah." She asked me the same question again, but this time her tone totally changed. "Who are you?" She couldn't believe that I was there. I don't think Karla Tucker or Danny knew anything about Debbie other than she was a witness to Jerry Dean's murder. They did not go to Jerry's house to kill Debbie.

Karla started to cry. I interrupted her. I said, "Karla, I want you to know this, for whatever it is worth, I forgive you and don't hold anything against you." When I said that, I felt like a great weight had been lifted off of my shoulders; I felt like a burden I had been carrying was gone. We didn't have a lot of time, but I could tell that the visit had helped both of us, so I suggested we keep in touch. I gave her my phone number, and she gave me her address. The entire visit lasted twelve minutes.

After meeting Karla, I went to the courtroom to watch the hearing. Since I had not watched the trial, most of what I saw and heard was new to me. Because it had been seven years since Debbie's murder I was able to watch the hearing with some degree of detachment, which would have been impossible at the time of the trial.

There were a number of different people in the courtroom, and I wondered what their interest was in the case. During the breaks, I talked to the other people attending. I introduced myself to two ladies from the victims' support group Parents of Murdered Children. I told them who I was, and I asked them why they were at the hearing. They said, "Oh, we're here for you." I said, "I don't even know you." They replied, "Well, we're here for all of the victims." One of them asked me what I thought about what was going on. I looked at the lady and said, "I'm not trying to be rude, but I don't support what is going on." I calmly explained that I didn't think it was right to have the death penalty. After that they didn't want to have anything to do with me, even though they were supposedly "there for me."

I also met a number of reporters covering the story. Once they learned that I was Debbie's brother, they all wanted to talk to me. A reporter from the national program *Primetime Live* asked me to appear on the show. I realized that if I was going to start talking about the case I needed to learn a lot more about it.

After the hearing I went downstairs to the clerk's office and asked if I could look at the transcripts from the trial. I figured it would be a few pages. They asked me if I wanted to see all of it, and I said yes. The clerk led me into a room filled with boxes that were filled with files. "Make yourself at home. Don't take any of it; if you want to, you can make copies." I spent three days going through the transcripts. I looked at all the photographs. I looked at microfilm. Then I asked to read the files in my father's case. I wanted to see what had taken place in those courtrooms.

I finally saw the photograph of Debbie's dead body with the pickax embedded in her chest, the one that the police refused to show me years ago. I felt nauseous looking at Debbie's mangled, bloody corpse. I was glad that Bill and the police had spared me from looking at the picture.

I started to read and became transfixed by what I was learning. I couldn't stop. I took three days in a row off from work and spent all day reading the hundreds of pages of transcripts. Then when I had to go back to work, I went to court every day after work to read, take notes, and photocopy parts of the transcripts. I felt this need to know what had happened. I was thinking about getting to know Karla and making a public statement against the death penalty, but I wanted to know exactly what I was dealing with before I said or did anything.

Everything pointed to the fact that Karla and Danny were vicious killers. The prosecutors had portrayed them both as monsters, which seemed like an accurate description. What I saw was enough to turn any person to the death penalty. But I didn't want any killings done in my name. I believed strongly, in spite of what they had done, that forgiving Karla and Danny was the right thing to do.

It was more than just not wanting to see Karla killed. I would say what influenced me was my religious background and what the Bible commands, "Thou shalt not kill." Jesus teaches that we should forgive our enemies. Of course the bad thing about the Bible is you can read it either way about the death penalty. It is a real hard call to make when you start making arguments out of the Bible.

After reading everything, I confirmed that in spite of it all I could not support the death penalty and that I must speak against it. I appeared on *Primetime Live* and spoke out against Karla's execution. I had never been on television before, let alone national television, but it was just something I felt I had to do.

Soon after Ron visited Karla, she wrote him a letter. He wrote back. They began corresponding regularly, then started talking on the phone. Eventually, Ron decided to visit Karla at Mountain View, in Gatesville.

Gatesville is more than 250 miles from Ron's home in Houston, a four-and-a-half-hour drive. To get to the prison in time for visiting hours, Ron left his house early in the morning.

RON: Going to see Karla involved a lot of effort and expense. First I had to go through the administrative hassle of getting permission to visit. Then I had to enter the prison, with tall fences surrounded by razor wire and electric gates and buzzing locks. Prison guards carrying guns and cameras all over the place. There is no privacy in prison.

I remember the feeling I had the first time I went inside and the gate locked behind me. I said to the guard, "You *are* going to let me out of here, right?" He said, "Yeah, when you're through you can leave."

Prison is not a place you would want to go. Contrary to stereotypes, it is sure not like any hotel I've ever seen. There is no air-conditioning in the summer and no heat in the winter. There are no pools or color TVs. The only parts of the jail that are temperature controlled are where the guards are, not the individual cells.

In spite of all the hardships, Karla had a good attitude about prison. She made it very clear that it wasn't a Holiday Inn, but she knew that she was there for a reason, that she was being punished, and she accepted her punishment freely. She said that like everywhere else, there were good people and bad people in prison. She talked about the work program that she was in, and she talked a lot about her Bible study. She talked about the other inmates. She was very concerned for their well-being, both physical and spiritual.

We didn't talk too much about the crime because it was too distressing for both of us. I did, however, ask her why she hated Jerry so much. She said, "He destroyed the only picture I had of my mother." I asked her what she meant and she said, "He took a knife and he stabbed the picture with it." She said that they hadn't gone over to Jerry's house planning to kill him, but one thing led to another and that's what happened. It opened my eyes as to why people act the way they do. From what I learned about the whole thing, the reason why the killing happened was simply revenge. And, without a shadow of a doubt, the death penalty is nothing but revenge.

Karla also told me that she wanted to tell me something that she hoped would bring me peace. She told me that Debbie's last words were "Oh God, it hurts, if you're going to kill me, please do it now." She wanted me to know that my sister had called out to the Lord before she expired from this world. To the average person who doesn't know anything about Christianity or about what is said in the Bible, that statement might sound cold or morbid. But it told me that my sister did know the Lord and in her last breath cried out to him. Whatever happened in the end, I know she made it to heaven.

Things happen spontaneously from time to time. One of the great philosophers, Newton, said that for every action there is an equal and opposite reaction. What I am going to say sounds hard, but I think everything happened just the way it was supposed to. I don't understand why everything happened the way it did, but I do know that through all of this a lot of people have looked at this one case and a lot of people have changed their lives. Many people tell me they are inspired to hear how

Karla changed and how the situation brought me out of despair to the point where I am today. All I can think of is the passage "The Lord works in mysterious ways."

I'm not saying that the murder was predestined, but I am saying that good can come from even the worst circumstances. If you study human history you will see that over and over again. The Christians use the image of warfare with God and Satan fighting a battle between good and evil. Satan makes things look bad, but God can take that same thing and make it look good. I might sound like a religious fanatic, but I don't think I am. I think the Lord is just showing me another one of his powers.

• • • •

Ron's public statement against the death penalty and the fact that he had forgiven and befriended Karla outraged Richard Thornton, his brother-in-law. Karla continued to get a lot of media coverage, and by now much of it was positive. Both the prosecutor and the investigating police officer had stated publicly that they believed she was a changed person and they liked her. Ron was speaking out against Karla's execution. The positive attention given to the woman who was an accessory to the brutal killing of his wife understandably upset Richard.

As the time of Karla's execution drew near, Ron tried to halt the execution by lobbying official authorities. Ron disliked angering Richard but believed he had a moral obligation to try to save Karla's life. (Danny's execution was not an issue because he died of liver failure on June 14, 1993, while awaiting a retrial.) Ron wrote letters to the governor and members of the parole and pardons board and sought opportunities to meet with them in person advocating that her sentence be commuted from death to life in prison.

On December 12, 1997, Ron wrote the following letter to Governor George W. Bush:

I write to you today concerning the fate of one Karla Faye Tucker Brown. I compel you to search your heart and do the right thing. I realize that this situation is a so-called sticky wicket. I myself would not want to be in your shoes at this time.

I ask that you would consider working with the Board of Pardons & Paroles and consider the facts of the case closely. I realize that according to law Karla should be executed. However through all of this I see one thing that just does not go over well with myself. That is the fact that executing Karla will not bring back my sister (Deborah Thornton Carlson Davis), nor will it bring back Jerry Lynn Dean. However the pain that I feel for the loss of my loved one will not be replaced with joy by the execution. I believe that the same pain will be felt by all of Karla's relatives. The fact of the matter is also that executing Karla will not bring me a sense of closure concerning this matter. If Karla is executed it would only add to the pain that I already have concerning this matter. I believe that killing is wrong, no matter how it is done. We as human beings do not have the right to take a life. As it is written, Vengeance is mine sayeth the Lord, I will repay. I have enclosed a copy of Chapter 12 of the book of Romans for your convenience.

The fact that I forgive Karla myself, along with Daniel Ryan Garrett, should not matter. However the fact does remain that having compassion towards them as I do, I feel that by executing those death row inmates, our society is not improved. If anything, it just makes the cycle continue and cause the pain to increase.

I personally think and believe that Karla is not a threat to society. I do believe that Karla is an asset to our society and a lot of people could learn a valuable lesson about how we should and should not live. I am referring to the use of drugs, alcohol, and the way we live in general. Our society is supposed to be based on loving one another, however the way things are today, that is theoretically impossible because of the fact that no one seems to care about anyone except themselves. You yourself are in a position where you can make great changes in our society and by doing so could make our world a better place to live. The bottom line is that we have to start somewhere. Without compassion for one another we are all doomed to our fate.

I leave you with this thought. Jesus of Nazareth walked upon the face of this earth for a very short period of time. It was through compassion for the people in this world that He gave his life on the cross. He himself was executed. He suffered a terrible death. However because of compassion he followed what his father in Heaven had to say. Through Him many changes were made, and are being made even today. Quite possibly by stopping the executions this will be another change that He wants. I am not saying that He said not to execute Karla. But He did say to love one another, and to forgive one another.

Search your heart and follow how the Lord leads you. Do not be compelled to follow the world, but follow the Lord. He will lead you in righteousness for His name's sake.

With deepest admiration,
Ronald W. Carlson

The governor's office sent Ron a form letter in reply.

January 7, 1998
Dear Mr. Carlson:

Thank you for your letter regarding the inmate Karla Faye Tucker's capital punishment sentence. I understand this matter is of great concern to you and your family.

Governor Bush supports the use of capital punishment for violent criminals who commit heinous crimes. He believes capital punishment is a deterrent and is one part of an effective criminal justice policy.

Capital punishment is the law in Texas, and Governor Bush is sworn to uphold the law. According to the Texas Constitution, the Governor has no independent authority to commute a death sentence. He may only commute a sentence if the Board of Pardons and Paroles recommends it. If the 18-member Board of Pardons and Paroles votes to recommend commutation in this case, the recommendation and file will be forwarded to the Governor for a final decision.

Governor Bush takes seriously his responsibility to uphold the law. The Governor will carefully evaluate this case, as he does all death penalty cases, by asking two questions: Is there any question about the individual's guilt? Finally, have the courts given full and fair hearing to all the legal issues involved in this case?

The Governor appreciates receiving your views on this issue.

Sincerely,
Shirley M. Green
Director of Correspondence and Constituent Services

Two days later, a friend of Ron's who had also written to Governor Bush on Karla's behalf received the same form letter from the governor's office. The only difference: it did not contain the sentence "I understand this matter is of great concern to you and your family."

**RON:** I felt betrayed that Governor Bush did not respond personally to my letter. I had thought that because I was a family member of the murder victim the governor would, at the very least, consider my requests and personally respond instead of putting my letter in the same category as any other letter.

I had the same kind of response from the Pardons and Parole Board. I wrote to Chairman Victor Rodriguez, but he refused to meet with me. I really felt like the government officials in charge of making the decision in Karla's case did not care about my opinion.

To help Karla, I needed to take her case to the public, so every opportunity I got I spoke to the media about it. I spoke to dozens of reporters from around the country and the world and even appeared on *Larry King Live*.

Although I prayed that the State of Texas would spare Karla's life, I did not feel optimistic. During an earlier conversation, the subject of the death penalty and her execution had come up, and I told her that if it ever got to that point, I wanted to be present for her. I wanted her to know without a shadow of a doubt that true forgiveness was possible. I believe that the Lord used me to reassure her that her faith was not a waste. I told her flat out, "Look, if this ever happens I want to be there, standing up for the Lord."

The fact that I was her friend moved her deeply. She told friends and reporters, "Ron didn't just forgive me, he loves me."

The State of Texas set Karla's execution date for February 3, 1998. The case had attracted attention from around the world—some positive and some negative. Many opposed her execution. Her petite, slender figure, freckled face, broad smile, and warm brown eyes caught the attention of millions. Texas had not executed a woman since 1863, and many found the idea distasteful.

Commentators remarked on Karla's "preferential treatment." Some claimed that her popularity stemmed from the fact that she was an attractive white woman. Some thought her life should be spared because she had genuinely changed. Others felt she had made up her religious conversion to gain sympathy. Celebrities, among them Bianca Jagger, took up her case. Even television evangelist Pat Robertson, an ardent death penalty supporter, personally appealed to Governor Bush to spare Karla's life.

Throughout all the controversy, Karla maintained her poise and serenity. On January 14, she appeared from prison on *Larry King Live* and told the world that she accepted her fate and responsibility for the crimes she committed. When King asked her how she felt about her impending execution, she said it was "exciting." King commented on her word choice, and Karla replied, "There's a lot going on, and it's going to affect a lot of people. And it's a blessing to be part of it and to know God has a plan for this."

In spite of everyone's efforts, time was running out for Karla. She began preparing to die. In the middle of January, Ron tried to visit, but the guards refused to let him see her. Karla learned about this and wrote to him apologizing.

RON: I got a letter from Karla dated January 15. She wrote that she was sorry that she didn't have a chance to see me. She asked me to please come and see her again before the execution. "You can be sure I want to see *you*, Ron. I believe there is a great need on both our hearts for this." She mentioned that she had seen me on *Larry King Live* with my brother-in-law. She told me I did a great job and said she was glad that Richard and I could appear together in public and respect each other's feelings.

She finished the letter by saying that she knew that Richard was still very angry with her. Richard had stated publicly that Karla had never said Deborah's name and had never apologized for her part in Deborah's murder. Neither of these things was true. She wrote, "Ron, I heard what he said about me not even being able to say Deborah's name, and never saying I'm sorry. I pray you do know this is not true. I have shared my heart with you and said I'm sorry, and I'll say it as many times as you need to hear it. I've also called Deborah by her name to you. I never want to disrespect her or you in anything I say or do. I would say this to Richard if I had a chance."

She wrote about having to live with the fact that what she did hurt so many people. "I know it hurts you and him and her children and Jerry's family every single day of your lives—because of *me*. I wish I could take it all back." She finished by saying, "I love you Brother, and I thank you for allowing Jesus to help you forgive me. It brought into my life a freedom to grow deeper with the Lord. *Thank you.*"

For a postscript she wrote that if she were to be executed she hoped that it would bring Richard some peace. She would like to talk to Richard personally to tell him how sorry she was, but she didn't think Richard would want to see her. She asked me, if I had a chance and thought it was appropriate, if I would communicate to Richard and the children what she wrote in the letter.

•　　•　　•　　•

The sun shone brightly on February 3, 1998. Ron woke with dread in his heart knowing that at six P.M. he would likely watch the State of Texas kill Karla. With great effort he dressed and prepared himself for the day. People started gathering in the early morning in front of the police barricade set up outside of the Walls Unit in Huntsville, the site of the state's execution chamber. Television stations staked out the prime viewing spots and set up their satellite dishes. A group of Italian abolitionists sat next to death penalty opponents from the United States. As the day wore on, others gathered.

At first, most of the people congregating opposed the death penalty, but as the execution hour approached, those in favor of Karla's execution gathered, bringing picnic dinners and coolers filled with beer. The scene outside the prison resembled a homecoming football game.

RON: I left my house at around two P.M. to make the hour-and-a-half drive from Houston. All of the witnesses for Karla had arranged to meet at the Hospitality House in Huntsville. The Texas Baptist Prison Ministry runs the Hospitality as a combination guesthouse and support center for the families and friends visiting people on death row. At 3:45 a staff person from the house briefed us on what to expect. Besides me the other witnesses were Karla's husband, Dana Brown; her sister, Kari Tucker Weeks; Jackie Oncken, wife of U.S. Attorney Henry Oncken, who had befriended Karla; and George "Mac" Secrest, her lead attorney. As I listened to the description of what to expect at the execution, I felt very nervous. When it was over, I prayed.

Richard Thornton would also be witnessing Karla's execution—as an official witness for the state. He arrived at the prison in midafternoon in a wheelchair, looking weary. In 1983, Richard had been a strong, virile man. The stress of the last fifteen years had taken its toll. Suffering from diabetes, overweight and weak, Richard could no longer walk or stand up for extended periods.

Reporters hurried to question him. Richard had advocated Karla's execution for years, and it seemed that he would finally get his wish. "Make no mistake," he said, loud enough for the crowd to hear. "This is *not* Karla Faye Tucker's day. This is Deborah Ruth Davis Thornton's day."

RON: At five P.M. we went to the Walls Unit. After we were searched for any weapons, cameras, or recording devices, a guard led us to a room that was empty except for a few scattered chairs. For the second time that day, we listened to a description of what to expect.

In contrast to the spartan surroundings provided Karla's supporters, the prison treated the victim's witnesses like VIPs, serving a lavish buffet meal. Richard, his daughter, Kate, Deborah's son, Bucky, and several reporters and state officials ate and drank in comfort waiting for the appointed hour.

RON: The execution was supposed to happen at six o'clock, but at six P.M. we were still in the waiting room. We hoped that the delay might mean that Karla had been granted a last-minute stay of execution. That hope was dashed at 6:20 when another guard escorted us to yet another building. We asked him about the delay, and he said that it was "normal." He said it might take another fifteen minutes. However, in less than five minutes another prison official came in to get us and took us to one of the viewing rooms. The state witnesses were in another room.

By the time we got to the viewing room, Karla was already strapped down to a hospital gurney with thick webbing. Intravenous tubes were inserted into both of her arms. Almost immediately, a voice came on over the loudspeaker and asked Karla if she had any last words. Karla turned her face toward Richard and said, "Yes, sir. I would like to say to all of you—the Thornton family and Jerry Dean's family—that I am so sorry. I hope God will give you peace with this."

She then turned to look at her supporters. She said to Dana, "Baby, I love you." Then she said to me, "Ron, give Peggy [Jerry Dean's sister] a hug for me. Everybody has been so good to me." Scanning the entire group, she said, "I love all of you very much. I am going to be face to face with Jesus now. Warden Baggett, thank all of you so much. You have been so good to me. I love all of you very much. I will see you all when you get there. I will wait for you."

Karla licked her lips and whispered a silent prayer. Within seconds she gasped twice and let out a loud wheezing sound as the air left her lungs. Her eyes remained open, and she had a smile on her face.

Her sister, Kari, cried out, "I love you, Karla." Dana said to Kari, "She loves you, too." Jackie Oncken turned to me and said, "She told me to tell you she loved you, Ron."

In the opposite room, Richard remarked, "Here she comes, baby doll. She's all yours. The world's a better place. So now Dana Brown gets to write his book."[4]

Four minutes later, Daryl Wells, the Huntsville physician, entered the chamber through a steel door. He shone a light in each of Karla's eyes, checked for a pulse with his fingers, then checked for a heartbeat using a stethoscope. He looked at his watch. "Six forty-five," he said. The warden repeated, "Six forty-five."

The steel door to the chamber opened, and a guard gestured toward it, saying, "Family members first." The five got into the van and returned to the Hospitality House.

Prison officials announced Karla's death to the crowd waiting outside. In contrast to the somber atmosphere inside the prison, the mood outside was celebratory among both Karla's supporters and her opponents.

Karla's supporters believed that she would go immediately to heaven, where she would meet Jesus and be at peace. At Karla's request, her friends from the StraightWay ministry had arranged to broadcast a music video of her favorite song at the time of her death. They had erected a stage with a public address system and a large screen. As soon as the official announced her death, the hymn "When the Time Comes" blasted through the sound system, and a life-size image of Karla signing to the song appeared on the screen. Her supporters cheered wildly. At the conclusion of the song, someone exclaimed, "Praise the Lord. Now she is in heaven at last."

The group of pro–death penalty supporters also cheered and sang. Many held signs and chanted slogans like "The bitch is dead" and "Good riddance to bad rubbish." One group broke into the chorus of a popular rock song, "Na na na na, na na na na, hey hey, good-bye."

A small group of death penalty opponents huddled together against the crush of the crowd, holding candles and standing in silence, attempting to create a dignified presence in the midst of the mania.

The media kicked into high gear. A tent set up with tables holding computer terminals and phones buzzed with activity as reporters hurried to meet deadlines. At least a dozen television stations covered the execution. Anchorpersons stood talking into cameras.

RON: Dana Brown, David Botsford, one of Karla's lawyers, and I had been asked to do the *Larry King Live* show, which was being broadcast from the prison. Richard was supposed to be on the show, too, but declined at the last minute. We were all pretty shaken up, especially Dana, who was fighting back tears.

The show was over at around ten, and I went back to the Hospitality House to get my car. I stopped at an all-you-can-eat barbecue restaurant and met up with some of my death penalty abolitionist friends. I paid for a plate but couldn't eat very much. They told me about what a circus it had been outside the prison. I told them what it had been like to watch from inside. After about an hour I got in my car and drove home.

It was an honor to witness her execution, to be requested by her to be there. I'd never ask any man to do this unless he really knows the Lord. He was there. I drew on all the strength that I could get from the Lord. He surrounded us all with his love. I felt a sensation, like tingles but amplified a hundred thousand times. I believe this was God reaching out of heaven to hold us in his hands and cradle us with love and compassion.

Ron has not seen Richard since the execution; nor has he seen his nephew, Bucky.

RON: I don't talk to Richard anymore. I may be wrong, but I don't think the execution helped him. He has brainwashed my nephew so that Bucky doesn't want to see me. I don't appreciate that, and I don't think my sister would like it one bit. I've tried to talk to my nephew so many times it's pathetic. I have written letters and called but he won't respond.

•　•　•　•

Karla's death did not end Ron's work for abolition. To the contrary, it increased it. He is helping to start a Texas chapter of Murder Victims' Families for Reconciliation. On occasion, he is asked to share his story; he always tries to do so. He also maintains a website dedicated to abolition: www. flash.net/~rwcarlso.

RON: I'll keep doing this work until we end the death penalty. Besides keeping up my website, I also write to some people on death row. Writing to death row inmates gives them hope and reassures them that they are not alone. There is a passage in the Bible where Christ talks about judgment day, and he refers to those who know him and those who know him not, and he makes a statement about being in prison, "When I was in prison you visited me." What it all comes down to for me is that I just can't see Jesus pulling the switch. I don't think the Son of God would destroy his own father's creation. I just don't think he'd support that.

# EXECUTING THE VULNERABLE

In theory, the death penalty is the punishment reserved for those people who commit the most heinous murders. In practice, it is meted out to those who are the most vulnerable and least powerful. Two groups that are particularly vulnerable are juveniles and mentally retarded people.

Chapters 4 and 5 highlight the issue of the juvenile death penalty. The first juvenile execution in North America took place in 1642, when Plymouth Colony in Massachusetts executed Thomas Granger.[1] Over the course of the next 350 years, at least 361 juveniles have been executed in the United States.

Despite legal challenges, the nation's high court continues to uphold the use of the death penalty against juvenile offenders. In *Thompson v. Oklahoma,* a plurality of the United States Supreme Court held that the death penalty as applied to juveniles over sixteen did not violate the Constitution. The Court reaffirmed this position a year later in the case of *Stanford v. Kentucky.*[2] Of the thirty-eight death penalty jurisdictions, fifteen do not have a juvenile death penalty. Of the states that do have one, eighteen use sixteen as the minimum age, and five use seventeen. The federal government does not have a juvenile death penalty.

Since 1973, two hundred death sentences have been handed down to juvenile offenders, half of them in just three states: fifty in Texas, thirty in Florida, and twenty-one in Alabama. Nearly two-thirds of juveniles sentenced to death were black (ninety-six) or Latino (twenty-two), compared to approximately one-third white (eighty-one) and one Asian American. Eighteen have been executed, with half of those executions taking place in Texas. At the end of 2001, eighty-four juvenile offenders awaited execution.[3]

The United States has one of the harshest juvenile justice systems among industrialized countries. In response to fear, the 1980s saw politicians and law enforcement agents wage a "war against juvenile crime." To fight the battle, many states enacted laws that allowed juveniles to be prosecuted in adult court and drastically increased the length of prison sentences for juvenile offenders.

The United States has received widespread international criticism for its practice of executing juvenile offenders. It is the only country in the world that has signed but not yet ratified the United Nations Convention on Human Rights. Nor has it ratified the Convention on the Rights of the Child. Both agreements contain express provisions that the United States would be violating if it continued its practice of killing juvenile offenders. Since 1990, only five countries besides the United States have executed juvenile offenders: Iran, Pakistan, Yemen, Nigeria, and Saudi Arabia, putting the United States in the company of some of the world's most notorious human rights violators. Of all the world's countries, the United States ranks second behind Iraq for executing the most juveniles during the modern death penalty era. Iraq executed a record thirteen juveniles in one year, 1987.

Chapter 6 involves a case with a mentally retarded defendant—James Bernard Campbell, who had an IQ of 68. As in many death penalty cases, the issue of retardation was not thoroughly presented to the jury that made the decision to sentence James to death. After more than ten years of advocacy by SueZann Bosler and others, substantial evidence of his mental incapacity was eventually presented to a jury.

At least thirty-five mentally retarded people have been executed in the United States since 1976. An estimated two to three hundred currently await execution. Some estimates indicate that as many as 10 percent of the people on death row in the United States are mentally retarded.

Offenders who are mentally retarded are particularly vulnerable to arbitrariness and error in capital trials and likely to be wrongfully convicted. One of the explanations for the error rate is that these defendants often withhold information from their own attorneys about their mental capabilities, either because they do not understand their own limitations or because they are ashamed. This seriously undermines the ability of their lawyers to defend them.

Another factor contributing to wrongful convictions is that retarded people are particularly vulnerable to police interrogation and therefore likely to confess to crimes they did not commit. A number of high-profile cases not covered in this book are noteworthy. For example, Earl Washington confessed after a lengthy police interrogation to a crime he did not commit. When his attorney moved to dismiss the confession, the court held that Earl had "knowingly" waived his right against self-incrimination, even though he had the mental capacity of a ten-year-old.[4] Earl was eventually exonerated and given an absolute pardon after DNA evidence proved his innocence—after he spent sixteen years on death row.

Another example of an unreliable confession is the case of Doil Lane, who, after confessing to murdering a young girl, climbed into the lap of the police officer who was questioning him. During his trial, Doil asked the judge for crayons so he could color pictures. Similarly, Jerome Holloway, convicted of murder in Georgia, had an IQ of 49 and could not tell the time, recite the alphabet, or identify the country he lived in.[5] Besides being retarded, these defendants also grew up poor with few resources to protect their legal rights.

The constitutionality of executing mentally incompetent people is coming under scrutiny. In 1989, the U.S. Supreme Court decided the case of *Penry v. Lynaugh.*[6] In this five-to-four decision, the Court held that executing persons with mental retardation was not a violation of the Eighth Amendment. In determining the "evolving standards of decency" necessary for deciding Eighth Amendment questions, the Court looks to what is happening in the states; at the time, only Maryland and Georgia prohibited executing retarded people. Writing for the majority, Justice Sandra Day O'Connor wrote that a "national consensus" had not developed against executing those with mental retardation.

In March 2001, the Supreme Court granted a stay of execution for Ernest McCarver and agreed to hear the case of *McCarver v. North Carolina*, revisiting the question of whether executing mentally retarded people violates the Eighth Amendment.[7] There is reason to believe that the Court might reverse its position on executing retarded people. In the twelve years between *Penry* and *McCarver*, the political landscape has changed significantly. At the time of the *Penry* decision, only two states prohibited executing mentally retarded offenders. When the Court agreed to hear the *McCarver* case, twenty-five of the thirty-eight death penalty states still permitted the execution of mentally retarded offenders, while thirteen prohibited it. Since then, several state legislatures have passed bills outlawing the execution of mentally retarded people: North Carolina, Missouri, Connecticut, Florida, Arizona, and Texas. These bills have been signed into law except in Texas, where Governor Rick Perry vetoed the bill. (It is noteworthy that Texas leads the nation with the most executions of mentally retarded persons—six since 1976.) With the newly passed laws, eighteen, or almost half, of the death penalty states oppose executing mentally retarded people. Adding that number to the twelve abolition states brings the total of states that forbid executing the mentally retarded to thirty.

In September 2001, the Supreme Court reversed its decision to hear the *McCarver* case on the grounds of mootness given North Carolina's new law banning executions of mentally retarded people. However, the Court accepted the case of *Atkins v. Virginia*, which addresses the same issue.[8]

By the time this book went to press, the Supreme Court had decided the *Atkins* case (*Atkins v. Virginia*, 122 S.Ct. 2242 [2002]). The Court held that executing mentally retarded people violates the Eighth Amendment's prohibition against cruel and unusual punishment. Now it will be up to the states to change their laws to comply with the Court's decision. Meanwhile, there are still many mentally retarded people on death row across the country at risk of being executed unless competent attorneys are successful at getting their cases reopened.

# CHAPTER 4

# The Answer Is Love and Compassion

Around noon on Tuesday, May 14, 1985, seventy-eight-year-old Ruth Pelke was at her home at 4449 Adams Street in Gary, Indiana. She had lived in the modest two-story white wooden frame house since 1944, when she married Oscar. Oscar had three children from his first wife, Dorothy, who died of leukemia in 1941. Although the children were grown when their father married Ruth, she always treated them as her own. Those three had nine children among them, and the nine had fifteen, so Ruth had a large family that loved her.

Ruth was attached to her home and her neighborhood, even though it had changed over the years. She used to know all her neighbors, but now she knew only a few. In the last several years, burglars had invaded her house four times. Her stepson Robert and daughter-in-law Lola had urged her to move many times. They had mentioned the idea the previous Sunday, when the family was together celebrating Mother's Day, and on Monday evening, when visiting at her home. Ruth dismissed any notion that she would move. "I like my neighbors. We look out for each other. I'm not leaving here until I go up there," she said, pointing toward heaven.

Ruth's greatest joy was sharing her faith with others, especially bringing the Bible alive to children in ways they could understand. She participated in two programs—Child Evangelism and Five Day Clubs—specifically aimed at teaching children about the Bible. To illustrate her lessons she used a felt-covered board, moving pictures of Bible characters around on it to make the stories come to life. Over the years she had taught her grandchildren and great-grandchildren, who had happy memories of spending time with her. Ruth also taught neighborhood children at her home.

On this Tuesday, only a few blocks away, four ninth-grade girls at the Lew Wallace High School decided during their lunch break to skip school for the

Front row (left to right): *Bill Pelke and sister Dottie McKay.* Back row (left to right): *Bill's parents, Lola and Robert Pelke, and grandparents Oscar and Ruth Pelke. Photograph provided with permission of the family.*

rest of the day. Fifteen-year-old April Beverly, fifteen-year-old Paula Cooper, sixteen-year-old Karen Corders, and fourteen-year-old Denise Thomas went to April's house, where they drank beer and wine and smoked some marijuana while discussing what to do with their day.

The four girls did not know each other well, but they all shared the burden of being kids who did not fit in. Karen had had a son when she was thirteen and still in junior high school. April was seven months pregnant. Paula often ran away from home to escape her mother's violent temper. Their young lives were too burdened by responsibilities and too unstable for them to excel at school.

They decided to go to an arcade a few blocks away, but none of the girls had any money. April told the others that there was an old lady in the neighborhood who taught Bible lessons. April, in fact, knew Ruth because she had taken them from her, and when April's mother died a few years earlier, Ruth brought meals to the family. "She lives alone and I think she has money," April said. She suggested that they go to her house under the guise of seeking Bible lessons and, once inside, rob her. The girls decided that it would be too risky for April to go inside at Ruth's, so she would stay outside to act as lookout. As they were leaving April's house, Paula grabbed a twelve-inch-long butcher knife.

At one o'clock the girls knocked on Ruth's door. She opened it, and they told her that they wanted to take her Bible lessons. Ruth let the girls inside and told them that she didn't teach the classes at home anymore but would get them the name and number of a woman who did. As soon as Ruth turned her back, Denise grabbed a vase from an end table and hit Ruth over the head, knocking her to the ground. Paula pulled out the knife and began to stab Ruth. While Karen and Denise ransacked the house looking for money, Paula continued stabbing her.

The girls found little for their efforts. After thoroughly searching the house, turning furniture over and opening bureau drawers, they found ten dollars and the keys to Ruth's 1977 aqua-blue Plymouth. At some point, Karen took over with the knife. Between the two of them, Karen and Paula knifed Ruth thirty-three times with such force that they frayed the carpet beneath her body and splintered the hardwood floor under the carpet. Before leaving, the girls covered Ruth's face with a towel to smother her and avoid looking at her. It took Ruth somewhere between twenty-five and forty minutes to die.

After they killed Ruth, the four drove back to their school, where they offered friends rides in Ruth's car. April and Paula decided to drive to Illinois. They picked up April's brother, Tony, and the three drove until they reached Harvey, Illinois, where the car ran out of gas. They used the ten dollars to buy soda and fast food.

On Wednesday morning, Robert Pelke called his stepmother about a house repair he had offered to do for her. Not able to get her on the phone, he stopped by the house at around 1:45 P.M. to make sure Ruth was okay. He walked in the front door and found her lying face down with a towel wrapped around her head. Blood covered the floor and had splattered on the wall. Frantically he grabbed the phone to call for help, but it had been torn from the wall. He ran outside and began knocking on neighbors' doors, but no one answered. Seeing a woman parking her car up the street, he ran to her, yelling that somebody had killed his mother and asking her to call the police.

Initially, most of the family assumed that a deranged drug addict murdered Ruth. But Paula had left behind a white denim jacket with a prescription for birth control pills in the pocket. The police went to the school in search of Paula, where they spoke with students who had ridden in the stolen car and named the four girls. Once confronted, the girls confessed to the murder. A few days later, police found the abandoned car in Illinois.

Bill Pelke, one of Ruth's grandchildren who lived locally, had just gotten off work when he heard the news.

BILL: I was at my girlfriend Judy's house when I got a call from my brother-in-law Frank: "Bill, I've got some bad news about Nana." Nana was my grandmother and the oldest person in the family, so of course I assumed that she had died. He went on to explain that my father had found her and it looked like her death was the result of a home invasion.

I turned on the TV, and the lead story was that seventy-eight-year-old Bible teacher Ruth Pelke had been stabbed to death in her home. I could see Nana's house in the background as the story unfolded. Four men carried her body on a gurney out the front door, onto the porch, and down the stairs. Her body was covered with a blanket. My father was standing to the side of the house talking with a policeman, but he declined to be interviewed by the media. I wanted very much to go be with him and comfort him.

Our family was in shock. Nana was the nicest, sweetest lady. We could not understand who would want to kill her. We were even more aghast when we learned that four girls had killed her, one from her own neighborhood.

• • • •

Because Karen Corders was sixteen, Lake County prosecutor Jack Crawford charged her as an adult and announced he was seeking the death penalty. The other three girls were charged as juveniles, but he immediately petitioned the court to have their cases transferred to adult court. In an interview on May 18 with a *Post-Tribune* reporter, he said, "I've been a prosecutor for seven years, and we've never had a case like this before. There is no evidence that adults took part in the killing." He added that as far as he knew, it was the first time in the county's history that four juvenile females had been charged with planning and carrying out a murder. If the juvenile cases were waived into adult court, he said, he would consider filing another death penalty charge against one or more of the other girls.[1]

The situation forced Bill, who had never thought a lot about the death penalty, to examine his beliefs.

BILL: I had never really thought about the death penalty in any kind of serious way. I attended Hyles Anderson, a conservative Christian college, and everybody there supported the death penalty. I figured if Indiana had a death penalty, then the girls that killed my grandmother should get it. Otherwise, that meant that her life was not as important as others'. In any event, my father and everybody else in the family supported the death penalty. It never really occurred to me to think differently.

The case focused attention on the issue of juvenile crime and the death penalty. The idea of a grandmother being stabbed to death in her own home by four girls shocked even a community accustomed to homicide. At the time, Indiana allowed children as young as ten years old to be prosecuted as adults and face the death penalty. Victor Streib, a law professor at Cleveland State University who specializes in the juvenile death penalty, was interviewed by a local newspaper. His remarks put the case into historical perspective:

Indiana is the only state that says ten-year-olds can be tried as adults. Only fourteen other states issue the death penalty to people who commit murder before they are eighteen. And these states have minimum ages of fourteen, fifteen, sixteen, or seventeen. Indiana has executed only three people under eighteen. . . . All three were seventeen-year-old boys. The latest was executed in 1920. Only nine girls have been executed in the entire history of the United States. The first was a twelve-year-old Indian girl who was executed for murdering a six-year-old white girl. The other eight were black girls, most of them slaves accused of murdering white children. The latest juvenile girl in this country to be executed was in 1912. Her name was Virginia Christian, a seventeen-year-old, mentally deficient black girl from Virginia. She was executed for killing her white female employer. Throughout history, blacks have received the death penalty more often than whites. All four girls in the Pelke case were black.[2]

The local media ran stories with provocative headlines and gory details about the murder, but they also presented the reality of the girls' troubled lives. None of the girls came from a stable home. Neither April nor Karen lived with her mother. Paula was a "chronic runaway," leaving home because, she claimed, her father abused her. None of the girls had succeeded in school, and each had been expelled at one time or another for poor grades and truancy. Keith Medved, Lake County public defender for juveniles, said in a June 17 article: "Sometimes I quit trying to find answers, but when you see kids raised with no father or no mother, or parents who can't read and write, the kids seem predestined to have problems. It's not a defense for killing anybody, but if from Day One you have that type of life, it seems the cards are stacked against you. My client, April Beverly, is fifteen and seven months pregnant. That tells you something. It doesn't ensure a very rosy future."[3]

All four girls ended up in adult court. Denise's case went to trial first. A jury found her guilty and on December 4, 1985, Judge James Kimbrough sentenced Denise to thirty-five years in prison. In his sentencing remarks he said, "Perhaps the community and parents are to blame for allowing school-age children to skip classes and roam the streets without supervision."[4]

Prosecutor Crawford decided to seek the death penalty for the other three girls but announced soon after that the state was entering into an agreement with April Beverly whereby she would plead guilty to robbery and the state would drop the death penalty. Only Karen and Paula still faced possible death sentences.

Karen's trial was scheduled to begin on March 26, 1986. Before the trial began, her public defender, David Olson, advised her to plead guilty to murder, so the judge would not hear all the gory details, and take responsibility for the crime. He believed that Judge Kimbrough would spare her life if she did. Karen pleaded guilty, and the judge set her sentencing date for May 29.

At the sentencing hearing, Karen pleaded for her life. She said, "I'm real sorry for what I done to Mrs. Pelke and her family. I pray for them and ask the Lord to have the family forgive me for what I have done. I know it was a terrible thing to do. I have a son who is four years old, and that's one of the reasons why I want to live. I also want to prove to society I'm not as bad a person as they think I am."

The judge recessed for twenty-four hours and then came back with a decision to spare Karen's life. He sentenced her to sixty years. He cited Karen's age, lack of other criminal convictions, and Paula Cooper's influence as mitigating circumstances that led him to reject the death penalty in favor of the maximum prison term. Jack Crawford said, "I'm disappointed, but we accept the court's decision. We will continue to vigorously pursue the death penalty against Paula Cooper."[5]

By this point in the legal proceedings, the state had taken the position that Paula Cooper was the most culpable. She had taken the knife from April Beverly's house, and she had dealt the majority of blows with it. The prosecution claimed that Paula went to Ruth Pelke's house planning to murder her. To the state's surprise, Paula did not contest the charge and offered to plead guilty to murder without any sentencing agreement.

The absence of such an agreement meant Paula's lawyer would have the difficult job of convincing the judge to spare his client's life. While awaiting sentencing, Paula had sex with two prison guards and a recreational counselor, all of whom lost their jobs. Some speculated that Paula had been trying to get pregnant in order to elicit sympathy and avoid a death sentence.

The press crowded the courtroom for the sentencing hearing on Friday, July 11, 1986. Many members of the Pelke family, including Bill, attended.

BILL: Paula Cooper entered the room wearing bluish-green prison garb. As the prison matron escorted her to her seat, Paula smiled. When I saw her smile I felt angry and offended. *You killed my grandmother and you are smiling. Well, you won't be smiling when this day is over,* I thought to myself.

Deputy prosecutor James W. McNew called my dad as a witness. He had to identify several gruesome photographs taken the day of the murder. I felt so bad for him. It was the fourth time he had had to do this. I was proud of him, too. He handled himself well. He finished his statement by saying that he wanted Paula to be punished to the fullest extent of the law.

Paula's attorney, public defender Kevin Relphorde, assumed that because my dad had not specifically mentioned the death penalty, he did not support it. Relphorde asked Dad point blank what he meant, and Dad said, "I meant the death penalty."

Relphorde tried to recover by bringing out the fact that Nana had been a deeply religious woman. Dad was prepared for that line of questioning. He pulled a piece of paper out of his pocket and recited thirty Bible references that called for the death penalty. Dad ended by saying that it would be a "travesty of justice" if the death penalty were not given.

Next, McNew called Frances Irons, a former corrections officer, who testified that Paula had once said to her, "Yeah, I stabbed an old lady and I'd stab the bitch again. I'd even stab your fucking grandmother."

I didn't like McNew's style. He reminded me of a bandy rooster prancing around the courtroom, smug and self-righteous. I wasn't impressed with Paula's lawyer, either. I wondered why her lawyer allowed her to plead guilty without a guarantee that she wouldn't be sentenced to death, but then I thought, *What the heck, I'm not on her side anyway.*

Then it was the defense's turn to try to save Paula. Paula's sister, Rhonda Cooper, testified. She told the judge that their father, Herman, had regularly abused them both. He beat them with his hands or an electrical cord. Once he beat and raped their mother, Gloria, in front of them. On cross-examination McNew asked her why she had not responded to the abuse like her sister had. Rhonda didn't respond.

Paula's uncle, Ronald Williams, testified that his sister Gloria was "crazy, a very sick person." Once she tried to kill herself and Paula and Rhonda. She put the girls in a running car in a closed garage until they passed out from carbon monoxide poisoning, but firefighters saved their lives. Ronald begged the judge to spare Paula's life.

At the very end, Paula spoke. She stood up and said, "I am very sorry for what I did. All I can ask you is not to take my life. I'm not a gang member or leader. I never denied what I did. Everybody put the blame on me. The other three girls didn't tell the whole story. They took full part in the crime and didn't get the death penalty." She turned towards my family and said, "I didn't kill your mother on purpose. I hope you can find compassion in your heart to forgive me. How will you feel when I'm in my grave? Will that bring her back?" She next looked at the prosecutor and said that his asking for her to be killed was just as bad as what she had done.

Just as the judge got ready to impose the sentence, an old man in the back of the courtroom began to wail and cry very loudly, "They're going to kill my baby! They're going to kill my baby!" The judge looked over at the bailiff and said, "Bailiff, escort that man from the courtroom. He's disrupting the proceedings." I watched as the old man was led out of the courtroom, tears rolling down his cheeks. I later learned that the man was Paula Cooper's grandfather.

Before imposing sentence, Judge Kimbrough made lengthy remarks. He found that the state proved beyond a reasonable doubt that Paula Cooper intentionally killed Ruth Pelke while committing a robbery. Noting that Ruth was seventy-eight years of age and that Paula inflicted thirty-three stab wounds in her body, he found no substantial mitigating evidence beyond Paula's age and the lack of history of any criminal convictions or conduct.

His remarks then took on a very personal tone. He confided that he opposed the death penalty but acknowledged that his view was in the minority. He spoke with despair about the rise in juvenile crime and how that factor might be contributing to people's support for the death penalty. He noted that this case had received extensive coverage because society was grappling with how to address the problem of youth violence. Then he read from a prepared statement:

I don't believe that I am ever going to be quite the same after these four cases. They have had a very profound effect on me. They have made me come to grips with the question of whether or not a judge can hold personal beliefs which are inconsistent at all with the laws we are sworn to uphold.

And for those of you who have no appreciation of it, it is not a simple question. It is not a simple question for me.

I would say to Mr. Pelke, I have read your letter. And I have heard you speak on two prior occasions. And I suppose I am at odds with almost everyone who has spoken at some point.

I do not believe that the failure to impose the death penalty today would be unbiblical. I believe that there are passages in the Bible that say a person who takes a life shall die by man's hand. I believe that there are other passages (but I don't profess to be an expert in religion) in the Bible which are merciful, and do not demand and mandate an eye for an eye. . . .

Stand up, Paula. All of the evidence in this case, including your statement, indicates that you stabbed Ruth Pelke 33 times. . . . The law requires me, and I do now, impose the death penalty.[6]

Bill looked at Paula and saw that her tears had caused dark blotches on her prison garb. Just fifteen years old, Paula Cooper had become the youngest death row prisoner in the country.

BILL: I walked out of the courtroom stunned. No one had actually thought the judge would impose death. A reporter asked me for a comment. I said, "The judge did what he had to do." Then, fighting back tears, I said, "But it won't bring back my grandmother." Rhonda Cooper came over and screamed at Jack Crawford and my family, "Are you satisfied now?" Nobody said anything.

The *Gary Post-Tribune* ran a profile of Judge Kimbrough, written from interviews taken after the Cooper sentencing. The judge confided to the reporter how difficult the case had been for him:

My responsibilities, as long as I'm in this job, are to enforce the laws of the state, no matter what I may personally feel. Yet all my being said don't do it. It's been a strain. I lost many nights sleep over this. I was not a particularly good father or husband. I was struggling with myself. I was trying to determine if I was capable of doing what I knew the law required me to do, in spite of how I personally felt. When I said in my sentencing [remarks] that I thought that I would never be the same, that's what I'm talking about. To come to that realization that you, in effect, allow your job to take over from you makes you look again at what your personal convictions are and ought to be.[7]

Although Bill and Robert didn't talk about the case much, at one point Robert said that he was glad that Paula had been sentenced to death—glad that the judge had the guts to do it. However, he said that Paula would probably never actually be executed. "Someday a 'do-gooder' will probably come along and get her off death row."

•   •   •   •

On a particularly cold night in November 1986, Bill was at work at the Bethlehem Steel Company, where he operated an overhead crane. The large million-dollar piece of equipment moved massive loads of steel throughout the plant.

When he reported for work, his supervisor told him to take his crane to the west end of the sprawling factory. Bill climbed the sixty-foot stairway to his crane cab and moved it to the west end. None of the other workers had shown up yet.

BILL: Like most nights, I felt pretty miserable. Since Nana's murder, my life had been unraveling, and now it was in complete tatters. I couldn't eat or sleep. The last blow came when my girlfriend Judy and I split up. Even though it had been a mutual decision to break up, I was still very upset about it. I felt so hopeless that I decided to pray, which is something I hadn't done in a long time.

As I prayed, I started to get this image of my grandmother and what she stood for. I began to think about Nana's love of Jesus, and then thought about all the things that Jesus had said about forgiveness. I felt like Nana's spirit was speaking to me through the prayer. I knew for certain that her response to the situation would have been to forgive Paula. She would have wanted our family to show Paula love and compassion.

The message I was getting was that I should be the one in our family to forgive Paula Cooper. I thought that forgiveness would be the right thing to do in this situation, but the problem was that I did not have an ounce of compassion for Paula. I sat in the crane, not knowing what to do, with tears streaming down my face, and I begged God to please, please, please give me love and compassion for Paula Cooper and her family, and to do it on behalf of Nana. It was just a short prayer, but I sensed right then it would change my life.

I decided that I could write a letter to Paula Cooper and tell her about Nana. I could share Nana's faith with Paula. As soon as I made this decision, I no longer wanted Paula to die. I suddenly felt horrified by the idea of the State of Indiana strapping her into the electric chair and jolting electricity into her. My heart was no longer filled with pain and sorrow.

It had been a year and a half since Nana's death, and until that night each time I thought of her I would picture her butchered body on the dining room floor—the same room where our family celebrated Christmas, Easter, Thanksgiving, birthdays, and other joyous occasions. But now I had an image of her alive—vibrant and filled with love.

I knew that God had done something wonderful for me. It was a miracle, an epiphany. It was my mountaintop experience. I felt like I was born again. That prayer transformed my life. I decided to do whatever I could to help Paula Cooper, and I promised God that for any success that came to my life as a result of forgiving Paula Cooper, I would give the honor and glory to God. I also promised God that any door that opened as a result of forgiving Paula I would walk through.

Bill wrote to Paula the next day. He told her about his grandmother's strong faith and love for humanity. He shared his experience in the crane and told Paula that he wanted to help her. He asked her to write back and send him her grandfather's address so that he could contact him. Bill mailed the letter not knowing what to expect.

On November 10, Bill received a letter from Paula. She thanked him for writing and told him she had been reading her Bible and praying for his family. A "lady in a wheel chair" had visited her in jail, she said, and told her "God would be pleased if I prayed for all of you." She told Bill that she was in isolation twenty-three hours a day and it was a "mental hell." She said that her family didn't care much about her and that she never really had a chance. If he wanted to keep writing to her, she told Bill, she would like to write to him. She finished by saying, "I know all of you wanted to get even. You may not be free until they execute me but you know, Bill, it won't help. I will die for all of you to make you feel better so you can live, but you know in the long run we all lose."

Paula included her grandfather's name, address and phone number. Bill called him right away.

> **BILL:** I called him and he invited me over. He lived in Gary, probably less than ten blocks from where my grandmother lived. Paula was living with him at the time of the murder. It was a three-level town house that he shared with other family members. It was right around Thanksgiving time of 1986. I took over a fruit basket. We sat there at his kitchen table and looked at family photo albums from when Paula and Rhonda were younger.

•　•　•　•

As he had promised God, Bill did all he could to help Paula. Every chance he had, he shared his experience in the crane. His family and friends thought he was crazy. Judy didn't understand Bill, either, but by Christmas they were dating again.

Since childhood, Bill had been raised in a conservative Baptist faith. The year he graduated from Hyles Anderson, Jerry Falwell delivered the commencement address. Many of his college teachers were graduates of Bob Jones University.

> **BILL:** I was taught the world was going to hell in a handbasket because of the bleeding-heart liberals. I prayed for love and compassion and became a bleeding-heart liberal overnight!
>
> I rarely met anyone else who opposed the death penalty, even for a young girl like Paula Cooper. One day I ran into an acquaintance named

Tom who Judy and I knew from the bar where Judy worked. Tom told me that he hoped "the bitch would burn." I told him about my experience in the crane, and his tone changed. He said, "You ought to let people know how you feel. You should write a letter to the Voice of the People section of the *Post-Tribune.*"

I took his advice and wrote a short article saying that I did not want Paula Cooper to be executed. I called it "The Answer Is Love, Prayer, and Forgiveness." I signed it "the grandson of Ruth Pelke." I didn't know if anything would come from the article. But one hundred days after the article appeared in the paper, an Italian journalist named Anna Guaita called and asked me for an interview. She was writing a series of articles about Paula Cooper's case, and she had called the editor of the paper asking for names of people to interview. The editor suggested that she call me. One of the articles in the series focused on me.

The articles generated a lot of publicity in Italy, and soon after I got a call from a TV producer at RAI-UNO, Italy's state television station, inviting me to appear on a popular variety program. Keeping my vow to enter any door that opened, I agreed.

Before Bill's departure for Italy, the Cooper case claimed another victim. Judge Kimbrough died when he fell asleep at the wheel and collided with a tractor-trailer truck. His blood alcohol level was 1.9, nearly twice the legal limit. The judge reputedly had a drinking problem, and a bartender at a place he frequented said that after the Cooper sentencing the judge had started drinking even more.

· · · ·

Bill looked forward to the trip to Italy, in part, so that he could be around people who shared his opposition to the death penalty. He felt isolated in northwest Indiana. He remained close to his family, but their disagreement over Paula caused strain.

BILL: One time we talked about it and it was just not a productive conversation, so we elected not to discuss it further. I will say that when I told my dad of my plans to help Paula, he told me that I had to "do what I needed to do." I thanked him for that. But we are so far apart on this question there is no bridging the gap. My dad thinks the death penalty should be expanded to cover more crimes.

Two days before his departure for Italy, the *Post-Tribune*'s banner headline read "Should Cooper Die? Victim's Family Divided." Although Bill's mother, Lola, would not talk to reporter Lori Olszewski, his dad did. Robert said that he was "very much opposed" to Bill's efforts to save Paula's life and that he wished Bill "wasn't going to Rome. My son is alone [within the family] in his belief that Paula Cooper should not go to the electric chair for killing Ruth." He added, "I believe my son is one of the so-called new breed who doesn't believe people should have to pay their debts. This is contrary to my philosophy. If you break the law, you should suffer the consequences."[8]

When asked to respond to this criticism, Bill replied: "My grandmother died a martyr for Jesus Christ, who forgave his enemies. My grandmother would want us to do the same. Christian principles mandate forgiveness."

The article concluded with a prediction: "Officials in the Lake County prosecutor's office said they do not think widespread interest in the Cooper case in Italy will influence the outcome of Cooper's appeal in the United States."

On the second anniversary of his grandmother's death, Bill flew to Italy. He arrived to a huge press conference assembled with international media including CNN. Bill had never spoken in public before.

> BILL: I wasn't really nervous. I felt I was going there with a message. The reporters asked me questions that were easy to answer. I didn't know a whole lot about the death penalty, only some statistics about the juveniles on death row. I talked about how Paula and I had developed a friendship. I thanked the people in Italy who had signed petitions on Paula's behalf. At that point, there were about forty thousand.

CNN ran the story in the United States, and other networks picked it up, showing pictures of Bill, a smiling, handsome man with thick hair and a full beard and mustache. His eyes peered deeply into the camera, shining with warmth and openness.

After the ten-hour flight and draining press conference, the RAI program director informed Bill that they would have to postpone the show because the cameramen were going on strike. She apologized and said that they would like to invite him back in the future.

Not sure when he'd be able to return, Bill suggested that he stay until the strike was over and spend the time traveling around the country talking about Paula's case. The director agreed and gave him a million lire to help cover his expenses. Bill didn't know the exchange rate, but it sounded like a good deal to him.

Bill spent the next nineteen days on a whirlwind tour of Italy. Two priests, Father Germano Graganti and Father Vito Bracone, founders of an organization called Don't Kill, escorted him and arranged for him to speak in churches and schools and give media interviews. At every stop, Bill and the priests collected signatures on a petition asking Indiana governor Robert Orr to commute Paula's sentence.

When the strike was over, Bill appeared on *Domenica In,* the RAI show he had come for. Hosted by the international celebrity Raffaela Carra, it had an audience of several million viewers.

Even more exciting to Bill was an invitation to speak on Vatican radio. With his conservative Baptist background, Bill never dreamed he'd go to the Vatican, let alone speak to millions of listeners on Vatican radio's national and international segments.

Bill found that speaking of Ruth kept her memory alive and helped redeem her tragic death.

· · · ·

The coverage of Bill's trip to Italy resulted in more requests to talk about the Cooper case in the United States. Soon after his return, Bill appeared on *Good Morning America.* On June 23, 1987, the Associated Press ran a sympathetic story about his efforts to save Paula. Four months later, RAI-UNO invited Bill to return to Italy to appear on a different program, *Crimes of the World.* The station also invited Lake County prosecutor Jack Crawford, but he declined.

Organizations were also inviting Bill to tell his story. In April 1988, Magdaleno Rose-Avila, director of Amnesty International's USA Program to Abolish the Death Penalty, asked Bill to speak at the annual meeting. Magdaleno was bursting with ideas on how to use Bill's story to spread the abolition message in the United States.

At the Amnesty meeting, Bill met a woman from Albany named Elissa, who was also a murder victim's family member who opposed the death penalty. Elissa told Bill that she and some other people had been talking about the possibility of forming an organization for murder victims' family members to speak against the death penalty. Bill had never met other victims' family members who opposed the death penalty, and he welcomed the chance to meet others who felt as he did. The two decided to organize a preliminary meeting to be held in Albany during the first week in August, when Bill had scheduled a vacation and could take the time to drive from Indiana to New York and back. A cousin of Bill's and a granddaughter of Ruth's, Judi Weyhe, offered to go with him.

Death penalty abolitionists and murder victims' family members from around the country gathered for a weekend-long meeting. One of the participants was Marie Deans, whose mother-in-law had been murdered in Charleston, South Carolina. Marie shared her experience of being treated poorly by many people in the community after she told the prosecutor that she did not want the killer to get the death penalty. Some even threatened her and her family.

This had so unnerved Marie that she began looking for people in her situation. If she read about another victim's family member who opposed the death penalty, she contacted the person and offered support and advice. She named her fledgling organization Murder Victims' Families for Reconciliation. However, Marie worked full-time as the director of the Southern Coalition of Jails and Prisons and did not have the time necessary to turn her ad-hoc group into a functioning organization.

Although the Albany participants liked the idea, they did not like the name, thinking it was too long. They brainstormed and came up with SOLACE, an acronym for Survivors of Loss Against Capital Executions. Elissa was named executive director, and another participant, Camille, was named president of the new group.

Bill left Albany excited and hopeful. As soon as he returned home, the Oprah Winfrey show called asking him to drive to Chicago the next day to appear on a program about forgiveness called "Forgiving the Unforgivable." Bill agreed.

BILL: I hoped to have the chance to talk about SOLACE, but I never did. I answered Oprah's questions, but after she finished with me I never had a chance to make any additional remarks. But there was another guest on the show, a woman named SueZann Bosler. (See chapter 6.) An intruder stabbed SueZann's father to death and nearly killed

SueZann in their home in Opa-Locka, Florida. SueZann was trying to spare her father's killer, James Bernard Campbell, from Florida's electric chair.

The meetings with Elissa and SueZann turned out to be pivotal moments both in my life and, although we could not have known it at the time, in the movement to abolish the death penalty. By establishing SOLACE we created a network for victims' family members who opposed the death penalty. Instead of feeling isolated and rejected by our families and communities, we could connect with others who shared our beliefs.

SueZann and I became close friends from the moment we met. She immediately joined SOLACE, and because her case drew so much national attention she was able to use that forum to tell others about our new organization.

After so many positive experiences, the year ended on a high note. Judy and I decided to get married. A journalist from Italy was in Indiana doing a story about Paula the weekend we got engaged. He told us if we took our honeymoon in Italy we could stay at his apartment for two weeks. All we had to do was pay our way to Italy and all our expenses would be covered. After seven years of dating, we got married on October 1, 1988.

·  ·  ·  ·

Contrary to the Lake County prosecutor's predictions, the Italian opposition was influencing the Paula Cooper case. Over several years, Italian activists organized a number of high-profile events. In July 1986, protesters from the Italian Radical Party demonstrated outside the U.S. embassy in Rome carrying signs that read "For whom the bell tolls" and "The death penalty equals barbarity."[9]

One of the major organizers was Father Vito, who had stayed in touch with Bill. By that time, Father Vito and Don't Kill had gathered two million signatures on behalf of Paula Cooper. Father Vito traveled to Indiana in May 1988 to deliver the signatures to Governor Robert Orr, but the governor who was out of town during his visit.[10] The next year, Father Vito's organization collected signatures calling for the abolition of the death penalty in the United States. He organized a delegation that delivered the petitions to the United

Nations in New York. During that trip, the delegation traveled to Indiana to attend Paula's hearing in the state supreme court in March 1989.[11]

Besides the activists, politicians were rallying to save Paula's life. Seventy-eight members of the Italian parliament signed a letter to U.S. Ambassador Maxwell Rob asking for Paula's death sentence to be commuted. In the letter they said: "The West should give to the world a concrete and constant example in the face of the darkness and barbarism, arrogance and absolute power. The death penalty can't represent an acceptable practice on the moral level nor is it useful in the fight against violence and criminal behavior."[12] Even Pope John Paul took an interest, telling reporters that he might talk to President Ronald Reagan about the case during a 1987 visit.[13]

Prosecutor Crawford responded to this outpouring of criticism by saying, "The Italians do not understand that America has a tremendous problem with murders committed by young people. I just don't think they're in a good position to judge our sentencing guidelines when, to my knowledge, they don't have anywhere near the crime problem that we do here." Media representatives from Australia, London, West Germany, and Holland had also contacted the prosecutor's office.

However, some in Indiana disagreed with Jack Crawford. Chagrined by the international attention, State Representative Earline Rogers (D-Gary) introduced a bill to raise the minimum age for the death penalty from ten to sixteen. "I have been in office for five years," she said. "I wish I had proposed this legislation last year in time to save Paula Cooper." With a great deal of debate, the Indiana legislature changed its juvenile death penalty statute, raising the eligibility from age ten to age sixteen. However, the legislature specifically stipulated that the law would not apply retroactively.

The Indiana Supreme Court disagreed. On July 13, 1989, the court commuted Paula's sentence from death to sixty years, declaring that "evolving standards of decency" made it intolerable for Paula Cooper to be the first and last person to be executed for a crime committed by a fifteen-year-old.

"Praise the Lord" was Bill's reply to a reporter calling him at work for comment on the court's decision. He talked about forgiveness, his grandmother, love, and compassion, taking the rest of the day off to handle all the press calls he received.

To Bill's surprise, he had mixed feelings about the outcome. He felt tremendous relief that Paula was off death row, but he also felt at a loss with himself. He had enjoyed the opportunity to talk about his grandmother. He assumed that since Paula was no longer facing a death sentence he would not be asked to talk about the case any longer. Events soon proved him wrong.

•   •   •   •

In May 1990, Bill moved from public speaking to public activism. He learned about the Pilgrimage of Life, a march "to ignite the consciences of the religious community around the problems of the death penalty." Several national groups organized it, including the American Friends Service Committee, the National Coalition to Abolish the Death Penalty, and the Southern Christian Leadership Conference. The march began at Florida's death row in Starke and ended at the burial site of Dr. Martin Luther King Jr. in Atlanta, Georgia. Since Bill's opposition to the death penalty grew out of his religious philosophy of love and compassion, he decided to attend, hoping to meet kindred spirits.

Judy was upset when Bill told her that he planned on using more of his vacation time to attend yet another death penalty event. She had tolerated his absences during his crusade to save Paula but had thought their life would return to normal once she was off death row. "Are you nuts?" Judy asked. "Isn't it enough that you forgave her and saved her life? Why do you want to try to get all these other assholes off of death row?"

Judy attempted to dissuade Bill from going. When that failed, she tried to convince him to go for one week instead of two. She asked him who was going to be at the march, where he would stay, and what he would be doing. Bill replied, "I don't know. I don't know. I just feel the need to be there."

After Judy finally gave her blessing, Bill drove the thousand miles by himself, stopping only once for rest. That evening, the marchers converged at the Pax Christi office to make plans for the march. Bill saw Mike Radelet, a professor from the University of Florida he had met at the Amnesty International event. Mike was talking with a woman who was crying. He introduced Bill to Mrs. Kathleen "Kay" Talfero, whose son, Jesse, had been executed at 12:01 A.M. that day, about the time Bill was driving across the state line into Florida.

Jesse, who had been convicted with his common-law wife, Sonia Jacobs, had always maintained his innocence. (Two years after Jesse's execution, Sonia was exonerated and released from death row after filmmaker Micki Dickoff made a documentary about the case.)

Jesse's execution was particularly disturbing because it had been botched. Executioners had to administer three separate applications of electricity before "Old Sparky" finally killed Jesse. While he was still alive, the force of the current ignited Jesse's skin, burning his head and face. Three foot-high flames shot out from the black mask covering his face.

> BILL: Meeting Mrs. Talfero really brought home for me how hard the death penalty is for the families of the people who are executed. Family members are put in the position of having to wait for the state to kill their loved ones, and being powerless to stop it. Everyone felt bad for our family, but the families of the executed are totally forgotten about or made to feel like criminals themselves.

The next day, May 6, 1990, two hundred people gathered at Starke prison to begin their long walk to Atlanta. Before setting off, the group stood in a circle and read the names of all the people on death row in Florida and Georgia.

Many of the participants had extensive experience with the criminal justice system. There were professors, attorneys, activists, and even former defendants. At that time, Bill did not know much about the criminal justice system or the death penalty beyond his personal experience. The march proved to be a crash course in death penalty education that convinced Bill more than ever about the righteousness of his opposition.

> BILL: The more I learned about the death penalty, the more I realized how wrong it is. Most people on death row are poor and did not have adequate legal representation. A disproportionate number of them are minorities who are on death row because they were convicted of killing white people. I also learned that there were a number of people who had been on death row for years before they could prove their innocence. It made me wonder how many were killed before they could prove their innocence.
>
> I started thinking that I should extend my love and compassion beyond Paula. At that time there were thirty-two juveniles on death row, so I started to pray for love and compassion for them. Then I started to pray for love and compassion for everyone on death row. I found I didn't want any of them to die, either.
>
> I met another murder victim's family member, Sam Reese Sheppard. Sam's father, Dr. Sheppard, was wrongfully convicted of killing his mother. The sensational case was the basis of the movie and TV series *The Fugitive*.

Because we were both family members of murder victims, we really bonded. Also, the media was very interested in talking to us. Sister Helen Prejean, who was acting as spokesperson for the group, kept referring reporters to us. They were intrigued to learn that family members of murder victims would oppose the death penalty. That experience showed me the power that victims' families had when speaking against the death penalty. I realized that I had something unique to contribute. I decided on that march to dedicate my life to ending the death penalty.

I called Judy every day and told her about all the people I was meeting. I really wanted her to join me, and I finally talked her into coming down for the second week of the march. By the end of her first day marching, she was chanting slogans against the death penalty along with everybody else. It made me so happy to finally feel like these two pieces of my life were coming together.

Unfortunately SOLACE was not taking shape the way Bill had hoped it would. Both Elissa and Camille were having personal problems that kept them from devoting enough time to the organization. They did not return phone calls or follow through with commitments. In frustration, Marie Deans called Bill to complain that SOLACE wasn't functioning and suggested returning to the original name of Murder Victims' Families for Reconciliation. Jonathan Gradess, one of the attendees at the original SOLACE meeting, found a lawyer who helped set up a nonprofit corporation. Marie Deans, Pat Bane, Sam Sheppard, Theresa Mathis, and Bill became the founding board members.

In April 1991, Bill drove from Indiana to Texas to take part in a two-week pilgrimage organized by Texans Against State Killing and Amnesty International.

BILL: At the last minute one of my best friends, Wayne Crawley, decided to go with me to Texas. Wayne and I had worked together at Bethlehem Steel for years, and even though he supported the death penalty, he also supported the work I was doing. Wayne had met me at the airport when I returned from the first trip to Italy. He supported me when I felt no one else understood me or cared. When Wayne agreed to go to the Texas march with me, I felt like I did when Judy went to Florida—the friends I cared about and loved the most were on my side.

I loved being on the road talking to people about the power of for-giveness. I found that many of the people we spoke to already opposed the death penalty, but my message helped them feel good about their work as abolitionists. People often criticize abolitionists, saying they only care about the criminal, not the victim, so when they heard my story it made them feel like they could be against the death penalty and support victims, too.

I decided on the Texas trip that we needed to organize an event led by murder victims' family members. We came up with the name "Journey of Hope" because we were offering hope to the people we met—hope in the power of forgiveness and hope in the possibility of a world without violence.

When he returned from Texas, Bill pursued his idea of organizing the Journey of Hope. The new board members of MVFR all shared his enthusiasm. Bill organized a steering committee in Indiana led by Bob Gross, then associate director of the National Coalition to Abolish the Death Penalty. Bill, Bob, and many other volunteers spent the next two years organizing the Journey, setting up events at schools, universities, churches, and civic groups. They agreed to speak to anyone who would listen. In July 1993, the Journey began a three-week tour, departing from Bill's house in Portage, Indiana. Murder victims' family members and death row inmates' family members, accompanied by other supporters, caravanned around Indiana and surrounding states. In seventeen days they spoke to 175 different groups. They were starting to get their message out.

In the fall of 1993, a professor at Southern Methodist University, Rick Halperin, invited Bill back to Texas to speak on a panel at the university with two other murder victims' family members, Marietta Jaeger and Kerry Kennedy Cuomo, the daughter of Robert Kennedy. Marietta and Bill clicked right away. Like Bill's, Marietta's journey had been about forgiveness. Both credited their faith with carrying them through their losses.

Rick also wanted to talk to Marietta and Bill about an idea he had: to hold an event at the Supreme Court that would commemorate the reinstatement of the death penalty in the United States.

BILL: Rick is a historian, and he is always talking about dates. For years he had wanted to figure out a way to protest the *Gregg* decision that reinstated the death penalty after a four-year moratorium. *Furman v. Geor-*

*gia,* the Supreme Court decision that outlawed executions, came down on June 29, 1972. *Gregg v. Georgia* was four days and four years after *Furman.* Rick wanted to hold an event during the four days from June 29 through July 2.[14]

We ultimately decided to hold a four-day fast and vigil in front of the Supreme Court. Fasting has been a traditional way to protest injustices. We came up with a list of people we thought would help and formed an ad-hoc group that we called the Abolitionist Action Committee.

We spent the next several months organizing the event. We spread the word throughout the abolitionist community. We contacted the Supreme Court police and requested permission to hold the event. The police told us that we could set up tables and signs on the sidewalk in front of the Court but could not do any type of protesting on the steps leading up to the Court. I was surprised to learn that freedom of speech stops at the first step of the Supreme Court.

There were four of us the first night—Rick, Marietta, Kathy Ford, a writer for the television show *Dr. Quinn, Medicine Woman,* and myself. We sat in front of the court with a card table and a couple of signs. We made pamphlets explaining our purpose. We were very careful to not go onto any of the steps leading to the Court when we were wearing political T-shirts or buttons or anything that made it seem like we were demonstrating.

The next morning, some more people joined us—people from the Catholic Worker House in D.C. and some members of Amnesty International. By the last night we had between twenty and thirty people for our closing circle. We had a big banner and took turns writing the names of all the people that had been executed since the *Gregg* decision. We decided to hold the event every year until the death penalty is abolished.

•   •   •   •

Since the first letter that Bill wrote to Paula in November 1986, the two had corresponded regularly. Bill made many requests to visit Paula in prison, but all were denied. At first the warden told him that he could not visit Paula because she was on death row. Once Paula was off death row, the warden told Bill that he could visit her after she had been in general population for a couple of months and had a chance to get acclimated to her new environment. By then, a new warden was in charge, and she would not honor the old warden's promise.

Some filmmakers working on a documentary about Bill and other victims' family members got permission to interview Paula in prison. While visiting, they interviewed the warden. They asked her why she wouldn't allow Bill Pelke to visit Paula Cooper. The warden denied that she had ever forbidden Bill to visit Paula. She said that if Paula put Bill on her visitors' list, he could visit her.

BILL: The warden lied when she said that she hadn't forbidden me to visit Paula, but after she told them that I could, she kept her word. I learned in November of 1994 that I could visit Paula, so I decided to go on Thanksgiving Day.

By the time of my visit we had exchanged hundreds of letters, so in some ways I felt like I knew her already, but I still wasn't sure what to expect. It was a two-and-a-half-hour drive from my house to the prison, and I would only be allowed an hour visit. During the drive, I thought about what I wanted to say. I learned from the people working on the documentary that she had told them that she wanted to be able to look into my eyes and know that I had forgiven her.

We sat in a visiting room, and she had to sit in a special section so that the guards could keep an eye on her from the observation deck. The first thing I did when I saw her was look into her eyes and tell her I loved her and I had forgiven her. I asked if I could give her a hug and she said yes. She looked just like a normal girl, not some hardened killer. I remember thinking that she looked smaller and thinner than I remembered from seeing pictures of her.

I bought her a soda and some candy, and we just talked about nothing in particular. We didn't talk about the crime. We talked about common friends that we had developed over the years, her attorneys, her sister and grandfather. I talked about my family and some of the traveling I had done.

I just didn't feel like bringing up the crime. She had written to me in a letter once that when we finally had the chance to visit there were things she wanted to tell me about it. She said that some of the things the paper reported weren't true. But I had long ago decided that there was no good reason why she killed my grandmother and Paula herself didn't really know why it had happened. I knew she was remorseful, and I didn't see any reason to bring it up.

Driving home the word *wonderful* kept running through my mind. It was amazing that I could visit someone who had done this to my grandmother and family and not feel any hatred towards her.

· · · ·

In the summer of 1996, Bill bought Judy a Harley-Davidson for her birthday. He often offered to pick her up after work as an excuse to ride the bike. On the road he drove, he passed an old Eastern Trailways bus parked on a lawn.

BILL: When I first saw the bus I thought it would be a great thing for our Journeys. We had just finished our fourth Journey of Hope. I thought that if we had a bus, we could all travel together instead of in a lot of separate vehicles. But I just figured there was no way I could afford to buy a bus.

One day, on a lark, I stopped and copied down the phone number posted on the FOR SALE sign resting in the bus window. I called the number and spoke with a man who turned out to be a deacon for the Baptist church that owned the bus. He said the church was asking $7,500 or best offer. That was a price I could afford. I went and got Wayne, and the deacon took us for a ride. The bus ran good.

I mentioned the bus to Judy even though I wasn't really sure how she would react. She said that for that price I should do it. I suppose it helped that I had just bought her the Harley. By November the bus was mine. I called a friend, George White, who I had met on the first Journey. When I told him about the bus he asked if he could name it. I asked him what he wanted to name it and he said, "Abolition Movin'," which seemed like a good name, so it stuck.

I figured I would fix the bus up, and after I retired I could spend time driving around the country talking about the death penalty. My plan was to work for another year and a half, and then I started thinking, *Why wait another year?* I had put in my thirty years and was eligible to retire. I decided I would retire on May 14, 1997, the twelfth anniversary of Nana's death. That seemed like an appropriate day to start my new full-time work as an abolitionist.

Life was going great. I had the bus to work on. Judy had graduated from nursing school and was working full-time, so between my retire-

*Sister Helen Prejean and Bill Pelke with his bus* Abolition Movin'. *Photograph by Abe Bonowitz.*

ment pay and her salary we had plenty of money to live comfortably. But before I got my first retirement check, Judy dropped a bomb. She said she wanted a separation.

I was shocked. I thought things were fine between us. All the traveling I had been doing had taken its toll, and by the time I realized there was a problem, it was too late. She said to me, "You've got your dream. You know what you want to do. I don't know what I want to do. I need to go away and figure it out." She said she wanted time. I asked her if there was someone else and she said no.

There was an event scheduled in Missouri for the first week of October. She told me that by the time I got back from the event, she would have her stuff out of the house. She was going to stay with a girlfriend's mom who lived in Valparaiso, about ten miles away. I said I wouldn't go to Missouri, but she said it wouldn't make any difference.

I took the bus to Missouri and somehow managed to make it through the event. After everything was over and I had delivered everybody to the airport, I pulled over at a truck stop. Usually after events I was always in a hurry to get home to see Judy. Now I wasn't in a hurry to get home, because there wasn't anyone to go home to.

I felt really crappy. All my dreams involved her. There wasn't really anything I wanted to do on my own. She figured in on everything I was doing. Even when I did stuff without her, she was always a big part of any decision I made or part of whatever goals I had for the future. I got very depressed. I had a hard time sleeping and eating. Sometimes I fell asleep on the couch too depressed to get up and go to bed. On those days Trixie, my great Dane, would come and lie down beside me like she could tell something was wrong. I got to know my dog really well then.

Even though Judy was living nearby, I wasn't seeing her too often. She'd come by the house once in a while, but that was about it. Our relationship had been through a lot of ups and downs, though, and I thought we'd still get back together. Then about six months later, February of 1998, I found out that Judy had been seeing someone else all along—a Harley-Davidson mechanic. I was upset and very angry that she had betrayed me and lied to me.

Forgiving Paula Cooper was one thing, but forgiving Judy Pelke was another. I found out on a Friday that she had been lying. I was supposed to fly to New York on Monday to be on the Sally Jesse Rafael show talking about forgiveness. I was wondering how on earth I could talk about forgiveness when I was so angry at Judy.

For about ten hours I really acted out. I pounded my fist into the wall a few times. I wrote FUCK YOU on some balloons I had given her that said I LOVE YOU. At some point during my ranting, I realized I had to practice what I had been preaching. I had been telling people for years that forgiving Paula Cooper had done more for me than for Paula. I suspected the same would be true with Judy. By about two o'clock the next morning I was able to feel that I had forgiven her. I still felt very sad about our separation. But the anger I felt at what she had done was gone. When I got to the Sally Jesse Rafael show I could talk about forgiveness and mean it.

• • • •

It is January 2002, and Bill sits in his small office in Anchorage, Alaska. His dark hair is just beginning to turn gray; his slightly too long bangs slide down his broad face, almost obscuring his twinkling dark eyes. He is still ruggedly handsome, with a slight belly put on since his retirement.

The room is in the basement of a town house where he lives with his new partner, Kathy Harris. Several file cabinets and a bookshelf dominate the room. A printer, copier, and fax machine sit on an L-shaped desk built into the walls. Mementos of Bill's journey of forgiveness adorn the walls. One three-by-five foot poster memorializes an international march and rally against the death penalty held at the Vatican on Christmas 1998. A calendar from Amnesty International marks the date. Bumper stickers with slogans like JOURNEY OF HOPE . . . FROM VIOLENCE TO HEALING and EXECUTE JUSTICE, NOT PEOPLE adorn the file cabinets. In one picture that Bill is particularly proud of, he is posing arm-in-arm with Tony Knowles, the governor of Alaska, wearing a T-shirt that reads FRY FISH, NOT PEOPLE.

As he tells his story, Bill admits that he wonders sometimes at the strange and twisted path that led him to leave his well-paid job at Bethlehem Steel in Indiana, choosing early retirement so he could dedicate his life to abolishing the death penalty. But he has no regrets.

When he is not on the road telling his story, he spends his days in his office sitting at the computer, responding to e-mails and keeping track of developments in the anti–death penalty movement around the world. He answers the phone and sends out information about his organization, Journey of Hope . . . From Violence to Healing. When he can find the time, he works on writing his memoirs.

He still tells his story whenever he can and has spoken throughout Alaska during the three years he's lived there. His story continues to move people. He says, "When I speak, I don't give a talk on the death penalty, I tell a story. People listen to stories. They open their minds, and then you can touch their hearts."

Recently he spoke at the Holy Family Cathedral in Anchorage. After he finished, a fifteen-year-old boy stood up and said that he had changed his mind about the death penalty. Now, after hearing Bill talk, he opposed it.

BILL: I preached at a church in Soldotna, and after the service, a lady approached me. Her father had been a leader in the Disciples of Christ and had supported the very first pilgrimage I went on in Florida over ten years ago. Her father opposed the death penalty, and he was always trying to talk to his daughter about it, but she wouldn't listen to him. But when she heard me speak, she saw the issue in a whole different light. She was excited and couldn't wait to get hold of her father and tell her about her conversion.

Bill supports the abolition movement by participating on a number of different boards of directors, including the National Coalition to Abolish the Death Penalty and Alaskans Against the Death Penalty. He admits, however, that his true passion is to be out talking to people about the cause he loves. "I don't like going to meetings. I'd rather be on the road telling my story and sharing my message of love and compassion for all of humanity."

# CHAPTER 5

# The Last Word

On Saturday, April 7, 1990, in Winnetka, Illinois—an upscale North Shore suburb of Chicago—Richard and Nancy Langert spent the evening with her parents, Lee and Joyce Bishop, and her sister Jeanne Bishop, celebrating Lee's sixtieth birthday. At around 10:30 P.M. the couple drove Nancy's parents home, then returned to the town house where they were living temporarily while waiting to move into a new home in fashionable Mount Prospect, a few miles to the west.

Nancy was pregnant with their first child, and both she and Richard were excited at the prospect of being parents. Their dream of starting a family and owning their own home was coming true. Nancy told friends that she thought 1990 was going to be a very special year for them.

The couple entered the town house through a sliding glass door that led into the living room. Since they would be moving into their new home soon, they had not unpacked many of their belongings. Boxes covered the floor, and the general disorder of the house may have obscured the fact that someone had broken in while they were out. As they walked into the kitchen, a sixteen-year-old boy pointed a .357 Magnum at them and threatened to kill them. Nancy offered the boy five hundred dollars, which she had because she had just cashed her paycheck. The boy refused the money. They told him to take the compact disc player or anything else he wanted. Nancy told him that she was pregnant and begged him not to hurt them.

Nancy and Richard had locked their cocker spaniel, Pepsi, in the bedroom upstairs before they left the house. Now the dog barked, startling the boy. He fired into a corner of the room, lodging a bullet in the floor. Hoping the noise from the shot would attract the attention of a neighbor, Richard advised the intruder to leave before someone came by to investigate. The boy agreed to go, but he insisted on locking the couple in the basement first so that he could

*Nancy and Richard Langert. Photograph provided with permission of the family.*

escape before they could notify the police. Nancy and Richard cooperated as the boy handcuffed them and led them down the stairs to the basement.

As soon as they reached the bottom of the stairs, the boy placed the gun at the back of Richard's head and pulled the trigger. Nancy watched her husband's head explode. She backed into a corner, covering her stomach protectively, and again begged him not to hurt her child. The boy took a step toward her and shot her directly in the stomach. She turned away from the killer and screamed, "No, not again." This time he shot her from behind. The bullet ripped through her left elbow and lodged in her back, paralyzing her legs. The boy left Nancy to die.

Using her arms to pull her body, she dragged herself to a set of metal shelves, where she got an ax out of a toolbox. She banged it on the shelves, hoping the loud noise would attract attention. No one came.

Knowing that she was dying, Nancy used her last ounce of strength to leave a message for her family. She dipped her finger in her blood and drew a heart with the letter *u* next to it, shorthand for "I love you," the way she signed letters to her family. It took approximately fifteen minutes for Nancy to die.

Nancy and Richard had planned to attend church with the Bishops the next day, Palm Sunday. When the couple did not appear at church, Lee called the town house several times, then decided to drive by to make sure everything was okay. Both cars were in the driveway. Worried, Lee let himself into the town house with his key. He heard Pepsi barking upstairs and rescued the trapped dog; letting it outside, he noticed that the patio door was open. The contents of Nancy's purse were strewn on the floor.

Seeing the light on in the basement, he descended the staircase. Before reaching the bottom, he saw his daughter huddled on the floor. His first thought was that Nancy had fallen down the stairs, but then he saw Richard. In shock, he ran up the stairs and called 911. The dispatcher, concerned because of Lee's extreme distress, kept him on the line until the police arrived.

•　　•　　•　　•

Eighty miles away in Kankakee, Nancy's sister Jennifer was puttering around the house, having just returned from a weekend retreat; she and her husband, Malcom, had chaperoned a group of twenty high school students from the Bishop MacNamara Catholic School, where Jennifer taught religion and social sciences. The retreat had been a wonderful experience for both her and Malcom. She came home feeling refreshed and energized.

JENNIFER: I had only been home an hour or so when I got the phone call from my parents. My father said to me, "Are you sitting down?" I said teasingly, "Oh no, do I have to sit down?" He said, "Yes." I said, "Okay, I'm sitting down." He said, "Nancy and Richard have been murdered." I said, "No, no, no." I didn't believe him. I remember distinctly thinking that he was playing a horrible cruel joke on me, and I was surprised because it was so out of character for him. Then I told him to wait a minute, and I got my husband. I held the phone up next to both of our ears and asked him to repeat what he had just said. I was shaking. Then my mother got on the phone and spoke in a voice I had never heard before. She sounded like she was speaking from another world. I could tell it took enormous effort for her to stay in control. She told me to pack a bag and come as quickly as possible. "Be sure to pack something black for the funeral, and bring enough clothes for several days." I said I'd be there within two hours.

I couldn't believe my sister was dead. It wasn't until about an hour into the drive when I heard the story on the news that it hit me like a ton of bricks. I felt a blow in my chest. I kept wondering what her last moments must have been like. If she had died in an accident I don't think I would have felt such horror.

Lee called his other daughter, Jeanne, at 6:30 in the evening at the Fourth Presbyterian Church in Chicago, where she was taking part in a Palm Sunday processional. The church secretary told Jeanne that she had a phone call. Jeanne looked at her as if she were crazy and asked her to take a message. "No," she said, "you need to come with me."

Jeanne knew something was very wrong but was not prepared to hear her father say, "Nancy and Richard have been killed. Someone murdered them." Lee told her that he had made arrangements for the minister from his church, Dr. Gil Bowen, to pick her up.

Forty-five minutes later Dr. Bowen arrived. They stopped briefly at her apartment, where she packed her things, then drove to Winnetka. Jeanne wanted to find out where Nancy's body was, so Dr. Bowen drove her to the police station. The police told them that Richard's body was already at the morgue, but Nancy's was still at the town house. An officer offered to take Jeanne to see her sister. He drover her to the town house, escorted her to a black body bag, unzipped it, and waited while Jeanne said good-bye to her baby sister. An officer then asked her to go to the morgue to make an official identification of the bodies. Meanwhile, Jennifer and Malcom drove to Winnetka as fast as humanly possible.

JENNIFER: When we arrived in Winnetka, we swung by the town house. I'm not sure why I wanted to go in. I guess I needed to know that it was real, that it was true. I needed to see it for myself. Yellow police tape surrounded the entrance, and I couldn't go inside. A group of reporters hovered near the scene. A well-known television reporter saw me and stuck a microphone in my face, asking, "Who are you? Why are you here? How do you feel about this?" Malcom, who used to work in radio, knew the guy and told him to fuck off. After that, they left us alone.

We drove to my parents' house. The first person I saw was Jeanne. I remember grabbing hold of her. It was the strangest hug. Jeanne said, "It'll never be just the two of us again." I knew exactly what she meant. From then on for the rest of our lives, whenever we would be together we would think of Nancy.

Jeanne told me about seeing Nancy's body. She said that seeing Nancy was unimaginable. Her eyes had a vacant look, there was blood coming from her mouth, and her skin was cold and hard. My mother, who had also seen Nancy, said the expression on her face looked like she was crying out when she died.

For me one of the most profoundly difficult things to deal with is that at the moment Nancy was murdered I was having a great time at this retreat sitting with twenty high school kids who were pouring out their hearts. Everybody was crying and hugging each other. While Nancy was being murdered, I was telling the kids how much I loved my sisters. There was a strange synchronicity about that experience. I both marvel and draw comfort from it.

The next day I went to the town house to help clean up. I didn't want my mother to have to do it, and I didn't want to pay someone else to do it. The police had tried to clean up somewhat, but there was still a lot of blood in the basement and black fingerprint dust all over the place.

We wanted to cremate the bodies as soon as possible and to have the funeral on Wednesday. When we told the police that we had decided on cremation, they panicked, thinking they would not have enough time to complete the forensic work. After we made the plans to have the funeral on Wednesday, they called to tell us that we couldn't. But then they told us they would try to finish the tests on time.

It was very difficult for my parents to wait. My father couldn't bear to think of his daughter lying on a cold slab, and my mother had horrible dreams about the bodies waiting in the cold refrigerator. As it turned out, the police finished all their work in time for us to have the funeral as scheduled.

On Tuesday, we went to the funeral home to cremate Nancy's body. After all the final preparations were complete, I cut a lock of Nancy's hair and kissed her good-bye. I waited for my mom to have a moment with her. She threw herself over Nancy's body. I have never heard anything so painful, a sob from deep inside.

We held the funeral at Kenilworth Union, a nondenominational Protestant church, which Nancy and Richard attended and where they were married. After the service our family and Richard's family buried the ashes in a beautiful memorial garden adjacent to the church, only half a block from Lake Michigan. My father kept lingering at the gravesite. He couldn't seem to bring himself to leave, as though once he did her death would be final.

·　·　·　·

The case attracted extensive media coverage in the greater Chicago area. The killing of a young couple in the affluent suburb of Winnetka shocked the community. The fact that Nancy and Richard were on the brink of starting a family made the deaths more tragic. It was the first double homicide in Winnetka, and only the second case of murder there in thirty years.

Early coverage was very sympathetic, describing Nancy and Richard as "happily in love." They were portrayed as an all-American couple: nice, hardworking, loved their families, and wanted to live the "American dream"— owning their home and raising a family.

The police ruled out burglary as a motive for the murders because the killer left behind the five hundred dollars in cash, credit cards, and a VCR. With virtually nothing to go on, the police began digging into the personal lives of the victims and their families. Any possible lead, no matter how tenuous, made it onto the evening news.

An article in the April 11 *Chicago Tribune* offered the first tentative theory. Police speculated that Richard had incurred a gambling debt and was killed when he couldn't pay it. There was, however, no evidence that Richard gambled; nor were Richard and Nancy in any greater debt than most young American couples.[1]

The next day's *Tribune* featured an article in which Winnetka police chief Herbert Timm announced that the investigation was now focused on Richard and Nancy's workplace. Both worked for Gloria Jean's Coffee Beans, a chain of gourmet coffee stores, Nancy as a sales representative and Richard as a warehouse manager. The story suggested that an employee Richard had recently fired might have had a grudge against him. Or perhaps Richard had uncovered evidence that the company was smuggling in drugs along with the coffee, and someone killed him to prevent him from disclosing his discovery.[2]

The police questioned Jennifer about whether there was anyone who could have wanted to kill Nancy. Jennifer mentioned a man Nancy had known while performing in a local theater production.

JENNIFER: I was racking my brain to think of anything that might possibly provide a lead to the murder. Assuming that what I said would be held in confidence, I told the police about a brief relationship that Nancy had with a man when she was performing in a local play. This happened very early in her relationship with Richard, and Richard knew about it. I didn't really think it would be useful, but then I thought I should tell the police because maybe this man was some kind of wacko and killed Richard and Nancy.

The police investigated the lead, and absolutely nothing came from it. But to my horror, an article appeared in the paper reporting on this relationship. It was very painful for my parents, Richard's family, and the other man. The only way the media could have found out was from the police leaking it.

Next the investigators turned their attention to Lee Bishop's law practice and learned that intruders had attacked one of Lee's clients, a pizzeria owner, in his home. The police publicly speculated that the beating of the pizzeria owner could be connected to the murders: someone seeking revenge against Lee for representing this client might have killed Nancy and Richard.

While the Winnetka police were combing through the personal lives of the victims and their families, they failed to pursue two early leads. A local pawnshop owner contacted the police, telling them that he had recently sold a boy a pair of handcuffs similar to the ones used in the murder. The police did not follow up to find out the boy's name. Additionally, a police officer on duty the night of the murders reported seeing a boy in a black trenchcoat walking in the neighborhood near the town house. The investigators did not try to learn who the boy was.

Within a week, the FBI helped police construct another theory of what happened and why: members of the Irish Republican Army (IRA) were out to kill Jeanne and had mistakenly killed Nancy and Richard instead. The basis for this theory was the fact that Jeanne had traveled to Ireland as part of a human rights organization, American Protestants for Truth about Ireland, whose purpose was to draw attention to civil and human rights violations. The group documented cases of people being held without being charged with crimes, tortured to obtain "confessions," and denied their right to a jury trial.

The FBI started questioning Jeanne about people she knew in Ireland. Jeanne refused to answer, fearing that if she named anyone the FBI would turn the information over to the British government, thereby placing those people in jeopardy of being detained or even killed.

Jeanne pointed out to the authorities how far-fetched their theory was. First of all, no American had ever been killed in the IRA conflict. Besides, the IRA always took responsibility for its killings. Why would it kill Nancy and Richard and not tell anyone?

There were also practical problems with the theory. Why would the IRA think Jeanne was living at the town house? Because Nancy and Richard were only temporary occupants, they hadn't even posted their name on the mailbox or door. Hardly anyone knew that they were living there. On the other hand, Jeanne's name and address were printed in the Chicago phone book, making it very easy for the IRA, or anyone else, to find her at her own home. To top it all off, the two sisters looked nothing like each other.

Despite all the holes in their theory, the FBI persisted in pressuring Jeanne, even telling her that the IRA had made a death threat against her—although they would not tell her when, where, or how this threat had been made. A more likely motive for the investigation, however, might have been the Freedom of Information Act (FOIA) request Jeanne had made the week before the murder to learn if the FBI had a dossier on her.

JENNIFER: I was at home in Kankakee when Jeanne called to tell me to turn on the television news. Carol Marin, a nationally known reporter, was "breaking the story" that Nancy's murder was connected to the IRA. The story mentioned that Jeanne had made a Freedom of Information Act request to the FBI. Turning on the television and learning that the police had decided that the murders were somehow connected to the human rights work Jeanne had done in Ireland was surreal. I was incredulous. I knew the IRA had absolutely nothing to do with the case.

The only thing that made any sense was that the FBI was trying to intimidate Jeanne. The only way that Carol Marin could have learned about the FOIA request was from the FBI, so we concluded that the FBI leaked the story in retaliation for Jeanne filing the request. We knew then that they were going to play hardball, so we steeled ourselves for what was likely to come.

You have to understand that at this point my whole family was still in shock about the murders. I can't stress enough how media attention interferes with the grieving process. We were overwhelmed by the media attention. Each day the theories seemed sexier and more bizarre.

My first emotional reaction was sympathy for Jeanne; for how painful it was for her to be blamed for our sister's murder. The whole theory was so ludicrous I didn't believe that the FBI believed it. I was also angry because this IRA tangent was going to misdirect the murder investigation. I remember having this image of the real killers, who I suspected were two men, sitting at a bar someplace watching the news and laughing to themselves thinking they had outsmarted the FBI and would get away with murder.

Our family decided that we would not answer any questions about Jeanne and her work in Ireland. We did not want to do anything to give the theory any credence.

One thing this experience taught me is not to believe everything you see on the news. I now have so much sympathy for people like JonBenet Ramsey's family. They always go after the family first.

Although Jeanne willingly met with investigators anytime they asked her to, she refused to give them names of anyone whom she had worked with in Ireland. Despite all the weaknesses of their theory, law enforcement officials said that without that information they could not solve the murder. Police Chief Timm publicly accused her of being uncooperative. A story in the April 25 *Tribune* reported, "While not ruling out less unusual reasons for the murders, such as domestic turmoil, drugs or a business deal gone bad, authorities say they are being equally vigorous about pursuing the possibility that Jeanne Bishop's activities may have a link in the April 7 shooting deaths. They want to question Jeanne Bishop, who read aloud at her sister's funeral, about her frequent travels to Ireland as a human rights observer. But Bishop has refused to cooperate with the investigators, according to Winnetka Police Chief Herbert Timm."[3] As the family feared, the FBI and Winnetka police launched a full-scale investigation into the IRA angle and dropped any serious inquiry into other theories. Soon coverage of the case spread outside the Chicago market into major national media outlets such as CNN and the *Wall Street Journal.*

The FBI intimidated Jeanne's family members in their effort to pressure her into "cooperating" with their investigation.

JENNIFER: They showed up at the small conservative Catholic school where I taught without any advance notice and told my principal to "get a substitute" because "we have to talk to her." My principal practically had a heart attack. In front of my students the agents came into my classroom and took me away for questioning.

Within two weeks my principal told me that the school would not renew my teaching contract for the following year. He told me I was "too controversial," but he said he would write me a good letter of recommendation. All I said was "You have really bad timing."

About a month later, at the end of May, I came home from work to find four agents waiting for me at my door. They told me that I needed to talk Jeanne into giving them information. Agent Buckley, in charge of international terrorism, sat in the living room of my house, held my hand, and told me with tears welling up in his eyes that he had been dreaming about my sister Nancy. He said he really cared about her and wanted more than anything to solve her murder. He was so persuasive I was almost convinced that maybe there was something in Jeanne's life that I didn't know about. He told me that the IRA had made a death threat against Jeanne. I later learned this is a common FBI tactic to get people to confide in them.

The FBI also called all Jeanne's friends and clients of the law firm where she worked. They leaked unfavorable information to the press. They checked family phone records, searched Jeanne's apartment and mail, and even went as far as wiretapping her parents' phone. As a last resort, they convened a grand jury investigation. Jeanne learned about it from her best friend, whom they subpoenaed to testify against her.

JENNIFER: Their strategy seemed to be to make it so difficult for Jeanne's family and friends that she would finally succumb to their demands. It was so hard on Jeanne because she had to be on guard all the time. Her battle with the FBI kept her from grieving for her loved ones. It was so hard for all of us to have the name of our murdered sister plastered over the evening news and all the newspapers, but it was hardest of all for Jeanne.

The worst part of all this was our fear that the real killer would never be caught. I remember sitting in the Winnetka police station—eight of them and five of us. They said to Jeanne, "We have exhausted every angle. You have got to talk to us about the IRA."

My mother tried to get them to focus on other possible lines of investigation. She asked them why the IRA would be at 722 Oak Street on a Saturday night. She asked them if they had tried using paid informants to snoop around and ask questions. She kept throwing out ideas that made a lot more sense than that the IRA had killed Nancy and Richard. The police claimed that they had investigated all of those angles, but as far as we can piece it together, once the FBI showed up they dropped other lines of investigation. I don't blame the Winnetka police. They had little experience investigating murder cases. The FBI dazzled them with its theory of international terrorism.

A task force comprised of police from four North Shore communities—Deerfield, Glencoe, Northfield, and Wilmette—assisted the Winnetka police with the investigation. An article in the May 1 *Tribune* reiterated the IRA theory, but this time with a slightly different twist: Jeanne was the real target of the killings, but whoever killed Richard and Nancy may have wanted to send a message to her without leaving any direct links to her activities. The task force speculated that Richard might have been the only intended victim, and that Nancy was killed when she resisted. The article concluded, "Police are convinced that the killings were done by a professional. The killer also left behind an article of clothing that is usually used by professional assassins, sources said. Police have not publicly identified the item."[4]

After two months of investigation, the media had gone from idolizing Nancy and Richard as a model American couple to portraying them as shady characters living lives of intrigue. The *Tribune* editorialized:

> When they were shot to death two months ago last Thursday, Richard and Nancy Langert were described by friends and relatives as an all-American couple who had the perfect marriage. With good jobs, a new home, and a first baby on the way, their young lives appeared full of hope and possibility, which made their brutal slayings in the basement of a Winnetka town house seem all the more tragic and shocking. Below the surface, however, the lives of Richard, 30, and Nancy, 25, were far less idyllic. Their relationship was tinged with indiscretion, and police have discovered several complexities and an intriguing amount of violence on the periphery of their small world.[5]

While the Winnetka police and the FBI searched for the IRA, sixteen-year-old David Biro, a junior at the prestigious New Trier High School, bragged to a classmate that he had killed "that couple," the one that was "all over the papers and the news," but then he added, "Just kidding." He told another classmate, "The police may never catch the guy who killed that couple."

David was a tall, thin youth with a reputation for being very smart but odd. He kept to himself and had few friends. He dressed mostly in black and wore a long black trenchcoat. David's behavior showed signs of his being a dangerous sociopath. He committed so many acts of delinquency that his parents retained John Lewis, a former FBI agent turned lawyer, to defend their son. Among his crimes: he shot out car windows with a BB gun, set a girl's sweater on fire, stole computer equipment from New Trier High, and tried to poison his parents by putting chemicals he got from school in their milk.

After the milk incident, the Biros committed David to Charter Barkley, a private psychiatric hospital, where he stayed during the summer of 1989. There his doctor diagnosed him as "dangerously psychotic." After he came home one weekend on a pass, his parents refused, against medical advice, to return him to the hospital, deciding instead to keep him at home so that he could continue school in the fall. David lived on the third floor of the family's spacious three-million-dollar home. He locked his bedroom door with a padlock and refused to talk to his parents.

David persuaded a twenty-five-year-old man he met at a bar to assist him in obtaining a firearm owner's identification card (FOID), necessary to buy a gun in Illinois. The man filled out the required paperwork using David's address, and David posed for the ID photo. When the card arrived in the mail, David's mother intercepted it. She confronted David and told him that she had mailed the card to John Lewis. David called him and demanded the card, which he refused to turn over. David threatened to break into his office to get it and reminded him that he knew how. The attorney evidently believed him, because when he left town a few days later he placed the FOID card in a locked filing cabinet.

On April 5, 1990, David burgled John Lewis's law office, using a glass cutter to get inside. He rifled through file cabinets, then, not having any luck, opened the desk drawers. There he found something better than an FOID card—a fully loaded .357 Magnum without a trigger lock. David took the gun.

•　　•　　•　　•

On Friday, October 5, 1990, Jennifer was eating dinner with a teacher friend at her favorite Chicago restaurant, the Heartland Café. The weather was mild, and the women sat outside. Jennifer was engrossed in conversation with her friend when the owner of the restaurant approached and asked her if she was Jennifer Jones. He told her that she had a phone call.

**JENNIFER:** It totally flipped me out. I had never gotten a phone call at a restaurant before, and I couldn't imagine who would be calling. It was Jeanne. She said, "Drop everything and come over here, they've made an arrest in the case." I went to Jeanne's apartment in downtown Chicago, and while I was there she got a call from somebody at Channel 7, the ABC affiliate, asking if we wanted to comment on the arrest. We didn't know who had been arrested, so we asked the reporter if he knew. He told us it was a kid named David Bira.

I said to Jeanne, "I wonder if they mean David Biro?" We knew the Biros. At that point we skedaddled out of the city to Winnetka. The phone calls were coming in like crazy. My husband, Malcom, was already at my parents' house doing his usual job of fending off the press. Then a phone call came from Nick Biro asking to speak to my father. Malcom handed me the phone. I said, "Hello, Mr. Biro, this is Jenny. My dad is in the other room with the police and can't talk right now." Nick Biro said, in a very broken voice, "Will you please tell him I said I am so sorry."

Our family had known the Biros for years. Both my dad and Mr. Biro worked for Wilson Meats, first in Illinois and then in Oklahoma City in the 1970s. Both families moved back to Illinois around the same time. Like our family, the Biros had three children, but their children were younger, so we didn't know each other. But our parents socialized together occasionally.

The murder of Nancy and Richard Langert was solved not because of the investigative efforts of the North Shore task force but because Phu Hoang, a friend of David Biro's, turned him in. When the police arrested David, they found a .357 handgun, a glass cutter, handcuffs, burglar tools, and a scrap-book full of clippings about the case. They told him that he was under arrest for the murder of the Langerts. He replied, "So what if I did kill them? How are you going to prove it?"

•     •     •     •

Six weeks shy of his seventeenth birthday when he murdered Nancy and Richard, David was not eligible for the death penalty under Illinois law. The day after the arrest, Cook County district attorney Cecil Partee held a press conference at the Winnetka police station. Partee, an African American, was part of the Cook County Democratic political machine. He was in a tough reelection race against a conservative Republican named Jack O'Malley. O'Malley was white, young, well educated, preppy, and ultraconservative with a message of getting "tough on crime."

JENNIFER: I was in the basement of the Winnetka police station when I heard someone, I believe a person working on Partee's campaign, mention David Biro. The aide said that Biro was too young to get the death penalty, so one of Partee's campaign promises was that, if elected, he would advocate lowering the age of the juvenile death penalty to sixteen. I heard this remark and thought that once again my sister's case was going to be used for a political platform. I walked over to him and said, "If you do that we will publicly oppose you."

I explained to them that I opposed the death penalty. I laid out all the intellectual arguments against it that I had formulated from studying the issue. But what really motivated me was that it made me sick to think that Nancy's murder would become a political event for the purpose of expanding the juvenile death penalty in Illinois. I stated very clearly that we would fight them every step of the way if they tried to use Nancy's case to further their political agenda. The issue may have come up again during the campaign, but it was not seriously promoted. I'd like to think that my conversation with his staff kept Partee from pursuing it.

The trial of David Biro began November 4, 1991, and lasted two weeks. Nancy's entire family attended. Jennifer and Lee were both witnesses. Lee testified about finding the bodies, and Jennifer, who was five months pregnant, testified about the location of various items in the basement that she found while cleaning the day after the murders.

Phu Hoang, the main prosecution witness, explained to the jury how he learned that David Biro had killed the Langerts. David visited Phu at the drugstore where he worked in July 1990 and told him that he needed to leave town, that he would wind up "in the morgue, in jail, or on the news" if he didn't leave Winnetka soon. Phu went for a ride with David and asked him why he needed to flee. David asked Phu, "What is the worst thing I could have done?" Phu replied, "Kill someone." David then said, "Who could I have killed?" Phu asked if it was the Langerts. David laughed. He told Phu, "They were pleading with me not to kill them. I considered taking the money and the Discman and running but decided not to because that is not why I was there."

Phu asked David if he regretted what he had done. David said, "No. There's no room for regret in this world." He added that the Langerts deserved to die because they were "annoying." David told Phu that after the murder he went to a fast-food restaurant and several Chicago bars.

Phu agonized about what to do, but at that time he did not tell anyone about the conversation. However, on September 21, 1990, David told Phu that he was planning another killing. He described a detailed plan to drill into the Bank of Winnetka in the middle of the night, wait until the staff arrived in the morning, and then kill them. David said he would leave a note taunting the police. Phu saw a drill, chisel, spikes, and hammers in a gym bag in David's bedroom.

Fearing that his friend was going to kill again, Phu sought the advice of his friend Kate Usdrowski. Kate told Phu to go to the police, and on October 4 the two contacted Detective Sergeant Patricia McConnell of the Winnetka police department.

JENNIFER: Watching the trial was very therapeutic for me. I never doubted that the jury would convict David Biro. I felt a certain satisfaction at seeing him exposed for who he was. He stupidly chose to take the stand and testify in his own defense, against the advice of his attorney. He had this "I'm smarter than everybody else" attitude. He was so cocksure, certain that he was not going to be convicted. He had read about Leopold and Loeb and was convinced he had committed the perfect crime. His lawyer had advised him to plead insanity, but we heard through the grapevine that David was running his own defense.

David admitted to taking the gun from his lawyer's office but said he gave it to his friend Burke Abrams, who killed Nancy and Richard with it and then gave it back to him to hide. David's explanation for Nancy's message in blood was that she had written the letters *b* and *u* because she was trying to write the name Burke.

The prosecutor devastated David during cross-examination. He calmly and methodically made him out to be the lowest thing alive. He asked him, "David, what did you say to the pregnant woman before you killed her?" I was cheering him on, saying to myself, "Yeah, you get him." I felt righteous anger. I felt like all of my need to see him suffer was satisfied by watching him be exposed for what he was.

A particularly gratifying moment came when the prosecutor recalled me to the witness stand to rebut David's explanation for the letters in the blood. He asked me what Nancy had been trying to communicate, and I explained that Nancy always signed notes and cards to us with a heart and a *u,* which was shorthand for "love you."

The trial also helped heal the animosity between the police and our family. The Winnetka police assigned Patty McConnell to lead the investigation against David. She finally did for us what we had wanted all along—she conducted a real investigation against a real killer. She was very professional. She won us over.

We had barely settled ourselves upstairs in the prosecutor's office when we got the news that the jury had returned a verdict. It took less than an hour and a half. We knew by the speed of the deliberations that the verdict was guilty. And of course it was. Not only was David convicted of two counts of murder for killing Nancy and Richard, he was also convicted of a third count of murder for intentionally killing an unborn child. Under Illinois law the judge had no choice but to sentence David to mandatory life in prison without parole. We considered the outcome a victory.

•   •   •   •

With the criminal case finally behind them, the Bishops tried as best they could to go on with their lives without Nancy and Richard. On March 2, 1992, Jennifer gave birth to her first child, Elizabeth.

JENNIFER: At the time of Nancy's murder I hadn't had children yet, so I didn't really understand what it had been like for my parents to lose a child. When Elizabeth was five days old, it was my first day alone with her. My mother had gone home, and my husband was at work. It was early in the morning, and I was nursing my baby, and she was all wiggly and cute, and I looked down at her and realized that if anything happened to this child I would die. The enormity of Nancy's murder hit me. I burst into tears, and I realized the depth of what my mother had felt. I called my mother and told her about my experience, and *she* burst into tears. She said that she and Dad didn't want to show Jeanne and me the intensity of their grief because they didn't want us to think that they didn't love us.

Looking back I realized that whenever we were with them they always asked us how we were doing and focused their attention and love on us. I guess it was selfish of me not to think about what it must have been like for them.

*Jennifer and Jeanne Bishop and children. Photograph provided with permission of the family.*

On April 3, 1992, just shy of the two-year statute of limitations, the Bishops and Langerts brought a civil suit against David, his parents, and John Lewis.

**JENNIFER:** David himself prompted our decision to bring the suit. We were pretty close to the two-year statute of limitations. We had originally decided not to sue, but then we learned about a plan for a made-for-TV movie script. Supposedly Holly Hunter had already been approached to play Jeanne. When I learned that, I jokingly said I'd agree to the movie if they got Meryl Streep to play me.

But all kidding aside, it was clear to us that David was intending to profit from killing Nancy and Richard. In the case of David Berkowitz the Supreme Court ruled that the First Amendment protects the right of a killer to tell his story and that he is entitled to keep any royalties.[6] In order for the family of the victim to prevent the killer from keeping that profit, the family has to sue civilly and get a judgment against the killer. We decided to sue David so if he made any profit from the murder, we would get the money instead of him.

We decided to sue his parents, too, because we believed that they had been negligent by failing to get psychiatric help for David. They didn't return David to the hospital after the doctors told them he was not ready to be released. We decided not to sue the hospital, even though it had deeper pockets, because nobody there made any decisions that contributed to Nancy and Richard's deaths. We felt the hospital had done everything that could reasonably be expected.

We also sued John Lewis, because he negligently provided the murder weapon. David had told him he was going to break into his office, and Lewis took the threat seriously enough that he locked the FOID card away for safekeeping. Unfortunately, he had left the .357 Magnum accessible. David broke into his office on Thursday, and on Saturday he killed Nancy and Richard.

We know that Lewis reported the theft, but the Winnetka police apparently did not look through reports of stolen weapons in an effort to locate the murder weapon. Had the police followed the lead from the pawnshop owner and investigated the theft of Lewis's gun more thoroughly, this crime could have been solved in days.

We got a judgment against David Biro for forty-one million dollars. Of course, we have not gotten a penny of the money. The judgment put an end to any further talk about a movie. We are unlikely to get any money from David except for any inheritance that he might get, which will be meager. David's case wiped out his parents financially. We settled the case with the Biros. Their homeowner's insurance paid a modest settlement.

•　　•　　•　　•

In the fall of 1992, some friends of Jeanne's from the Unitarian church in Evanston invited Jeanne and Jennifer to address the congregation about their sister's murder and their opposition to the death penalty. Neither had felt free to speak publicly about the case while the criminal case was pending. The invitation provided them with their first opportunity to talk about Nancy. Word spread about Jennifer and Jeanne and their opposition to the death penalty.

A few months later, Bill Pelke invited Jeanne to speak at a Journey of Hope rally he was organizing in downtown Chicago at Daly Square, part of a two-week event in which members of Murder Victims' Families for Reconciliation would be traveling throughout Indiana and surrounding states speaking against the death penalty. (See chapter 4.) Neither Jeanne nor

Jennifer had heard of MVFR or met other victims' family members who opposed the death penalty. They were eager to meet others who felt as they did.

JENNIFER: The rally was only the second or third time I had spoken publicly. There were about a hundred people in the audience. Jeanne spoke before I did, and she just came out and told the entire story of Nancy's murder. She talked about the details of how David murdered her and her heroic efforts to protect her baby and send a last message to her family. I was greatly relieved and surprised when I heard Jeanne tell the chronology of events of that evening. I had never heard anyone go into such detail about a murder in public. She moved the audience deeply. It really amazed me. That is part of the power of the story. I had been unsure of how much of the story to tell, but Jeanne's honesty freed me up to speak from my heart. And I saw the power that murder victims' families have to move people on the issue of the death penalty.

The *Chicago Tribune* covered the demonstration and published an article on June 13, 1993, stating the sisters' opposition to the death penalty. Jeanne is quoted as saying: "Executing murderers will not make the victim's family feel better" and "We're here to say: 'Don't kill in our name.' We've suffered from killing and violence, and we reject it." The article concluded with Jennifer explaining the message Nancy left in her own blood—a heart with a *u* inside, meaning "love you." Jennifer added, "[Nancy] had the last word that day, not the murderer, and the last word was love."[7]

Shortly after her Chicago speaking debut, Seth Donnelly from the Illinois Coalition to Abolish the Death Penalty asked Jennifer to serve on the board of directors. Surprised and flattered by the invitation, she said yes. Once on the board, she was asked to join the "visiting team," a group from the coalition that regularly visited death rows, monitoring conditions and providing support to the inmates. Jennifer reluctantly agreed.

JENNIFER: I had mixed feelings about visiting death row, but eventually my curiosity and need to understand won out. Ron Frederickson organized the visits to the Pontiac row, the largest one in Illinois. I told him I only wanted to meet with people who had really struggled with their consciences, people who had changed or were interested in changing. I wasn't interested in talking to people like David Biro who were just going to make me feel hopeless about the possibility of real change. He assured me that I would meet a lot of really good people, and he was right.

I remember my first trip to Pontiac. It was one of the most transforming days of my life. I saw about three-quarters of the ninety guys there. I saw kids from poor communities, with no education, who committed their crimes while whacked-out on twenty different kinds of chemicals and now at age twenty-five were sitting on death row. For every white face, I saw three or four black faces.

I saw mentally ill people—some just staring at the ceiling. For example, one man, Robin Owens, refused to wear clothes or use a toilet. He ate his urine and feces. I passed by his cell very carefully trying to check on him. I sort of had a conversation with him. I asked him if there was anything he needed. He started masturbating, so we had one of the male visitors go talk to him instead.

I was not prepared for all that I had seen. I remember saying to Ron at the end of the day, "Ron, this is unbelievable. Every American should see this." He nodded at me and said, "Yup, pretty powerful."

As a result of her visits to death row, Jennifer became involved in opposing Ray Lee Stewart's execution. Ray had killed six people on a rampage and was facing a September 17, 1997, execution date. What drew Jennifer to the case was the fact that Connie Mitchell, the mother of one of the victims, opposed the execution. Connie wrote a letter to the editor saying that she had forgiven Ray and asking that he not be executed.

JENNIFER: After reading her letter in the paper, I telephoned Connie to tell her about MVFR. Connie was a very poor, elderly shut-in who lived in public housing in Rockford and had cancer. She was thrilled to know that anyone cared enough about her to reach out. I decided to help Ray by helping Connie to speak out on his behalf. I drove Connie to Pontiac to visit Ray and accompanied her to Springfield to testify before the legislature.

Although Ray committed a horrible crime, my heart went out to him when I learned about the circumstances surrounding it. Ray lived in a home with an alcoholic father who sexually abused his five daughters. Each night he took one of the girls off to a room to have sex with him, including his five-year-old. One night Ray confronted his father after he watched him beat his mother and push her down the stairs. His father's reaction was to beat Ray and throw him in a Dumpster. Ray left home after that incident and started living on the street. By age nineteen, he was regularly using drugs. One night he became delusional and went on a shooting spree, randomly killing six people. In his paranoid state he believed he was retaliating for President Kennedy's assassination. All of the victims' family members, with the exception of Connie Mitchell, wanted Ray executed.

We also used Ray's case to bring several legal challenges against Illinois Department of Corrections (DOC) policy. The first challenge involved the right of the condemned person to have a spiritual advisor of his own choice, which DOC policy forbade. A person facing execution had to use whichever chaplain happened to be on duty at the time of the execution, regardless of whether the condemned person knew the chaplain or shared the same religious faith. Second, Ray requested that he be permitted to donate his organs, also forbidden by the DOC. Lastly, Ray had made a tape apologizing to the families of the people he murdered, and he asked that it be sent to them, but the DOC denied this request as well. By challenging these policies, Ray hoped to make legal inroads for other persons on death row.

I also helped raise the profile of Ray's case by convincing both Reverend Jesse Jackson and Joseph Cardinal Bernadin to visit Ray. The cardinal, who was dying of cancer, literally left his deathbed to meet Ray to give him his blessing. The story of the dying man meeting the dying man made a powerful statement against the death penalty. Reverend Jackson offered the support of his Rainbow/PUSH organization. All of our efforts proved futile, though. The state went ahead with the execution.

Ray wanted me to witness his execution, but the warden denied his request. DOC policy does not require them to allow witnesses other than the DOC chaplain. Ray's mother and sister visited on the last day, but they left at six P.M., and he wasn't executed until midnight.

The only witnesses permitted were family members of the victims, the media and elected officials. Carol Marin, the reporter who broke the IRA story, watched the execution. By then we had become friends. I arranged for her to interview both Ray and Connie Mitchell.

While the execution took place, I attended a candlelight vigil outside the prison. It was after midnight when Carol finally came out. She walked to me and gave me a huge hug, and we just hugged each other for half an hour, crying together. She described the execution to me. The experience greatly disturbed her.

It was Ray's case that really convinced me to devote myself to being an abolitionist. Ray wasn't a really bright guy, and he committed horrible crimes, but at the end of his life he tried to make a difference. He tried to redeem himself, and it broke his heart that he failed in his efforts. Denying his requests was part of the DOC's effort to totally dehumanize him. Their policies seem to be designed to prevent people from doing any small action that might help the convicted person gain a shred of humanity. It was heartbreaking.

Their decisions were wasteful and sad and reaffirmed the evil of the system. As a victim, I would be angry if I was a family member who didn't get to hear the apology. Ray wanted the families to know how sorry he was. He was a changed man, and he was begging for their forgiveness. I would give anything to hear David Biro ask for my forgiveness.

During one of her visits to Pontiac, Jennifer met with a death row inmate named Leonard Kid who told her that he had met David Biro while serving time at the Menard correctional facility, where David is housed. Although he had not met Jennifer at that time, Leonard knew about her and her story, as did all of the men on Illinois's death row, because of her work against the death penalty. He made the connection that the David Biro he knew at Menard was the one who had killed Jennifer's sister.

One day while in the exercise yard, Leonard said to David, "You killed the sister of those two wonderful women who are trying to save our lives." David responded, "I don't give a shit about those bitches." At that remark, several of the men on death row beat David so badly he had to be hospitalized. When Leonard told Jennifer this story he was very proud of himself. Jennifer told him, "I appreciate your chivalry, Leonard, but you know how I feel about violence."

JENNIFER: I would like very much to meet with David, but I am not willing to approach him unless I think that he has taken responsibility for what he did. It would mean the world to me to hear him apologize, but I don't see that happening anytime soon. I have asked the prison chaplain at Menard to let me know if David says or does anything to indicate that he has taken responsibility for the crime or if he has any interest in meeting me. So far, there has been no sign of either.

. . . .

More than a decade after their sister's death, Jennifer and Jeanne are both actively speaking and organizing against the death penalty. Jeanne left her job with the large law firm to become a Cook County public defender. She married and now has children. After trying very hard to keep their marriage together, Jennifer divorced Malcom. As a single mom, she does not have much time to visit death row, but she still keeps in touch with some of the men and regularly speaks to audiences around the country. In January 2001, she was elected president of the board of directors of MVFR.

JENNIFER: There is no way I would be spending so much time speaking against the death penalty had Nancy not been murdered. The depth of feeling on the issue wouldn't have been there. What motivates me is the power of my ability to make a difference on this issue. I know that I have an impact. If a religious leader or abolitionist speaks against the death penalty, nobody is surprised, but if someone in your family has been murdered and you oppose it, you have a different type of credibility. People listen more.

It is very healing for me to talk about Nancy. I get to remember her and share with others how she loved life and repeat the message she left in her blood. Whenever I am asked to give a title to my talks, I always say, "How do we respond to evil?" Nancy watched her husband murdered in front of her, felt her baby die inside of her, and still with her last gasps of life left her family a message telling us she loved us. We all get so busy with the details of our lives that we lose sight of what is important. "Love you" were her last words on life. Those words are sacred to me. That is how I am going to live my life, and that is how all of us should live.

# CHAPTER 6

# Keep Hope Alive

On Saturday, December 22, 1986, the Reverend Billy Bosler and his twenty-four-year-old daughter, SueZann, spent the morning shopping for last-minute Christmas presents at the Swap Shop, a large flea market in Fort Lauderdale, Florida. They planned to fly on Christmas Day to Warsaw, Indiana, to join the rest of the family at the home of Jill Bosler Best, Billy's oldest daughter. Jill had recently given birth to a girl named Lindsey Marie Best, the first grandchild in the family. SueZann's mother, Phyllis, and younger sister, Lynette, were already in Warsaw.

At around two o'clock in the afternoon, Billy and SueZann returned to their modest coral-colored home—a Church of the Brethren parsonage at 18200 N.W. Twenty-second Avenue in Opa-Locka, a suburb of Miami. Located north of Liberty City, the neighborhood was considered dangerous. People often asked Reverend Bosler why he chose to work in a drug-ridden neighborhood where violence and murder were commonplace. He would reply, "These are God's people and I love them. We Christians must show God's acceptance, not just talk about it."

SueZann and her dad were in a good mood after their shopping expedition. They laughed and joked with each other while unloading their treasures. Most of the presents were for the new baby. SueZann had more shopping to do, so she telephoned a friend to make arrangements to go to an area mall. Reverend Bosler settled into a comfortable chair in the living room, planning to spend the afternoon reading.

SueZann took a shower and was putting on her makeup when she heard the doorbell ring. People visited the parsonage at all hours of the day and night seeking food, shelter, clothing, and spiritual guidance. The family always made them welcome. SueZann assumed the visitor was for her dad, but out of curiosity she opened the bathroom door to see if she could recognize who was there.

*Reverend Billy Bosler. Photograph provided with permission of the family.*

**SUEZANN:** I heard my dad open the door, and then I heard strange noises, like grunts and groans. I knew something was wrong. I ran into the hallway, and by that time my father was by the kitchen doorway holding onto the molding and facing me. A man I had never seen before was stabbing him. I screamed and ran towards them trying to stop the man but by the time I got there my father had been stabbed multiple times and collapsed to the floor.

The man came towards me to stab me in the front, but I turned quickly enough that he stabbed my back—three times. I fell to the floor. My father tried to get up to his knees to help me, but the man started attacking him again, stabbing him repeatedly until my dad collapsed again.

I got up from the floor and started backing into the living room, and the intruder put his hand on my right shoulder. He was about a foot away from me, staring into my eyes, and he had the knife in his right hand up by his head, preparing to thrust it in my face. I turned my head to the right, and he stabbed me three more times. Each time the blade was embedded in my head. I collapsed on the floor facing my father.

I felt the man's presence above me as though he was trying to figure out if I was dead or alive. I pretended to be dead by holding my breath.

He must have thought I was dead because he went into my bedroom in the back of the house. It sounded like he was dropping things and pushing stuff around, probably looking for money and valuables.

I started wondering if this was really happening or if I was having a bad dream. I asked God, "Is this for real, is this really happening?" Warm blood was running over my face and eyes. I was watching my father, and I could tell that he was gasping for breath, desperately trying to get air into his body. I was talking to God, asking him what I should do. "Should I wait or go try to help him?" I just lay there and watched my father try to breathe. Finally the man came out of my bedroom and went into my sister's bedroom. I just started praying, "Please hurry, please get out of here so I can get help for my dad."

It didn't take him long to search Lynette's room because she had just left for college, so there was hardly anything there. He came out of the room and seemed very angry, but he was mumbling and I couldn't tell what he was saying.

I heard him go into the kitchen. It sounded like he got into my purse, because I heard keys drop to the floor. He stole thirty-one dollars. I saw my father's shoulders collapse to the floor as if he had stopped breathing. I prayed, "Oh God, please don't let him be dead." I knew deep within myself that he had died, but I talked myself out of it because I had faith and hope that I could save him. I asked God to please save my father's life. I said, "If something happens to me, that is okay, I know I am going to heaven, but people here need him. Please don't let him die." My dad was such a good person he deserved to live. He would give the shirt off his back to anybody.

The man came out of the kitchen, grabbed a chair and threw it on top of me, then went back into the kitchen. I heard a noise like a thump, and then he came back into the living room and paced back and forth on the terrazzo. He didn't touch me any more but instead went into my parents' room. He was in there for a long time. I wondered why it was taking so long. When he finally came out I could see that he had something wrapped around his hand. He pulled open the door, hitting my dad's body, then locked it and pulled it shut.

As soon as I heard the door click, I looked out the window to see which way he went so I could tell the police. I dialed 911, and the person who answered acted like she thought I was a prank caller. I told her my number and address five times, and she kept asking me off-the-wall questions. I got upset and hung up and called back. The next person I got helped me to calm down. She made me stay on the phone. I said to the person on the phone, "Oh my God, I am going to die." I remember holding my head and holding my knee, although I'm not sure why. There was a river of blood running down me, and I was getting weak.

Finally I saw someone in a uniform go by. The operator told me to get up and open the door for the police officer. When I opened the door, I sat back down. He pulled his gun out, and he caught my head and the phone as I blacked out, now that I knew help had arrived.

Detective Hank Ray Jr., one of those who responded, had rarely seen such a gruesome crime scene as the Bosler home. It looked like a hurricane had gone through the house raining blood in its path of destruction. Furniture was tipped upside down and scattered around the room. Blood covered the lime green carpet and the terrazzo patio floor. A number of bloody paper towels littered the kitchen area.

**SUEZANN:** The next thing I remember was waking up in the ambulance. A paramedic was cutting my underwear off. I asked about my dad and he said, "Your dad is okay." I remember being pushed across four lanes of traffic to get to a helicopter that was waiting to take me to Jackson Memorial Hospital. Detective Rickie Smith stayed next to my side. I drifted in and out of consciousness. Each time I became conscious, he was there asking me questions about the crime.

En route, SueZann described her assailant to Rickie as a black, clean-shaven man, about her height—five feet, two inches.

**SUEZANN:** I remember at one point I woke up in the emergency room and looked down at my naked body covered with different shades of blood—dark red for the older, dried blood and a lighter red for the fresh blood. I said to Detective Smith, "I am going to pass out. I am going to throw up." He just stood there and looked at me. I turned my head to the other side of the stretcher and threw up before passing out again.

At the hospital, it took medical personnel eight hours to stabilize SueZann. At midnight, a team of surgeons led by Chief Surgeon Howard Landy opened SueZann's skull and removed hundreds of pieces of shattered bone, the entire left side of her skull, and two pieces of mangled brain. Now only a layer of skin covered one half of SueZann's brain, making the risk of further brain damage great.

Each time SueZann woke, she'd ask about her father. No one told her the truth: he had died before the ambulance arrived at the parsonage. Her family and the doctors agreed that SueZann was more likely to survive if she did not have to deal with the added emotional trauma of her father's death.

While the doctors and nurses fought to save SueZann's life, Metro Dade police officers began the laborious process of preserving evidence from the crime scene. Officer Carl Bennett, assisted by technician Susan Bowman, painstakingly collected twenty-three latent fingerprints from furniture and other objects that the assailant probably touched, such as paper towels and a package of cigarettes. Given the amount of blood throughout the house and on the doorjamb outside, crime scene investigators determined that the attacker had serious cuts on his hand, probably caused when the knife slipped while he was stabbing his victims.

The coroner's report indicated that Reverend Bosler died of multiple stab wounds—twenty-four total. Many of the wounds were superficial and defensive. But several were serious: a blow to the left arm that penetrated three and a half inches and shattered his left humerus; a blow to the stomach that penetrated five and a half inches and perforated the fifth, sixth, and seventh ribs, punctured the liver, and filled the right chest cavity with blood; and one that punctured the left lobe of the lung, filling the left chest cavity with blood.

Even though it was the Christmas holiday, Metro Dade police worked around the clock to catch the killer. Detective Jeff Geller was assigned as the lead investigator. Tall, with dirty blond hair, Jeff was both an intensely driven investigator and a compassionate person; he cared deeply about solving crimes but also respected the rights of the accused. Jeff informed all officers to be on the lookout for a short black man with cuts on his hands and ordered any officer who found someone meeting that description to contact him personally.

A week to the day after the murder, Detective Hank Ray Jr. responded to a call at Hearns Market, a small convenience store in the Opa-Locka neighborhood near the Boslers' home, where many locals congregated. He found a black man peering into an unoccupied police car with his hand on the driver's door. When the man saw Hank, he tried to get away, but Hank detained him and asked what he was doing looking into the police car. Hank noticed deep gashes in the man's hands that cut into the bone, so he asked the man how he had gotten them. He had been in a bar fight, he said. The man identified himself as James Bernard Campbell. Hank ran a record check and found that James had two outstanding juvenile warrants. His address was listed as 2250 N.W. 178th Street—four blocks from the Boslers' home. He had recently served a twenty-eight-month sentence for burglary and assault in Hardee County and had been released from the Avon Park Correctional Institute the previous October. Hank arrested James on the warrants and took him back to police headquarters.

There, Detective Jeff Geller advised James of his *Miranda* rights. He ascertained that James could read and write and was not under the influence of any drugs or alcohol. James said that he had been in a bar fight and a day or so later had gone to the hospital for stitches, but the emergency room personnel refused to treat him, since his wounds had started to heal. Jeff took photographs of James's hands. He told James that he did not believe him and accused him of killing Reverend Bosler. James denied the murder, claiming that he spent the day doing yard work at his stepfather's house.

Jeff questioned James for three hours, then gave up and told James that he would return for further questioning once the lab finished analyzing the fingerprints taken from the crime scene. As Jeff started to leave the room, James started hitting him on his back. With the help of another officer, Jeff restrained James, handcuffing him to a ring on the floor. Eventually James fell asleep.

At about nine P.M., an officer woke James to tell him that his fingerprints matched those found at the scene. At first James denied committing the crime. He admitted that he had gone to the church to get money but said that he had gotten into a fight with the minister when he refused to give James money. Eventually, however, James admitted to stabbing both Reverend Bosler and SueZann.

On January 14, 1987, accompanied by two assistant state's attorneys, Malcom Purow and Dennis Siegel, Jeff showed SueZann a photographic lineup while she lay in bed at Jackson Memorial Hospital. SueZann looked at the five photographs, and a smile spread across her face as she pointed to number five. "That's him," she said. SueZann identified James Bernard Campbell.

·     ·     ·     ·

While the state prepared its case for trial, SueZann focused on her physical and emotional recovery. She spent the first month after the attack in the hospital recovering from surgery. She then moved to a studio apartment a block away from the hospital so that she could easily attend physical and occupational therapy and have regular neurological examinations. Her mother moved in with SueZann and focused all her energy on her daughter's recovery.

SUEZANN: The recovery process was very long and painful. I had to wear a plastic cap with padding on my head for the next eight months to protect my brain. There was only a thin piece of skin between my brain and the world. I had to be very careful about what kinds of things I did, and I had to sleep in a certain position with my head propped at an angle; otherwise it would swell.

My mother was really great. She lived with me for at least a year and a half before I could live on my own. I didn't have any medical insurance, but our congregation established a fund and people made enough contributions to pay about one-third of the medical bills.

After my father's murder, the people in our congregation really pulled together to keep the church going. They managed to hold the church together until a married couple, both ministers, replaced Dad. They were really wonderful to my mother and me. They attended court proceedings with us, visited, and took us out for meals.

The police officers were really fantastic, too. They visited me a lot, and several became friends. Hank Ray Jr., the officer who first found me at my house, is an artist. He gave me a beautiful piece, a black-and-white seal, and titled it *Survive*.

It really was a miracle that I survived the attack. The blow right below my shoulder blade was half an inch from my spine—it nearly paralyzed me. Another blow was millimeters away from severing the big vein that goes to your arm. If the wounds had been in slightly different positions, I would have bled to death or become a vegetable. When my mom flew back from Indiana, she thought that she would have to take care of me the rest of my life.

In August 1987, eight months later, SueZann returned to the hospital for her second round of surgery. This time, Dr. Landy implanted a plastic plate to replace the lost skull. After several weeks in the hospital, SueZann returned to intensive physical and occupational therapy.

**SUEZANN:** I had to relearn how to do a lot of things, like how to talk again. I had a very difficult time speaking. Sometimes I'd be talking to someone and get frustrated because I couldn't get the word I was looking for from my brain to my mouth. I was taking three different kinds of medication, and they affected my memory, too. The funny thing is that my memory of what happened the afternoon of the attack was perfect. I recalled every small detail.

•　　•　　•　　•

The trial of the State of Florida versus James Bernard Campbell began on January 4, 1988. Besides the murder of Reverend Bosler, the state charged James with five other crimes: attempted murder of SueZann Bosler, armed robbery, burglary while armed, use of a weapon in the commission of a felony, and assault on Detective Jeff Geller. The state dropped the assault charge before trial.

Lead prosecutor Michael Band knew his case was strong: matching fingerprints, a confession, and serious knife wounds on James's hands at the time of his arrest. But his ace in the hole was SueZann's testimony. SueZann horrified the jury with the details of watching her father being stabbed to death and being left for dead herself.

It took the jury only ninety minutes to convict James Campbell on all counts. On February 17, he returned for sentencing. Under Florida law, the jury decides whether to impose the death penalty, and then the judge either follows or rejects that recommendation.

The particularly heinous nature of the murder and James's prior criminal record supported imposing a death sentence. To try to spare his client's life, the defense attorney called a psychiatrist who testified that James had an IQ of 68, which meant he was borderline mentally retarded. James read at a third-grade level, suffered from chronic alcohol and drug abuse, and had a borderline personality disorder.

The defense called Willy Bell Lance, James's aunt, to testify about his early childhood. She told the jury that James had never had a relationship with his father and that his mother physically abused him. When he was ten, James ran away from home, arriving at his aunt's house with bruises all over his body and bleeding from his ear. The state intervened and took custody of James, who then lived at various times with his grandmother, with his aunt, and in foster homes. By the time he was a teenager, James was committing crimes to support his drug habit.

SueZann testified, asking the jury and the judge to spare James's life. She had also collected letters from many of Reverend Bosler's parishioners asking for mercy.

**SUEZANN:** When it came time for me to testify, I stood up in front of the jury and looked James in the eye and asked the jury to spare his life. "It's not right to take a life; no matter what." That is what my father preached. I told the jury about a conversation that my father and I had had years earlier in which he said that if anyone should ever take his life, he would not want that person to get the death penalty.

I also told the jury that I did not want James to get out of prison. If he was in prison for only twenty-five years, then there was always a possibility that he could get out of jail and come after me again. I wanted him in a place where everyone in the world would be safe from him, where he would stay for the rest of his natural life.

Reverend Bosler's mother, Nora Dickerson, asked the jury to "put him in a position where he will never be able to do this to anyone else."

The jury came back with its recommendation—nine to three in favor of death. Judge Alfonso Sepe continued the sentencing hearing until May 12, 1988, at which time he would impose the final sentence.

In the intervening months, SueZann publicly re-stated her opposition to the death penalty. On April 13, the *Miami Herald* carried a story quoting both SueZann and Phyllis Bosler. Speaking to a group of eleven local clergymen, SueZann shared her feelings about James Campbell and the outcome she hoped for at sentencing: "I do not hate him at all. But right now, I do not love him. I have not forgiven him totally. I have prayed for him." She went on to add that she did not believe in the death penalty and believed that life-and-death decisions were God's to make. "This is not easy for me yet," she said to the quiet audience. "I do believe it is God's decision. I don't know everything about life and death, but I am learning more." Phyllis echoed SueZann's opposition to the death penalty—"Vengeance is mine, sayeth the Lord." She added, however, that she was afraid of James Campbell and hoped that he would never get out of prison.[1]

When the court reconvened in May, SueZann appealed to Judge Sepe to spare James's life. Florida law requires a judge to determine whether there are aggravating and mitigating factors, and then to weigh all factors, before imposing a death sentence. Judge Sepe found five aggravating factors: the defendant was previously convicted of a felony involving the use of violence; the crime was committed during the commission of a felony; the crime was committed for pecuniary gain; the crime was especially heinous, atrocious, and cruel; and the murder was cold, calculated, and premeditated. The judge did not find any statutory mitigating factors. He did note, however, that the victim's family did not want James to be sentenced to death.

James Campbell's retardation and childhood abuse made little impact on Judge Sepe. In his opinion he wrote that the defendant had an "evil mind" and that "science had yet to learn how to predict, uncover, or cure" that evil. He acknowledged that James had had "difficult formative years" but said that there was no indication that he was "incapable of distinguishing between right and wrong and good and bad." Judge Sepe said that he was impressed by SueZann's statement, but he nonetheless sentenced James Campbell to death.[2]

The *Miami Herald* ran a story on May 14 that quoted prosecutor Michael Band as saying that it was the first time in his career that a victim's family, one member of which was a victim herself, had asked for mercy. He added, however, that the state "cannot be as charitable as SueZann."[3]

A few months after Judge Sepe sentenced James Campbell to death SueZann appeared on the Oprah Winfrey program "Forgiving the Unforgivable." Bill Pelke (see chapter 4) was there, too.

SUEZANN: Before I met Bill, I did not know that there were other people who felt like me—people who had family members murdered but opposed the death penalty. I was so inspired by all Bill had done for Paula Cooper, how he had written to her and told her he forgave her and then how he took up trying to save her life. He was the sweetest man I had ever met. Bill told me about a group of murder victims' family members who were starting up an organization to oppose the death penalty. It was so wonderful to know that I wasn't the only person who felt the way I did.

It helped to have the support of Bill and other family members, because once I was able to take care of myself again, my mother moved back to Springfield, Illinois, where she grew up. I returned to my job working as a hairdresser at the Eden Roc Hotel on Miami Beach. I wasn't able to work full-time, but I was able to make enough money to live on my own.

It was very hard when my mom left, but I understood her need to leave. She had put her grieving on hold to take care of me. For a year and a half she did everything for me. It was like caring for a small child again. She cooked for me, helped bathe and dress me, took me to my doctor's appointments. Her love and support saved me, but I know it took a toll on her. She needed to leave Miami. I grew up in Miami and did not have any connection to Springfield and did not want to live there. But it was hard for me to have her move so far away.

SueZann got her next opportunity to speak publicly on James's behalf when the Church of the Brethren asked her to speak at their annual conference.

SUEZANN: Being with my church community was bittersweet. I felt so much love and support from these people that had done so much for my family, but it also made me miss my dad more than ever.

I spoke for half an hour to a crowd of several hundred people. I told them about my father and his beliefs about the sacredness of life and how these values sustained me during this terrible time.

I asked people to pray for me and for James. I told them about an idea I had to give James a Bible. I had gotten the idea from Bill Pelke, who took a Bible with him to Italy, and everywhere he spoke he asked people to sign it and write messages for Paula Cooper. When Bill finally met Paula, he gave her the Bible. I wanted to do the same thing for James.

I really loved speaking about my dad. It helped me feel connected to him. I was able to tell people what a wonderful man he had been. It brought me out of my own pain and helped me feel more forgiveness for James.

· · · ·

On June 14, 1990, the Supreme Court of Florida issued an opinion reversing James's death sentence on the grounds that Judge Sepe had not properly considered the mitigating circumstances of mental retardation and childhood abuse before sentencing him to death. The court wrote: "Evidence of impaired capacity was extensive and unrefuted—Campbell's IQ was in the retarded range; he had poor reasoning skills; his reading abilities were on a third-grade level; he suffered from chronic drug and alcohol abuse; and he was subject to a borderline personality disorder. We note that he attempted suicide while in jail and was placed on Thorazine, a high-potency antipsychotic drug."[4]

**SUEZANN:** I was very glad that the death sentence was reversed, but I really didn't want to go through another sentencing hearing. It would have been so much simpler and less traumatic if the state had just agreed to a life sentence without parole. But Michael Band really wanted James to get the death penalty.

By the time of the second sentencing hearing, Judge Sepe was no longer the judge. He had been removed from serving as a judge because of some impropriety. The case was assigned to Judge Leonard Glick. Also, James had a new attorney, Mr. Houlihan.

Just like the first time, Michael called me as a witness and led me through the details of the crime. He made me identify large colored photographs of the crime scene. Finally, when he was done with questioning me, I read a statement I had prepared:

"Judge Leonard Glick and to all others present here today, thank you for letting me have this opportunity to get up here and express the way I feel and what I believe.

"Why am I doing this? There are several reasons. Number one: I am doing it to have peace within myself. Number two: I know it is what my father would have wanted. Number three: The most important thing right now at this time is James Bernard Campbell's life.

"Why kill people who kill people to show that killing people is wrong? To me that says it all. What happened that day seven years, three months, and three days ago I will never forget, and the pain may never go away, but I am putting it on hold right now to think about someone else and not just myself.

"Pleading for this human being's life to be spared is one of my purposes right now. It's not very easy but it's something that I want to do. I am not condoning what he did to my father and me and how it affected our lives and others. I will ask you this question: will it bring my father back? No."

SueZann repeated that her father had told her that if he were ever murdered, he would not want the killer to get the death penalty. She asked Judge Glick to sentence James Bernard Campbell to life, not death.

SUEZANN: I finished up speaking to James: "James, your life at this time is in Judge Glick's hands, and maybe, just maybe one day you and I might be able to come face to face together. As my father looks down to show you and tell you through me, not only I but he forgives you.

"One last thing that I will never forget is my father's favorite hymn. It associates with the situation and to me can be very universal. My father sang this song every time he had fears in his life. The name of the song is 'Let there be peace on earth and let it begin with me.' Thank you. God bless you."

Michael Band called Nora Dickerson, Billy's mother and SueZann's grandmother, to the stand. Whereas her testimony at the first trial was ambiguous about whether she wanted James Campbell sentenced to death, this time she made it clear:

Bill was my only child, and he planned to care for us in our old age. My husband is 90. I am 83. As a result of Bill's murder, we have had to move to retirement homes sooner than we had planned. Since the murder, I have had two strokes and severe cases of shingles.

Reverend Bosler by choice dealt with large numbers of people who closely identified with the background and character and social habits of the defendant, Mr. Campbell. Bill's murder has deprived many people in similar situations as [the] defendant, James Campbell.

These strung-out court episodes are taking further toll on us as well as on SueZann, our granddaughter. She will never be whole because of the repeated stabbings and attempted murder resulting in the loss of her retentive memory.

Because of Campbell's history of criminal recidivism and the fact he was free on early release from prison and on parole for a previous trial before he heinously stabbed my son the Reverend Bill Bosler to death and injured SueZann for life, I plead with you, Judge, to retain the original death penalty for James Campbell so he can never, never hurt anyone else as we have been hurt. Thank you.[5]

After the state finished with its presentation, the defense called Dr. Jethro Toomer, a psychologist, who testified about James's emotional problems. Michael Band attacked the doctor's credibility during cross-examination by bringing out the fact that Toomer had testified for several defendants who had been charged with killing police officers.

Q. You have testified for at least three individuals who killed police officers at sentencing hearings; is that correct?

A. I am unsure as to the number, but I have testified in those types of proceedings, yes. . . .

Q. You have testified on behalf of Manny Valle who killed a Coral Gables police officer? . . . You have testified on behalf of Manny Valle and you found mitigation?

A. Yes.

Q. You have testified on behalf of a Mr. Patton who killed a City of Miami police officer?

A. That's correct. . . .

Q. You have recently testified on behalf of Leonardo Fronki on a first-degree murder at the penalty proceeding?

A. Yes.

Q. You found mitigation?

A. Yes, I did.

Q. And Mr. Fronki is facing yet another first-degree murder for the murder of Officer Baur, a North Miami police officer; is that correct?

A. I believe that's correct.[6]

In his summation to the jury, Michael emphasized Dr. Toomer's association with "cop-killers," pointing out that the doctor had testified on behalf of at least ten defendants charged with killing police officers. He also urged the jury to "send a message" to the community by sentencing James Campbell to death:

The question you have to answer is does the mitigation change the circumstances of Billy Bosler's murder. The death penalty is a message sent to a number of members of our society who choose not to follow the law. . . . The death penalty is a message to certain members of our society who choose not to follow the rules. It's only for one crime, the crime of first-degree murder. It is for those who choose to violate the sacredness and sanctity of human life.[7]

This time the jury voted ten to two for the death penalty. Judge Glick followed their recommendation and sentenced James to death by electrocution.

**SUEZANN:** By the time of the second sentencing hearing, I had forgiven James at a different level. When I got on the stand in the second trial I said, "Mr. Campbell, I forgive you. Whether you accept it or not, I forgive you." This time I really meant it. At the time of the first trial, I still had bad feelings and anger and hatred towards him, which I now can understand. It took me all those years not to just say the words *I forgive you* but to really mean it. I felt this lifting of a burden from my shoulders—this emptiness being filled by peace and tranquility. After that I was finally able to really go on with my life.

I didn't really know that I hadn't fully forgiven James until that second trial. It's not like I lied when I said I forgave him before. I was just beginning the process; I didn't realize how far I still had to go. After the second trial, I felt so lighthearted. After all those miserable years of wanting to feel better, the healing was finally coming true. I went through the phases, and I was finally able to open my heart to him.

Speaking publicly about James helped me to forgive him at a deeper level. Each time I spoke, I saw him more and more as a wounded human being and less as a killer. Also, asking people to write messages in the Bible for him was healing. I asked people to pray for him and write him messages of hope, and they did.

I had prayed for him before, but it never really felt right. Now I feel really good about praying for him. Each year that goes by I feel more lightness towards him. I have no hate, no bad feelings; it is all just forgiveness and love and being able to go on with my life. It is very important for me that he gets forgiveness from God before he dies.

Ironically, as my heart softened towards James, I began to feel increasingly bitter towards the prosecution. They misled me to believe that what I said in court would matter, but really it did not. Michael had a lot of control over what I could say by the way he questioned me. But he didn't respect what I wanted. Neither did the judge. Before imposing sentence, Judge Glick said, "We respect you, but we are not going to do what you ask."

I was also angry at the prosecutors at the state attorney's office for lying to my grandmother. They convinced her that the only way to make sure that James never got out so that he could kill me was to give him the death penalty. That is not true. Sentencing James to life in prison would also keep him from killing again. I felt like Michael used her to get his death sentence. I felt like he tried to turn our family against each other.

Despite the state's best efforts to kill James, the Florida Supreme Court again reversed his sentence. On June 27, 1996, it issued a stinging opinion reversing the sentence due to "improper conduct by the prosecutor." The court focused on Michael's "cop-killer" statements and "message to the community" arguments:

> The "cop-killer" rhetoric and "message to the community" statements played to the jurors' most elemental fears, dragging into the trial the specter of police murders and a lawless community that could imperil the jurors and their families. These arguments, which were emphasized at closing, were fresh in the jurors' minds when they retired to consider Campbell's sentence. . . . On this record, it is entirely possible that several jurors voted for death not out of a reasoned sense of justice but out of a panicked sense of self-preservation.[8]

Although SueZann was elated by the news, it meant she had to go to yet another hearing.

•　•　•　•

By the time of the third sentencing hearing, SueZann's attitude toward the prosecutors had completely changed. She was no longer a frightened young woman who had nearly been killed. She was tired of the state using her for its ends without regard to her values. She decided to hire an attorney.

SUEZANN: I knew that I could not use the same tactics at the third sentencing hearing that I had used before—obediently answering all of Michael's questions with answers that he wanted to hear and then making my statement at the end that everybody discarded. So when an attorney named Melodee Smith contacted me through a friend and offered to help me, I gladly accepted. Melodee had been following the case. She told me that I had certain rights as a victim under Florida law, and she offered to make sure those rights were protected. Besides being a lawyer, she was also a minister, so that made me have even more confidence in her.

The Reverend Melodee Smith, Esq., was a force to be reckoned with. Large and imposing, she wore a minister's collar and a plain black smock with a suit jacket, combining the uniforms of her legal and pastoral trades. Melodee liked to work on death penalty cases because they combined her legal interests with her religious opposition to the death penalty.

Melodee's first tactic was to ask the state to drop its efforts to seek the death penalty and agree to a life sentence for James Campbell. She wrote a letter to Attorney General Katherine Rundle requesting a meeting and asking her to intervene and forbid Michael Band from seeking the death penalty a third time. In the letter she wrote:

> While you cannot make the decision to seek a life sentence for Mr. Campbell based solely on the concerns and opinions of the victims, the witnesses or the family, Ms. Bosler urges you to give her position, in this case, a greater degree of weight than someone who was merely a family member, merely a witness or merely a victim. She believes that you have good cause to do so, and that the community will certainly support you.[9]

Melodee pointed out several cases where the State of Florida did not seek the death penalty under comparable circumstances. She also questioned Michael Band's motive in continuing to seek the death penalty against James:

> Ms. Bosler has expressed grave concern over the continuing involvement by Michael Band in the prosecution of this case. Ms. Bosler, as well as Mr. Band, indicated to me that they have more than a professional relationship—not surprising because of the continuing need to litigate the issues in this case for more than 10 years, but somewhat disturbing. While not getting into the details at this point, she has asked me to alert you to her concern that the prosecutor Mr. Band may be pursuing the death sentence in this case for reasons that he would not be allowed by law to argue in Court. Mr. Band has already demonstrated this "overzealousness," a term used by the Florida Supreme Court in its most recent decision to reverse Mr. Campbell's death sentence. Ms. Bosler is concerned that Mr. Band . . . is not doing what the law requires of him—to seek justice.

The state refused to drop its quest for the death sentence, and the court set a date for the third sentencing trial, June 2, 1997. Before the court date, Michael asked SueZann to meet with him to go over her testimony.

**SUEZANN:** When I went to the meeting with Michael, I brought my attorney with me, and Michael did not like it. We went over the previous deposition, and I had to answer him exactly as I had before. I asked him again to spare James's life. He said, "SueZann, I hope you are still going to love me." I said, "Of course I'm still going to love you, but I don't like what you are doing." He said, "I am not going to change my mind, because this is my job." I said, "But you have the power to give him life instead of death." He said, "I know that, but I am not going to do it."

His answer made me so angry. He has so much power. He is one of the three top attorneys in the state's attorney's office. I picture the three of them together sitting around a table, drinking their coffee and deciding which case to seek the death penalty in. It's almost like "eeny, meeny, miny, mo." It is like they are playing God.

Besides Melodee Smith, SueZann had another new ally in her fight against the death penalty—former lead investigator Jeff Geller. Over the years he and SueZann had become friends. By now, Jeff had left the department and gone into private investigative work, in part because of his growing dislike of the death penalty. He agreed to attend the third sentencing hearing, not for the state but as SueZann's friend.

SueZann's efforts to save James Bernard Campbell generated national press attention. The television magazine program *48 Hours* was producing an hour-long segment on the case. Crew members would be filming the sentencing hearing.

The first day of the third sentencing hearing, June 2, 1997, was a typical Florida day. By the time court started at nine A.M., it was already hot. Fifty jurors lined the second-floor corridor of the Metro Justice Building. They brought their jury summonses and paperbacks, schoolbooks, briefcases, and cell phones, all things to keep them busy during the long waiting periods. Yet another judge was assigned to preside this time, Judge Marc Schumacher.

The big news was the case of Timothy McVeigh. A federal jury in Denver had already convicted him of killing eight federal employees during the April 24 bombing of the Murrah Federal Building in Oklahoma City. Timothy McVeigh's sentencing hearing was scheduled for today, the same day as James Campbell's.

The jury selection process alone lasted several days. To sit on a jury in a death penalty case, the juror has to be "death qualified," meaning the person must support the death penalty. Opponents of the death penalty are disqualified from service on the grounds that they would not be able to "follow the law" and impose a death sentence.

**SUEZANN:** I felt anxious about going through another sentencing trial. I would have to look at the gory pictures of my father again. Seeing them always brought back the whole event. But this time, I felt prepared. I was not going to be a willing participant in helping the state execute James Campbell.

Melodee advised me how to handle myself in court. She gave me advice like to look at the jurors and the judge, not at Michael Band. She told me not to be too emotional: "They want you to be emotional so the jury can play upon that emotion to give James the death penalty." She was right. That was exactly what happened before, and I never realized it.

On Monday morning, SueZann entered the courtroom of Judge Marc Schumacher with Melodee at her side. In prior court proceedings, SueZann had sat in the side of the courtroom behind the prosecutor's table; this time she sat behind the defense. The first-row bench is reserved for family and friends, but no one had shown up to support James. SueZann, along with her supporters—her sisters Jill and Lynette, Pat Bane from Murder Victims' Families for Reconciliation, Jeff Geller, and others—sat in the second row.

When Michael saw SueZann sit on the opposite side of the room, he ordered a marshal to sit in front of her, giving the jury the impression that she needed to be protected from James. Another indication of the strain between SueZann and the prosecution was that in the past a victim's advocate from the state's attorney's office had always been there to offer her emotional support; this time they would not go near her.

**SUEZANN:** Michael knew that I did not want to cooperate, so he tried to figure out how to control what I was going to say. Before the jury was brought in, Michael asked the judge to "prequestion" me. He asked me, "What would you say if we let you say anything you wanted to say?" I replied, "I would say that I am against the death penalty. It won't bring my father back. Speaking against the death penalty is one of the most important things in my life to me and my father." The judge went through my statement and took out everything that referred to the death penalty. He told me that I could not tell the jury how I felt about the death penalty. The judge then called the jury back into the room.

But Melodee had prepared me for how to handle the death penalty issue without violating the law. When Michael first called me to the stand, he started off by asking me really basic questions like what was my name and what was my address. Then he asked me, "Are you employed?" I said, "Yes. I have several jobs. I am a hairdresser, but for the past ten and a half years my main job has been working to abolish the death penalty."

I looked right at the jury as I said this. It was quiet in the courtroom. Michael was not expecting me to answer like that. He said, very slowly, "Okay," then he asked the judge for a sidebar. The judge ordered the jury out of the room and turned to me and said, "If you say anything about the death penalty again, I will put you in jail for six months and fine you five hundred dollars, and if it keeps up then it will get worse."

I was shaking from head to toe, but I refused to let them see it. I refused to cry. I did not want to show any extreme emotions, which is what they wanted the jury to see. But I hadn't done anything wrong. Michael had asked me a question, and I answered it truthfully. They can't take that away from me. I just didn't give them the answer they wanted to hear. My only purpose was to try to bring out information that the jury had not been able to hear before.

After the state finished questioning SueZann, defense counsel Remberto Diaz tried to elicit more information from her about her opposition to the death penalty. Each question brought an objection from the state, sustained by the judge. Finally, he walked to his chair as though he were finished questioning her and then turned around, pointed to James Campbell, and asked SueZann, "Do you hate this man?" Michael Band jumped to his feet shouting, "Objection!" The judge said, "Sustained," but SueZann firmly replied, "No!"

SUEZANN: I felt like Diaz had read my mind when he asked me that question. It was exactly what I wanted the jury to know.

The defense, having uncovered further evidence of the abuse James received from both his parents as a young child, called a series of witnesses who testified to it. Two psychologists testified that James was beaten by his mother with extension cords, water hoses, and pool cues until he would say, "Jesus, I repent." At age eight or nine he swallowed bleach in his first suicide attempt. Witnesses described how his mother spit in James's face in front of other people. One testified that James saw his mother stab his stepfather.

After calling all his witnesses, Remberto Diaz recalled SueZann to the stand.

SUEZANN: The judge again ordered the jury to leave the room and then he said to me, "SueZann, you are not to mention anything about the death penalty or your feelings toward the defendant. If you violate my order, you will be in criminal contempt and face six months in jail. Please don't push me on that."

I felt like a criminal instead of a victim. I felt that if I said one wrong word, I would go to jail.

Before Diaz was allowed to ask me any questions in front of the jury, the judge made him go through what questions he wanted to ask. Diaz asked me what impact my father's death had had on my life. I knew from Melodee that "victim impact" evidence was admissible and normally introduced by the state to elicit the sympathy of the jury to encourage it to impose the death penalty.

I answered that all I wanted to say was a very simple thing: "I forgive James Bernard Campbell for what he has done. I respect his life and value it here on earth. I believe in life. I've tried for ten and a half years to bring some good out of this. I'm doing it the best way I know how. I'm at peace with myself. That's all I wanted to say."

The judge said, "I respect your feeling and your opinions, but there is no place for them in this proceeding." Diaz decided not to call me as a witness.

In their final arguments, both attorneys passionately argued their positions. Michael Band adamantly declared that James deserved the death penalty, pointing out the twenty-four stab wounds that killed Reverend Bosler and the fact that Campbell had ransacked the house for money and then had the presence of mind to remove his blood-soaked clothes and change into some of the dead man's. He concluded by saying, "Has murder lost its ability to horrify us? This was a premeditated, savage, unprovoked, and random murder. Children grow up in bad homes every day and don't go out and slaughter people."

Remberto Diaz made equally compelling arguments. He pointed out that the prosecutors had introduced poster-size photographs from the crime scene, but he asked the jurors to consider other images not in the room. "There are no pictures of the violence that this young man grew up with, but the pictures that live in his mind." He gestured toward the chairs reserved for Campbell's family. "Look at those empty chairs. That's his family. Look at those chairs and you see his life. His only support comes from the second row," pointing to the chairs where SueZann and her supporters sat.

He closed saying, "I'm not asking you to let him walk out of here today. I'm asking you to stop the violence in his life. Cooking his brains is not the way to end it." Then he turned toward the audience in the courtroom and said in a voice loud enough for the jurors to hear, "Thank you, SueZann," as he sat down.

The jury adjourned for its deliberations on Friday the thirteenth. SueZann anxiously paced the hall with her sisters, calling friends and well-wishers for support. Approximately three hours later the jury returned with a verdict. SueZann studied their faces as they entered the courtroom. Several looked at her. The bailiff handed the judge a piece of paper. He read the verdict—eight to four in favor of life, not death. Judge Schumacher quickly imposed a life sentence with a mandatory minimum of twenty-five years without parole, to be served consecutively with his three other life sentences from the same case.

After imposing sentence, the judge invited SueZann to address the jurors and say what she had been forbidden to say before. Holding the Bible she planned to give to James, she finally had a chance to speak directly and openly to them.

SUEZANN: Thank you for giving life and not death to James Bernard Campbell. No matter how mad I could be at James Bernard Campbell, I still don't believe in the death penalty for this man. I'm so overwhelmed. This is the happiest moment of the past ten and a half years for me. I can't thank you enough. I have worked hard for his life to be spared. Now I can go on with my own life. And I thank you very much for that. God bless you all.

Several jurors clutched tissues wet from drying their teary eyes. Some hugged each other. Reporters asked jurors for their opinion on the verdict. One said it was "a fair, humane decision." Another said that the crime was heinous, but "the mitigating factors were strong." However, one admitted, "If something like that happened to me, I don't think I could forgive."

Though he had fought hard for years for James's execution, Michael Band handled defeat with grace. "The prosecution accepts the jury's deci-

*SueZann Bosler. Photograph provided with permission of SueZann Bosler.*

sion," he said, adding, "It's easier to discuss the death penalty at home than looking at a human being twelve feet away when your decision may alter his life."

SueZann gave Bruce Fleisher, one of James's attorneys, the Bible she wanted James to have. Bruce agreed to give it to James, but security would not let James take it back to prison with him. Bruce promised to make sure James got it. He also told SueZann that James had agreed to let her visit him in prison, something she had wanted to do for a long time.

• • • •

Four years later, SueZann Bosler has still not met James Campbell. She is philosophical about it, believing that someday she will be able to talk to him and ask him the question that plagues victims' family members: "Why?"

SUEZANN: I still haven't met James yet. I heard through the grapevine that he was interested in meeting me but because of his low IQ he changes his mind very often. He is borderline mentally retarded, so it is hard for him to make decisions.

I have tried talking to one of his aunts, but she did not want to speak to me. James did not have a lot of family support. Some of his family showed up at the first trial, but they wanted him to be executed. At the second trial a friend showed up but no family, and by the third hearing nobody showed up. I was the only one supporting him.

At first his family was reluctant to talk to me because they believed that James was innocent, in spite of all the evidence against him, including his confession. He hadn't told them all the details. After the *48 Hours* show came out somebody from his family called me. She made a tape of the show and showed it to the whole family. It was the first time all of them knew and understood what happened. Now they no longer believe him when he says he is innocent.

I have tried writing to him many times but have never been able to find the words to express what I want to say. I have sat for hours and days with a legal pad and I start writing and crumple it up and throw it away until I have a big pile of paper next to me. I am trying to find the right words so that he'll understand. It is not as easy as I thought it would be. I have thought about writing to a chaplain at the prison who might be able to help me correspond with him.

Reconciliation for me is a beginning, not an end. When the day finally comes that I meet James, I would prefer that it be private. This is important to me personally, but I don't want it to be a media event. I believe that someday I will meet him. I just have the feeling that something is going to happen. I know it will.

SueZann continues a busy schedule traveling and speaking against the death penalty. Along with other MVFR members, she spoke out against Timothy McVeigh's execution.

**SUEZANN:** It is really tragic to me that the victims from the Oklahoma City bombing thought that executing Timothy McVeigh was going to help them get on with their life and their grieving process. It isn't true, unless they forgive him. As long as they are still vengeful and hateful, he will always have a hold over them.

I don't think the government has made its case for the death penalty. The justice system has had twenty-six years since reinstatement of the death penalty, and they have not proven to us, the people that oppose the death penalty, that it works as a deterrent. It won't bring our murdered family members or friends back. But killing them will make their families and friends suffer the way we have. There will just be more victims. We should live without the death penalty for a while and see what happens.

When I talk to people, I try to keep an open mind and learn from them—even the people that don't agree with me. One time I was speaking to a group and there was a cop at the back of the room and he asked me a question. "SueZann, if there had been a gun on the table when you were going through that situation, would you have picked it up and shot James?" I didn't know what to say. I had never thought about that before. But his question really stuck with me, and later on I thought, "You know what? I bet I would have." I have normal human instincts.

The most important thing is to always try to keep hope and faith alive. You just keep learning more, trying harder, and you can never lose. Each time you try, it will be better.

My dad always had hope. He was a terrific human being. He wasn't perfect. He wasn't a saint or anything. But he always had hope. I remember when I was a little girl my father gave me a heart locket with a little mustard seed inside. He explained how the little mustard seed grows into a strong plant that can move mountains. Even the faith of a mustard seed can accomplish great things. Sometimes I wonder what I could accomplish if I had the faith of an orange, or a pineapple. I keep that locket—it reminds me every day that there is hope within each and every one of us to find peace in the world.

# GRAVE INJUSTICES

At its core, the American criminal justice system is premised on the ideal of fairness. The United States Constitution provides every person charged with a crime with due process—a fair trial and the right to be represented by an attorney. We also believe in equal protection: people should be treated the same regardless of their race or gender. Even people who support the death penalty want a system that is fair.

No issue highlights the flaws within the criminal justice system more than the issue of wrongful convictions, the subject of chapter 7. As of the end of 2001, a total of ninety-eight people from twenty-two states had been released from death row after establishing their innocence.

Ten of those ninety-eight had their innocence exposed by DNA (deoxyribonucleic acid) testing. Over the past decade, this has emerged as the most reliable forensic technique for identifying criminals—or exonerating suspects—when biological material is left at a crime scene. DNA testing can even be used on biological material that is decades old. However, before 1994, DNA testing was not widely available, and many people convicted of crimes before that time did not have access to it.

Federal and state legislative efforts are attempting to make DNA testing more available to persons with reputable claims of innocence who did not have access to testing at the time of their conviction. The Innocence Protection Act, a bipartisan bill with strong support from many members of Congress originally sponsored in the Senate by Senators Patrick Leahy (D-VT), Susan Collins (R-ME), and Gordon Smith (R-OR) and in the

House by Representatives William Delahunt (D-MA) and Ray LaHood (R-IL), would require states to provide DNA testing to inmates who have credible innocence claims and did not have access to DNA testing. Many states have passed similar measures; in 2001 alone, Idaho, North Carolina, Oregon, and Washington did so. In addition, Senator Russ Feingold (D-WI) has introduced legislation, the National Death Penalty Moratorium Act, that would establish a two-year congressional commission to study the death penalty nationwide and impose a moratorium on federal executions. One task of the commission would be to look at the problem of executing the innocent.

There are national litigation efforts to address the problem as well. A number of Innocence Projects have sprung up around the country, beginning with the one started by Barry Scheck and Peter Neufeld at Cardozo Law School in New York City. Now dozens of law schools around the country are offering free legal support to help inmates pursue claims of innocence through DNA testing.

Death penalty proponents claim that the fact that so many innocent people have been exonerated and released from death row shows that "the system works." Yet many cases of innocence were discovered not by the criminal justice system but rather through the work of investigative journalists, filmmakers, and family members. Most death row inmates are not fortunate enough to have this type of extralegal help. One can only speculate on the number of innocent people who have been executed.

Many factors contribute to wrongful convictions: official misconduct, often brought about by the enormous pressure placed on law enforcement to solve high-profile murders quickly; pretrial publicity that prejudices the jury and judge; and reliance on jailhouse snitches and single eyewitnesses without corroborating evidence.

In the book *Actual Innocence,* based on their work at Cardozo Law School, Scheck and Neufeld report a number of disturbing cases. In one, a medical examiner included in a death report the weight of the gallbladder and spleen from a man from whom both organs had been removed. The book also cites a survey released in 2000 by the Texas Defender Service that found 160 cases of official misconduct. Among them were 121 in which expert psychiatrists testified "with absolute certainty that the defendant would be a danger in the future," often without even interviewing the defendant.[1] One of the persons predicted to be a future danger was Randall Dale Adams, whose innocence was brought to light in the documentary movie *The Thin Blue Line.*[2] Besides being innocent of the crime for which he was sentenced to death, Adams has no history of violent behavior, either before or after his wrongful conviction.

However, the most common factor leading to wrongful convictions is ineffective assistance of counsel and inadequate defense resources. This problem is so severe that two Supreme Court justices have spoken out about it. In an address before the Minnesota Women Lawyers Association, conservative Justice Sandra Day O'Connor stated: "Perhaps it is time to look at minimum standards for appointed counsel." She added that all nine men exonerated the previous year all had been inadequately represented.[3] Justice Ruth Bader Ginsburg criticized the "meager" amount of money spent to defend poor people: "I have yet to see a death case among the dozens coming to the Supreme Court on eve-of-execution stay applications, in which the defendant was well represented at trial."[4]

Despite the serious flaws in our system, most recent legislative and judicial actions have increased the likelihood of wrongful convictions, with the exception of the Innocence Protection Act (which as the 107th Congress draws to a close had not become law). Congress and the federal courts have adopted measures to speed up the appeals process and limit access to counsel. In 1996, Congress passed the Anti-Terrorism and Effective Death Penalty Act (AEDPA), which severely curtailed habeas corpus, making it more difficult for state court defendants to have their cases reviewed in federal court. Many of the people who have been released from death row would not have been able to prove their innocence under the AEDPA and would have been wrongfully executed. The AEDPA also cut off all federal funding for capital resource centers, which helped provide legal representation to indigent defendants in capital cases. Despite the likelihood that the AEDPA will lead to more innocent people ending up on death row, the Supreme Court upheld its constitutionality.

Chapter 8 draws attention to the problem of racial inequality in the application of the death penalty. Since the days of slavery and Jim Crow justice, capital punishment has always been affected by race. Although Jim Crow laws are no longer officially on the books, in many jurisdictions people of color are subject to one kind of justice and whites to another. The race of the defendant certainly plays a role in whether a person is charged, prosecuted, and sentenced for capital murder, but equally important is the race of the victim. In the late 1980s, the General Accounting Office conducted a review of twenty-eight studies that examined the outcome in capital cases accounting for the race of the defendants and victims. In 82 percent of the cases, people who murdered whites were more likely to be sentenced to death than those who murdered blacks. In Georgia, the odds of a defendant receiving a death sentence were four times greater if the victim was white rather than black. In Florida, the odds were nearly five times greater, and in Mississippi, nearly six times greater.[5]

According to the Death Penalty Information Center, recent studies bear out these results. Two of the country's foremost researchers on race and capital punishment, law professor David Baldus and statistician George Woodworth, conducted a careful analysis of the death penalty in Philadelphia and found that the odds of getting a death sentence were 3.9 times higher if the defendant was black. The data were controlled for factors such as severity of the crime and background of the defendant. A study by Professor Jeffrey Pokorak at St. Mary's University Law School in Texas provides part of an explanation for these disparities. Of the chief district attorneys in counties using the death penalty, nearly 98 percent are white and only 1 percent are black. In 1996, *all* of Kentucky's death row inmates were there for murdering a white victim, despite the fact that more than one thousand blacks had been murdered in Kentucky since the death penalty was reinstated.[6]

The following statistics compiled by the National Coalition to Abolish the Death Penalty underscore the problem of racial inequities in criminal justice systems throughout the country:

- As of January 1997, thirteen people had been executed by the State of Alabama since 1976—eleven of them African Americans.
- African Americans make up half of the death row populations in North Carolina, Ohio, Delaware, Mississippi, and Virginia and over two-thirds of the death row populations in Pennsylvania, Illinois, and Louisiana.
- More than three out of four people waiting to be executed in U.S. military prisons are people of color.
- Sixty percent of the persons on death row in California and Texas are either black, Latino, Asian or Native American.[7]

The federal system is plagued with similar biases. Justice Department numbers indicate that 90 percent of the people U.S. attorneys seek the death penalty against are black or Latino, as are 90 percent of the people on federal death row.[8]

Despite overwhelming evidence of discrimination, the courts have continually denied relief, holding that patterns of racial disparities are insufficient to prove discrimination in any individual case. In the landmark case of *Gregg v. Georgia,* the Supreme Court stated that a defendant must prove intentional discrimination by the government to establish a constitutional violation, despite the fact that statistical evidence is admissible to establish discrimination for every other type of civil rights violation.[9]

It is extremely difficult for an individual to prove intentional discrimination. However, even in cases where racial bias is demonstrated, courts frequently deny relief. For instance, in preparing for the penalty phase of an African American's trial, a white judge in Florida said in open court, "Since the nigger mom and dad are here anyway, why don't we go ahead and do the penalty phase today instead of having to subpoena them back at cost to the state." The defendant, Anthony Peck, was sentenced to death, and the sentence was upheld by the Florida Supreme Court.[10]

Even more blatant, a Texas police officer said to defendant Clarence Brandley, a black man charged along with a white man for the murder of a white high school girl, "One of you two is gonna hang for this. Since you're the nigger, you're elected." Clarence was wrongfully convicted and sentenced to death row. Ten years later he was exonerated and released from prison.[11]

Race may have played a role in the case of Randy Reeves, the defendant in chapter 8. Randy, a Native American, was convicted in Nebraska of killing two white women, Vicki Zessin and Janet Mesner.

All three people executed in Nebraska since the death penalty was reinstated there were people of color. Concerned about this apparent racial disparity, in 1999 the Nebraska legislature commissioned David Baldus, a well-known death penalty expert from the University of Iowa, to study the state's death penalty system. Baldus said that the study did not show any real disparity in the application of the death penalty based on race but did show that minorities were adversely discriminated against by more aggressive prosecutorial actions. For example, white defendants were more likely to be offered plea agreements than minority defendants, but he attributed that to the fact that urban prosecutors, who saw more minority defendants, were more aggressive about seeking the death penalty than rural ones. He also pointed out the arbitrary manner in which the death penalty is imposed. Of the twenty-seven cases he studied in which the death penalty was sought, the circumstances of the thirteen people sentenced to death were similar to those of the fourteen who were not.[12]

# CHAPTER 7

# Rush to Judgment

The alarm clock woke Gary Gauger at his normal time—six o'clock—on April 8, 1993, a Wednesday. Gary planned to spend the day planting tomatoes. But when he looked out his bedroom window and saw a blustery, rainy morning, he opted instead to sleep in. He quickly fell back asleep.

Gary lived with his parents, Ruth and Morris Gauger, on a farm in Richmond, Illinois, that had been in his family since 1923. Morris grew up on the farm and raised his three children there: Greg, born in 1948, and twins Ginger and Gary, born in 1952. The modest white farmhouse with a beige roof sat five hundred feet off the main road. Attached to the original structure was a five-room garage where Morris ran a side business selling classic British motorcycles and parts. His shop had a solid reputation throughout the Midwest and was known by many motorcycle enthusiasts. Ruth also ran a side business: out of a trailer on the property, she sold imported rugs that Ginger bought while traveling around the world as a ski instructor.

Gary moved away from home in 1972 when he married Ronda, a woman he met in high school. The couple settled in Texas, opening a midwifery school and raising three children. Gary and Ronda divorced in 1985, in part because Gary had a drinking problem. In 1989, Gary moved back to the family farm.

The routine and discipline of farming provided Gary the structure he needed to take control of his life. He worked hard to build up the vegetable farm and obtained state certification as an organic farm. Gary laboriously practiced his principles of gardening without harming the environment. He never used pesticides on his plants, instead picking insects off the leaves by hand. When raccoons ate the sweet corn, instead of shooting them he played the radio, hoping to scare them away.

Left to right: *Morris Gauger, Ginger Gauger-Blossom, Gary Gauger and Ruth Gauger.*
*Photograph provided with permission of the family.*

Gary and his parents lived together companionably. During the day, they each carried out individual responsibilities. Gary planted, harvested, and sold his vegetables at his roadside stand. He also worked part-time fixing motor-cycles for his father. Besides his motorcycle business, Morris tended to the rest of the farm, maintaining all the property and caring for the chickens and ducks. Ruth ran the household and the rug store. They ate dinner together most evenings and then read or watched television, usually going to bed by ten o'clock.

Gary finally got out of bed at about nine o'clock and went to the kitchen. He expected to see his mother cleaning up after breakfast but instead found a pile of dirty dishes stacked in the sink. His parents were usually up and breakfasted before eight, and his mother promptly washed up after the meal. Gary walked around the house, then looked outside, but found no sign of them.

Gary assumed that his parents had taken a day trip away from the farm. Earlier that week, Morris and Ruth had planned to drive to Sugar Grove with their friend Windy to look at an antique tractor, but Morris had gotten a cold, so they postponed the trip. Gary thought that his dad probably woke up feeling better and decided at the last minute to make the trip to Sugar Grove. He did think it was strange that his mother had left without washing the dishes or leaving a note, but he assumed he would see them by dinner.

When they didn't return for dinner, Gary started to worry, but not too much, because they sometimes went out to eat, especially after an excursion. However, when there was still no sign by nine P.M. Gary knew that something was wrong. He worried that they'd had car trouble or been in an accident, but he didn't know what to do. He didn't know Windy's real name, so he couldn't call him. He thought about calling the police but knew that he could not file a missing person's report for twenty-four hours. He contemplated calling his brother and sister, but they couldn't do anything, so he didn't see the point in worrying them, too. He considered calling around to hospitals, but he didn't know the names of the hospitals between Sugar Grove and Richmond.

Gary went to bed around midnight but didn't sleep soundly. He woke frequently, hoping to hear the sound of the car driving up the gravel driveway. He finally dozed off and was awakened at around ten o'clock when a customer arrived wanting a part from the motorcycle shop. Gary offered to unlock the shop for the customer. He pulled on his boots and walked to the garage. When he opened the door, he found his father lying face down in a pool of blood.

GARY: At first I thought my dad had had a heart attack and maybe fallen and hit his head. I called the paramedics, and they called the police. We walked around looking for my mother. When the police arrived they started asking me all kinds of questions. I was in a state of shock. They asked me what I had been doing the last twenty-four hours. They asked me what my mother was wearing. They asked permission to search the rug trailer, where they found my mother's body, covered in rugs and blankets that were soaked in blood.

From the very beginning the police believed that I killed my parents, and they built their entire case around that assumption. I was arrested and held in the squad car for three hours, then taken to an interrogation room at four P.M. where Sheriff's Detectives Eugene Lowery and Beverly Hendle questioned me for hours. I was exhausted and hungry and asked if I could go, but they said no. After many hours I requested a polygraph, which they said was a good thing to do, and they agreed to let me go if I passed. They started the test at midnight. It took about an hour. They told me I did not pass the test.

At this point, the interrogation took a dark turn. They told me they had stacks of evidence against me a foot and a half tall. They said that they had searched the whole house and found bloody clothes and a knife belonging to me. When I questioned them about these things, they told me that they couldn't lie; otherwise they'd lose their jobs. It never occurred to me at any time that the police were lying to me. They were senior police officers investigating a capital case, and I believed that they must have been telling the truth. They were very effective. They wouldn't let me go, even when I asked them to stop. There was one officer at each side of me. They said, "You did it. We can see it in your eyes. The machine wouldn't lie." I asked to be able to stop for the night because I was so exhausted, but they wouldn't cut off the interrogation.

Between 2:00 and 2:30 A.M. they slapped down graphic photographs of my mother and asked me, "How could you do this to your mother, the woman who gave birth to you?" I was so distraught. I was crying. At this point they had convinced me I must have killed my parents. I asked if I could possibly have killed them in a blackout. I agreed to go through a hypothetical account of what must have happened using "facts" the police had given me.

Some time later they came back with the autopsy results. My father had been hit on the head with a blunt object and then stabbed. Both my parents had had their throats slit repeatedly. The physical evidence didn't match my "confession." For one thing, I didn't know the details of how they were killed. At first I said they had been shot, but then the police informed me that their throats had been slit, so I changed my story to say that I must have approached them from behind to cut their throats. I did not know that they had actually been hit on the head and knocked to the ground first.

They asked me about the weapon, and I said I must have put the weapon in the garage, but the police never found a knife there. There were other incorrect details, like I said that I had woken up, looked out my window, and seen my mother in the rug shop. If the police had done any kind of investigation, they would have learned that it wasn't even physically possible for me to have seen my mother through any of the windows in the house.

After an hour of this, they asked me for a motive. We couldn't come up with a motive. I threw out a couple of theories that didn't make sense, but that didn't seem to matter.

At 5:30 in the morning they stripped me naked in the interrogation room and put me in a prison uniform with COUNTY JAIL printed on the back. Another officer joined them. I started to tell him how I had slept late, then walked across the fields, but he didn't want to hear any facts that didn't fit with their theory.

I was in emotional shock, looking to the police for help. I was sleep-deprived and subjected to a constant barrage of misinformation. They had me thinking I must have done it. I repeated the hypothetical account again and they took notes, but never wrote out a statement, because I said I would not confess to something I had no memory of. I finally said that I must need a lawyer, so they stopped questioning me. The police did not record any of the interrogation, even though it is standard procedure to do so.

During their initial search, the police took three knives—two found in the greenhouse and one in the kitchen—which they claimed could have been the murder weapon, yet none of the knives had even a trace of blood on them. However, none of these inconsistencies seemed to matter to them. They had their confession and their killer. As far as they were concerned, the case was closed. I was charged with two counts of capital murder.

Gary's sister, Ginger, and her husband, Evan Gauger-Blossom, returned to Illinois immediately to deal with the family farm and help Gary. They left a twenty-year career traveling the world teaching skiing, which they loved. Back in Illinois they were like fish out of water. Nothing was familiar—they were jobless, and there were no mountains. Ginger and Evan took on the responsibility of running the farm and the businesses. Initially, both Ginger and Greg believed Gary was innocent. They cobbled together a thirty-thousand-dollar retainer that they used to hire two attorneys—William Davies and Russell Miller—who had been recommended to them by a lawyer who did some business for their parents. As it turned out, neither had ever defended a homicide case before, let alone a capital case. However, they charged four hundred dollars an hour, including charging for travel time to the courthouse and jail and time spent eating lunch.

GINGER: I was so busy during this time I can't believe I lived through it. I was starting out from scratch taking over the farm and the administration of the estate, and trying to get Gary out of jail. We asked questions of victims' services, but that door was closed. We were considered pariahs because we weren't helping or cooperating. The prosecutors shunned us, ignored us, or intimidated us.

The irony of the situation is that none of us wanted the death penalty. Even my brother Greg, who changed his mind and decided Gary was guilty, didn't want him to get the death penalty. My parents' other family members didn't want it. The prosecution wanted it because they wanted to be perceived as "tough on crime."

•　　•　　•　　•

Judge Henry Cowlin of the McHenry County Court scheduled trial to begin on October 8, 1993, a mere six months after the murders, nearly unheard-of speed for a capital murder case. Ginger knew that her brother was innocent and believed that any jury who saw the facts would acquit him. There was no physical evidence tying him to the murder, nor was there a plausible motive. The best motive the police could come up with was that Gary couldn't stand disappointing his parents because of his drinking, so he killed them. The only evidence the police had was the "confession," which, it seemed clear to Ginger, should have been suppressed because it was obtained under duress.

GINGER: I remember my first conversation with Gary's lawyer Bill Davies. I told him that I thought my brother was innocent and that it seemed like the evidence against him was very weak. I asked him what his strategy was to prepare for trial, and he told me that the other lawyer assigned to Gary's case, Russ Miller, was brilliant so he didn't need to study the stuff to get ready for trial. As though preparing me for the worst possible outcome, Bill told me, "These cases (meaning death penalty cases) are never won at trial, they are won on appeal." I had the impression they did not even want to win at trial.

From the very start, we feared that he was not going to get a fair trial. Murder was uncommon in this part of the state. The brutality of the crime shocked the local community, and the police felt pressure to solve the case quickly. There was a lot of public outcry to bring someone in immediately. Once they got started on my brother, they couldn't stop it or turn it around, they had to keep going.

It had been twelve years since the octogenarian Judge Cowlin last presided over a capital case from that area. Ironically, that case also involved a family slaying. In 1982, Charles Albanese, a fifty-six-year-old man from Spring Grove, was convicted of poisoning his father, mother-in-law, and wife's grandmother in order to inherit the family's trophy-making business. Judge Cowlin had imposed death sentences for the murders.

To make up for their lack of evidence, the police and prosecution trumped up their case against Gary.

GARY: During pretrial hearings the police admitted they had no evidence against me. But what they lacked in evidence, they made up with emotion.

The police really used the local press to its advantage. They played it like a violin. The stories basically parroted the police theories of the case, even to the point of printing an article two days before jury selection, "Gauger Beats Mother," by a person named Al Eastridge who knew my parents. The story said that I had beaten my mother on a couple of occasions, which was completely ridiculous. I can only speculate that Al made these stories up to help prove that I was guilty. After all, I had been arrested and confessed. Everybody thought it was an open-and-shut case.

During jury selection the article about me beating my mother was in the jury room. Somebody put it there to try to influence the jurors. When my attorney objected, the judge ruled that exposing the jurors to the story was "harmless error."

My attorney didn't do a good job representing me. I don't know why. He had thirty years' experience. He wasn't incompetent, just lazy. I think he was greedy, too. I think he wanted to lose at trial so he could get more money from the estate by handling the appeal. I think after thirty years he had become so jaded that he didn't care what happened to me.

The prosecution bolstered Gary's "confession" with the testimony of jailhouse snitch Raymond Wagner, a twenty-six-year-old man from Crystal Lake who was serving an eight-month sentence at the McHenry County Jail for driving on a revoked license. Wagner testified that Gary had admitted committing the crimes to him during two conversations, one on April 21 and the other on June 24. Not surprisingly, Wagner received favorable treatment on his case in return for his testimony. The rest of the state's case was weak, too. The prosecution went with the theory that Gary killed his parents because he could not stand disappointing them with his drinking, even though in truth Gary had a good relationship with his parents. Another weakness was that the prosecution never identified a weapon. In fact, Detective Chris Pandre admitted during testimony that of the twenty-five knives seized from the two-hundred-acre farm, not one had visible traces of blood.

Ginger attended every day, and from the start her fears that Gary would not get a fair trial were confirmed.

GINGER: Judge Cowlin was very confused. It seemed like he should have been retired about fifteen years earlier. He made statements that were totally incoherent. He looked to the prosecution for guidance when he made rulings. Also, he had facial tics, which make him raise his eyebrows and grimace. When Gary was testifying it looked like he was making expressions of disbelief. Instead of explaining this to the jury he turned his back on Gary, making it look like he was disgusted.

One of the disputed facts in the prosecution's case was the source of the thirteen hundred dollars that the police found in Gary's room. The money was leftover proceeds from last year's vegetable stand. The police never specifically stated that Gary had stolen the money, but they just left the box of money sitting on the evidence table in the courtroom. At one point during Gary's testimony he was explaining to the jury that he made the money selling vegetables but had never put it in the bank. After Gary said this, the judge rolled his eyes and threw up his arms as if to say, "Can you believe this guy?"

It seemed like the defense attorneys wanted to do the least amount of work for the most amount of money they could get. There were a lot of things that should have been done but never were. Russ Miller, the one that Bill had said was brilliant, kept making careless errors, liking getting names wrong.

In spite of the weaknesses in the state's case, the jury deliberated for less than three hours before finding Gary guilty. Jurors later said that they convicted him because they could not believe someone would confess to a crime he had not committed. Judge Cowlin set a separate sentencing date for January 11 and ordered a psychologist to examine Gary to determine whether he was competent to be sentenced to death.

GARY: The prison psychologist, Ramesh Vemuri, examined me to decide whether I was competent enough to be executed. He asked me to name the last five presidents, and when I could name them all he said I was sane enough to execute.

❧ Gary's lawyers spent less time preparing for his sentencing than they did for trial. They made two crucial mistakes. Under Illinois law the defendant is permitted to decide whether he wants a judge or the jury to decide the sentence in a capital case. Gary's lawyers advised him to let the judge decide, which was strange advice given the bias Judge Cowlin had shown during trial. Additionally, the lawyers offered no mitigation evidence, even though Gary had no history of violent or criminal behavior. Ramesh Vemuri reported to Judge Cowlin that Gary did not suffer from a thought disorder but was a chronic marijuana user who would go on drinking binges for several days, stop for a few weeks, and start drinking again. It came as no surprise to Gary or Ginger when Judge Cowlin sentenced Gary to die. ❧

> GARY: My attorneys did not offer any mitigating evidence. Many people wrote letters on my behalf. In the middle of the hearing I asked if the judge had read the letters, and he excused himself for twenty minutes to go read letters that he had never read; then he returned and sentenced me to death. My attorney assured me that was good because it would hasten the appeals process.

Gary continued living at the McHenry County Jail while his attorneys filed postconviction motions on his behalf. Ginger ran the farm and did everything she could to help her brother.

> GINGER: The whole experience was horrible. I used to wake up in the morning filled with dread at the idea of facing another day, but then I would think to myself, *I have to get up because the state is planning on killing Gary and I have to stop it.* I visited Gary at McHenry every week. It was horrible and depressing.

While Ginger worried about Gary, he feared for her.

> GARY: The police never conducted a real investigation, so I knew there was a killer or killers on the loose who for some unknown reason killed my parents. There was a rumor that my parents had been pressured to

sell their farm. I wondered if someone would have gone so far as to kill my parents in order to be able to buy the land. I worried they might kill Ginger, too.

I stayed in the county prison under a death sentence for nine months while my lawyers exhausted all postconviction motions. My sister formed a task force where my friends tried to brainstorm different ways to help me. Altogether I stayed at the McHenry County Jail for twenty months. They had a lot of rules designed just to make us uncomfortable. We were forced to wear light cotton jail suits with short sleeves, so we were cold all the time.

If we left our cells we couldn't take a blanket or pad out, so all we could do was sit on the floor or the metal benches. They only gave us enough food to keep us reasonably healthy, but it was greasy and horrible. I gave away my burgers and stuff. Partially they treated us badly as punishment, but also as a way to pressure people into making plea bargains.

Most people were borderline delinquents there for a vast range of minor crimes, but not everyone. I contemplated the eclectic nature of the place during one of our regular spades championships [a card game], one of the jail's favorite pastimes. I looked around the table. My partner was there for growing marijuana. There was a seventeen-year-old arrested for carrying a BB gun in town, and a federal prisoner busted for growing marijuana. Then there was myself, a guy sentenced to death for killing his parents.

Of course I felt anger and frustration. They were the only two emotions I managed to keep intact. My sister thought she would have to sell the whole farm. I slipped into deep, dark depressions. I was disillusioned that three senior police officers could do what they did to me and it was sanctioned by the state. The officers were fairly high ranking —between the three of them they had fifty-three years' experience. Throughout the investigation and trial I counted about 150 instances of police perjury, but instead of getting fired or reprimanded, all three officers received promotions, one to chief detective. It is very appalling what passes for justice in this country.

They blatantly lied to me. I was naive about how much trouble I was in. I didn't realize how hard it is to get someone off death row. When I was in prison, the United States Supreme Court decided that even though they thought a man might be innocent, they allowed Texas to go ahead with the execution anyway. That is the kind of weight they give jury decisions, and juries want to convict. I just kept thinking that if I could put together some kind of record and show police perjury, then some judge would let me out. My naiveté helped me out because I kept some hope alive.

I felt like my life was all about putting messages in bottles. Any name or address I'd learn about I'd write to and try to get their attention. I wrote to the TV news show programs, newspapers. I must have written at least forty letters, trying to elicit some aid. But I knew I was pretty much powerless to stop them from killing me. I was resigned. Even though I didn't want to die, I was ready for them to kill me. The situation was totally out of my hands.

•   •   •   •

In the summer of 1995, attorney Larry Marshall answered Gary's plea for help. A professor at Northwestern University Law School, Larry had successfully defended a number of innocent men who had been wrongfully convicted and sentenced to death.

At the time he entered the case, William Davies and Russell Miller had already filed a number of post-conviction motions, including a motion to reconsider the death sentence. Larry Marshall attended the court hearing on the motion, and informed the judge that he would be taking over as Gary's lawyer. Before ruling on the motion, Judge Cowlin asked him whether he would continue to represent Gary if Gary's sentence were modified from death to a life sentence. Normally Larry did not represent clients unless they were facing death sentences, but Judge Cowlin's question made him suspicious that the judge didn't want Gary's case looked at too closely. He told the judge he would represent Gary even if his sentence were to be modified. As it turned out, Judge Cowlin reversed Gary's death sentence, admitting that he had not adequately considered mitigating evidence—especially the fact that Gary lacked a prior criminal record—before sentencing him to death.

After Judge Cowlin modified Gary's sentence, the state moved Gary out of the county jail to a more permanent location. After an eight-day stay at Joliet, the transfer prison where inmates live while they wait for permanent placement, the state sent Gary to Statesville, one of the facilities where Illinois carries out death sentences. Despite the fact that Gary was no longer facing a death sentence, when he first arrived at Statesville he was placed in what served as the death house, which had been the home of several notorious killers.

GARY: I lived in the X house, which stood for "execution," an old brick building with high ceilings. I was put in the same cell where the notorious John Wayne Gacy, the sex offender and mass murderer, had stayed before they killed him. Eventually they moved me out of the X house, which ironically turned out to be worse.

The conditions at Statesville were unbelievably bad. The inmates ran the cellblocks. Gangs were always fighting each other for control. There was an ongoing war between the gangs and the warden. People were getting beaten or stabbed. While I was at Statesville, nine inmates were killed—five were executed, four others were killed by prisoners. This was a very violent time. I saw beatings almost daily. It was normal for guards to use guns to keep control. There are guard towers every two or three hundred feet around the wall. Guys in a cage armed with a shotgun. The first thing they are supposed to do at the sign of trouble is fire on a steel target. If that doesn't calm things down, then they fire at the ceiling to bring plaster down. The last step is to shoot somebody.

The first time I saw a near-riot was at Joliet over stolen Kool-Aid. I had never experienced anything like it. Thirty or forty people had their thumbs up or down. That signaled that there was going to be a fight. I had never seen anything so ugly. The noise level, the violence level, the tension, was extreme. My cellie [cellmate] got up on a table and established peace and order. His gang was the one that stole the Kool-Aid barrel, so it's a good thing he was able to take control.

Another time the skinheads attacked a bunch of black guys and the black guys were retaliating. The guards fired shots. This particular incident was at the chow hall. The back wall of the cafeteria and the fiberglass windows were all shot full of holes. The ceiling is all shot up, and the target is all shot up. There is a sign in the cafeteria that says, "If shots are fired, sit down."

Because I wasn't part of a gang, they put me in protective custody, which is an isolated part of the prison that does not have much contact with the general population. People who were not part of gangs were called "Neutrons" because they were neutral.

Protective custody was a strange mix of people. It turned out that there were a disproportionate number of innocent people in protective custody. The prison authorities seemed to sense that some people did not really belong in prison and would not be able to protect themselves.

On the other hand, they sent some really bad troublemakers to protective custody for their own safety. Or sometimes people were put in PC for disciplinary reasons. A lot of the sex offenders were in PC, and a lot of crazy, violent guys. Because it was such a strange mix, nobody could take control, so there was an uneasy truce between the gangs there.

Although we were living under very restricted conditions, at least the stress levels were a little less, because you were not always living in fear of violence. There were only twenty-five people on each wing. We were on lockdown the first month, so I didn't have to deal with any of the prison politics for a while. Lockdown is when there is no prisoner movement. You stay in your cell all the time. The only time you get out is if someone comes to visit. Otherwise once a week you got one phone call and one shower.

In the twenty-two months I was in Statesville I was on lockdown 70 percent of the time. In that sense it was worse than death row because on death row people got out for one hour a day. But at least it was safer being in PC. The cell doors were solid steel, not open with bars. Cells with bars could be very dangerous. Inmates stabbed one another, and guards, too, through the cell bars. It is amazing the things that people can make weapons out of. Guys got ahold of broom handles, broke off the head, and then waited for the guard to go by and stabbed him.

It was rumored that the Cubans could make a shank out of anything—even dried newspapers. You could do a lot of damage with those weapons. They would soak newspaper in salt brine, twist it tight to a point, and dry it. After they stabbed you, the salt would get into the wound. One of my cellies was making shanks, which is dangerous because you can get a year in segregation if you are caught.

We would be shaken down at least once a week, sometimes two or three times. A shakedown is when the guards come to your cell and rummage through all of your possessions looking for any type of contraband. They'd go through all your stuff, shake it down on the floor, and you would be outside your cell in shackles. In some pods where the guards were getting paid off, the guards would just slip a note, "You have been shaken down," but not actually do it.

Sometimes runners would warn us that a shakedown was in the works. Runners are inmates that get special privileges from the guards.

The guards allow them to move between the pods to deliver stuff—they keep the prison commerce going. They bring stuff from the commissary. They also brought the dope in. The guards bring in most of the drugs. The guys that are paying off the guards get to go wherever they want. They distributed the contraband.

Fifty-one percent of the inmates in Statesville were there for murder with either death sentences, life sentences, or very long sentences. They were just trying to figure out some way to have some kind of a life. People did all kinds of things in their cells. They'd make hooch out of ketchup and sugar and keep it hidden under their cot. I read newspapers, wrote letters, and got really good at killing cockroaches with rubber bands. I had about an 85 percent hit rate. Also, the Bible studies were great. I was singing in the choir. There is some life in prison, but you have to look for it.

Gary lived at Statesville for about a year and a half waiting for the appeals court to rule in his case. He settled into a routine, trying to keep a low profile, and dreamed about returning to his garden. Gary spoke regularly with his new lawyer, and Ginger visited when she could. He tried to find meaning in the day-to-day-life at the prison. Sometimes he got very angry and depressed, but he always maintained a glimmer of hope.

Since the prison was located two and a half hours from the farm, Gary had infrequent visitors. Ginger visited about every other month, making a special trip each year at Christmas. Friends visited less often. Sometimes Gary made calls, but he could only call collect, and the rate averaged about a dollar a minute, making it prohibitive for long conversations. Larry Marshall visited occasionally, communicating primarily by mail and phone.

There were other innocent men on death row at Statesville at the same time as Gary. Anthony Porter, who was exonerated after Gary's release, came within two days of being executed. He was mentally retarded and had been framed by Chicago police. Anthony's case made national news when some enterprising students from Northwestern University School of Journalism tracked down the real killer and got him to confess on videotape. Also, two of the "Four Heights Four," Willie Raigns and Vermeal Jimmerson, innocent men who were also wrongfully convicted due to police misconduct, went to the same chow hall Gary did.

During his stay, several men were executed at Statesville.

**GARY:** Executions were very depressing—very dark. They'd put us on lock-down for the day of the execution and the day after. After an execution the guards were afraid of rioting. Gradually they'd let people out of the pods one building at a time to see if anything happened. I was on lockdown most of the time anyway, so it didn't really matter. The first two times they executed someone, they gave everybody a box of sugar cookies as compensation for being unjustly locked down. The cookies were meant to appease us. If you didn't like sugar you could trade them for a pack of squares [cigarettes]. I don't usually eat sugar, but I ate it in prison. Then somebody on the street complained about us getting cookies, so they stopped doing that.

Hope sprang to life on March 8, 1996, when the appeals court granted Gary a new trial on the grounds that he had been illegally arrested and the confession had been unlawfully obtained. The state immediately petitioned for a rehearing. In its petition, state appellate prosecutor David Bernhard argued that the judges ignored Gary's "ridiculous" and "incredible" account of why he failed to look for his parents when he first noticed that they were missing. "It defies belief that anyone who had lived with his parents for years and worked on the same farm as they did every day would not immediately go to the two most logical places they would be found. The defendant's contention that he did not enter those areas because the doors were locked is more than merely suspicious, it is an outright lie."[1]

The state acknowledged that without the confession it had no case against Gary. After the appeals court denied the petition for a rehearing, the state appealed to the Illinois Supreme Court. While the appeal was pending, Gary sought release, and on August 2 Judge Cowlin approved his return to the farm, where he was confined by an electronic monitor.

**GARY:** There is a picture of me in front of the McHenry County Courthouse when the court released me. I am standing with my arms stretched up in the air as though I am getting ready to take flight, with a huge smile on my face.

It felt great to be out of prison, but also strange. There are a lot of little things that you get used to with prison life. I got used to a lot of noise and light all the time so that when I got out I slept with a radio and a light on. Even though I had an electronic monitor, I could move freely inside the house. In prison you can't walk anywhere without having to wait for someone to unlock the door for you. There were nine locked doors between my cell and the chow hall. Each one you'd have to stop and wait for a guard to let you through.

On October 2, the Illinois Supreme Court denied the state's appeal, allowing the lower court's decision to stand. Saying it had no choice, the state finally dismissed Gary's case on October 4, 1996.

GARY: Even though I was out of prison, the state persisted in claiming that I was guilty. It said that it would not reopen the case to look for a new killer because "they had the right man." I didn't really get any favorable press. I lived with this cloud over me all the time. Except for people closest to me, it seemed the rest of the world thought that I killed my parents and got away with it. I returned to living and working on the farm and just tried to keep a low profile.

• • • •

In June 1997, U.S. attorneys in Milwaukee indicted James Schneider and Randy Miller, members of the Outlaws, a notoriously violent motorcycle gang, for the murders of Ruth and Morris Gauger. The thirty-four-count indictment capped two and a half years of investigating the Outlaws for crimes throughout the Midwest. A dozen police agencies took part in the investigation coordinated by the Bureau of Alcohol, Tobacco, and Firearms.

Law enforcement only solved the Gauger case after listening to wiretapped conversations of gang members talking about the murders. The motive for the murders was robbery. James Schneider knew of Morris's reputation as a motorcycle dealer and assumed he was wealthy. According to newspaper accounts, the members of the Outlaws believed that Morris kept as much as thirty thousand dollars in cash on his property. In truth, the murders netted James and Randy fifteen dollars.

Murdering Ruth and Morris was only a small part of the Outlaws' crime spree, which lasted years. U.S. attorneys believed Randy Miller had killed at least six people.

News of the indictment thrilled Ginger and Gary.

**GARY:** It wasn't until charges were brought against Miller and Schneider that I started to get favorable press. Nobody really listened to me until the true killers were found. I was finally able to start putting my life back together again. I eventually learned that the Illinois prosecutors got wind of the connection between the Outlaws and my parents as early as September 1995. Even so, they continued prosecuting my case on the theory that there was some connection between the Outlaws and me.

Despite the cruel treatment he had endured at the hands of police and prosecutors, Gary harbored no feelings of vengeance. He told a reporter that he had been telling people for years that he hadn't killed his parents, and it was nice that people finally believed him. He added, "Whoever is convicted, I don't believe it's right to take their life. That reduces us to the same level as the killer. There's no reason to do it."[2]

Eventually, James made a deal with the U.S. attorneys to testify against Randy and other gang members in exchange for a more lenient sentence. In November 1998, he secretly pleaded guilty, then worked for nearly a year and a half as an informant before finally testifying against Randy in March 2000.

James confessed to killing Ruth Gauger. He told the jury about how he sought Ruth out and, when he found her, pulled a gun out of the back of his pants and hit her over the head twice. She fell to the ground and moaned. He lifted her head up by her hair, then slit her throat. Once Ruth was dead, he signaled Randy, who confronted Morris and then killed him using the same method. Afterwards the two headed north to Wisconsin. They stopped at a restaurant for breakfast, where they used the fifteen dollars from the robbery to pay for the meal. James told the jury that he lost his appetite after the killings, so he only ordered chocolate milk.

His testimony helped convict Randy, who stood for trial in U.S. District Judge J. P. Stadtmueller's courtroom in October. Gary did not attend, because he was considered a possible witness by the defense. However, both Ginger and Gary attended the sentencing hearing where Judge Stadtmueller sentenced Randy Miller to two life sentences, remarking as he did that the crimes were "nothing short of barbaric." The judge added that Randy was lucky that he had not been prosecuted in Illinois where he could have faced the death penalty.[3] Ginger declined to comment about the sentencing at length but said through tears, "It's a tragic situation for everybody."

Some months later, in March 2001, James Schneider faced sentencing in front of Judge Stadtmueller. He told the court that he hated the way he had acted and all the pain that he had caused. He asked forgiveness of the Gauger family but admitted he did not think he could forgive someone who had killed his parents. The judge commented again about the brutal nature of the crimes, saying that the trials left him with feelings of "disgust" and "revulsion" and that some days he had even been unable to eat because of the things he heard. The Gaugers "were just honest, upright, small-town folks trying to live the dream of being Americans," and Randy Miller and James Schneider "snuffed out those dreams."[4]

The government asked the court for leniency in light of the assistance James provided in bringing other gang members to justice. Judge Stadtmueller sentenced him to forty-five years in prison.

When asked to comment on the sentence, Gary graciously said that James showed remorse and took responsibility for what he did. "I believe his apology was genuine," he told reporters.[5]

•   •   •   •

With the cases finally behind them, Gary and Ginger are leading busy, full lives. Both live at the farm with their partners. In November 1999, Gary married Sue Rekenthaler, a woman he had known since grade school. They run the organic vegetable business together, specializing in hard-to-find species of produce. At their stand you can find things like Heirloom tomatoes and fifteen types of sweet corn, along with green beans, beets, carrots, lettuce, and pumpkins.

Ginger runs the business she used to share with her mother. She has expanded the inventory beyond rugs and travels around the world looking for interesting merchandise for her shop. Ginger is a member of the Fair Trade Industry, which buys goods made by microproducers and cottage industries where the people work for decent wages in a safe environment. Evan coaches skiing in the winter and works construction in the summer.

•   •   •   •

Gary's resiliency is inspiring. He is philosophical about his ordeal.

GARY: People have a hard time understanding why someone would confess to something they did not do. But what happened in my case was not

*Ginger Gauger-Blossom and Gary Gauger. Photograph provided with permission of the family.*

so much a confession as it was brainwashing. The police overstepped the boundaries of honest police work.

I do not believe the police had a personal vendetta against me. I did not have a long criminal record. I think they were motivated by the horrific nature of the crime—two elderly people killed by being hit in the head, stabbed, and then having their throats slit. If I had gotten out of bed that morning, or if the killers had come into the house, I would have been killed, too.

Not politically active before his conviction, Gary now leaves the farm eight or ten times a year to speak against the death penalty and the injustice that some experience within the criminal justice system; he considers it his duty. He has met with and testified in front of legislatures in Massachusetts, Kentucky, Michigan, and Illinois.

Besides traveling, Gary shares his experience with reporters from around the country and the world who go to his farm to interview him; in the year 2000 alone, reporters from Germany, France, England, and Egypt visited. His television appearances include *60 Minutes* and Geraldo Rivera's and Oprah Winfrey's talk shows. In July 2001, his story was featured in an Arts and Entertainment Network special on wrongful convictions.

GARY: We have a duty as citizens. Democracy is an active thing. We have a duty to express our views on how our representatives are conducting themselves. There is no statistical evidence that the death penalty reduces crime. In fact, in some cases it increases it. There is a brutality factor—during the month of an execution and following an execution, the homicide rate actually rises. The death penalty is very expensive, more expensive than life in prison. We don't save money by killing prisoners. There is no rational reason to keep it. It is murder. It is socially sanctioned murder, and that is wrong.

# CHAPTER 8

# Making Choices

Vicki Zessin and her two-year-old daughter, Audrey, spent the evening of March 28, 1980, at the home of her friend Janet Mesner. Janet lived in the Quaker meetinghouse in Lincoln, Nebraska. Both women were natives of Nebraska, but Vicki had fled her home state in 1972. With two friends, she had driven her Volkswagen Vannagon out west in search of a new life. She landed in Oregon, where she met and fell in love with Gus Lamm while working as a nurse at Woodland Park Mental Health Clinic in Portland. The couple had been together for five years and had been married for three. All of the pieces of Vicki's life seemed to be coming together. She enjoyed her job and was very good at it, had a husband and daughter she loved, and was fifteen weeks pregnant with their second child. She had made this trip home with Audrey to visit family and friends before the birth of the new baby.

Vicki and Gus had decided that Gus would not go along. He needed a dose of city life, so instead, he flew to New York City and spent the week with an old friend. Besides, Gus was glad to avoid visiting Vicki's family. She and her parents had very different values, which clashed and caused tension during their visits. Like many children who came of age in the seventies, Vicki opposed the Vietnam War, while her parents supported it. Vicki supported equality between the races, whereas her father feared that affirmative action might threaten his job at the Goodyear plant.

Vicki and Audrey stayed the week at Vicki's parents' home, but the visit had ended on a sour note. On the last day, Vicki and her parents fought so Vicki took Audrey to stay their last night in Nebraska with Janet.

Sometime after the women had gone to sleep, Randy Reeves let himself into the house through a kitchen window. A lifelong friend of Janet and her family, he was in the habit of staying with Janet occasionally when he needed someplace to stay. No one knows why, but Randy took a knife that he found

Left to right: *Gus Lamm, Vicki Zessin, and Audrey Lamm. Photograph provided with permission of the family.*

in the kitchen and went to Janet's bedroom and attacked her. It is likely that Vicki heard Janet's screams, woke up, and went to her friend's assistance. Randy stabbed Vicki in the liver, severing major arteries and killing her instantly with one blow.

Janet lived long enough to call 911. When help arrived, Janet told a rescue worker, "It was Randy, he had a knife. I don't know why he did it. I don't understand." She asked the rescue workers if her friend was okay. Although they had found Vicki dead upstairs, they told Janet she was all right. Soon after arriving at the hospital, Janet died.

On the kitchen table lay a note apparently left by Janet for Vicki: "Sorry your parents bummed you out. Just remember it is their loss. Enjoy your last night in Lincoln." Walking through the house, a man opened a bedroom near the storage closet and found a small towheaded girl who asked, "Where's my mom?" The man quickly closed the door so that the child would not see the bloodied body of her mother.

The morning of March 29, Gus, who had returned to Oregon, was waking up after spending the night with his friend Norman Malbin on Norman's houseboat on the Columbia River, a few miles from the Portland airport. Gus had driven down from his home in Tillamook the night before so that he would be close to the airport to pick up his wife and daughter. He had missed his family and was looking forward to seeing them. This was the longest time he had gone without seeing Audrey, and he wondered how she had changed. Gus was looking forward to a leisurely morning drinking coffee, reading the paper, and visiting with Norm when his friend walked into the room carrying the phone. "It's your brother," he said.

GUS: Norman handed me the phone. I said, "Hi, what's up?" My brother said, "Don't go to the airport. I want you to come to my house." I knew something was wrong. I said, "Tell me what's going on." He said, "I don't want to talk about it on the phone." I could tell he was really having a difficult time, but I could not stand the suspense. I said, "Just tell me what's going on." With great reluctance he told me, "Vicki's been killed. Somebody broke into the place where she was at last night and killed her and Janet." And I said, "And Audrey?" And he said, "Audrey is okay."

I drove to my brother's in a state of shock. My little dream life had just become a nightmare. I felt traumatized, nauseated, like someone had just sucker-punched me. I felt like I had been physically assaulted without anybody being there. I can remember driving to my brother's screaming and crying. Yeah, I was angry. I was furious at Vicki. I screamed, "God damn it, how could you go back to Nebraska and get yourself killed?" I kept screaming, "Oh fuck! Oh fuck!"

By some miracle I made it to my brother's house, and my folks showed up soon after. We discussed travel plans. I needed to go to Nebraska to get Audrey and deal with Vicki's funeral. My dad said he would go with me.

It's impossible to know how a person is going to react when someone they love is murdered. My immediate reaction was to try to make sense of it all. I wanted a logical explanation. I wanted a rationale for something that was irrational. I needed to figure out how to put this event into the context of my life. I started ruminating, obsessively replaying in my mind over and over what happened. I wondered what her last moments were like. I wondered if she thought of me. I wondered if she knew she was going to die. Somebody gave me a Valium. I'm sure that my sleep was very fitful if I slept much at all. The nightmares began that night and continued for years.

Gus flew to Lincoln to retrieve his daughter and bury his wife. Vicki's family made the funeral arrangements. They wanted a traditional religious service, even though Vicki had abandoned her childhood religion. Gus thought the service reflected not so much who Vicki was but who her parents wanted her to be. They ordered a headstone with the name Victoria Lamm engraved on it, because they had never accepted the fact that Vicki had kept her maiden name when she married. Gus didn't have the energy or desire to argue about the details of burying his wife.

Although it was very difficult, Gus made a concerted effort to focus on the positive. It could have been worse, he thought; Audrey could have been killed, too. Instead, she survived, and she had apparently slept through the murders and been spared the horror of seeing her mother dead.

·   ·   ·   ·

Born Randolph Blackbird, Randy Reeves was an Omaha Indian. The state took custody of Randy away from his mother when he was three, after judging that his mother and grandparents could not provide a "suitable home." Don and Barbara Reeves adopted him.

Randy and Janet had known each other since childhood. They lived in the same small town of Central City, Nebraska. They played together and prayed together at the same Quaker meeting. Janet's mother, Mildred Mesner, taught Randy Sunday school. The Reeves and Mesner families had cousins in common. Every summer the two families held a joint family reunion.

On March 28, Randy, who made his living working construction, had shown up for work, but it was raining hard, so the crew was told there would not be any work that day. Randy and some others decided to wait around until their paychecks were ready; to pass the time, they went to a bar and grill for breakfast. They started drinking that morning and kept at it all day. Randy, who was known by his friends as the designated driver because he did not normally drink, consumed large amounts of alcohol and by evening was extremely intoxicated. He also ingested some peyote. By the time he entered Janet's apartment, he literally did not know what he was doing. Janet must have been very surprised when Randy pulled a knife on her, because she knew him as a gentle man.

There was no doubt, however, that it was Randy. Janet lived long enough to name him as her attacker. He left his wallet behind at Janet's apartment. He was found walking near the meetinghouse wearing clothes covered in blood. At the time of his arrest, Randy's blood alcohol level registered .24 percent, two and a half times the most common threshold for driving-related intoxication—a level at which most people would be unconscious. When he attacked the women, Randy was in an alcoholic blackout. He did not remember committing the murders.

·   ·   ·   ·

After the funeral, Gus returned to Tillamook. He could not bear living in the home where he had lived with Vicki, so he sold it hastily incurring a significant financial loss. Gus did not care about the money. His sole focus was to try to provide Audrey with a stable, loving environment. They moved into an apartment, and Gus returned to work.

GUS: When I came back from Nebraska and returned to work, I exemplified diminished capacity. I was walking around, but there was nobody home. Every day that I went to work, I had to drive by where Vicki had worked. Every day I was reminded and surrounded by places we had been, people we knew, associations we had had in the community. It seemed like she was everywhere and nowhere at the same time. I was so ruminative and perseverative there was not anything else going on in my mind. I thought about her last moments of life. I wondered why she was killed and not me.

During that time Mount St. Helens blew up. Even the earth was revolting and purging. I thought, *I know just how that feels.* That eruption encapsulated my experience.

I was functional at some level. Some things you can kind of do on automatic. Loving Audrey was never a chore for me.

Life felt surreal. Other people did not inhabit the world that I was in. There is a character out of *Li'l Abner* named Joe. Wherever Joe went, he had a rain cloud over the top of his head. That is what it was like for me. Everything was tinged with this noir, this blackness. I had my black beast. The event was so enormous. It impinged on every part of my life. I wasn't sleeping well. I wasn't eating well. I wasn't seeing my friends or family. I was in a huge funk. So there was the world that other people had and then there was mine, and mine was very sad.

I'm sure there was probably a time when I felt angry with Randy, but the other feelings were so much more powerful they demanded more attention and time. I thought constantly about what had happened. People would ask me if I hated Randy and I told them, "No, I don't even know Randy. How can I hate him?" I hated what he did, but you have to know a person before you can really hate him. I could separate what he did from who he was. Since I didn't know him, I didn't bother to put any energy there. I had a limited amount of energy, and I couldn't spend any of it on Randy.

I was obsessed with trying to figure out what had happened. I kept thinking it should have been me that got killed. I had gone to New York City, a place with one of the highest crime rates in the world, and Vicki was in Lincoln, Nebraska, with one of the lowest crime rates in the world. It didn't make any sense. Everything was wrong. Life was turned upside down. My mind kept playing through scenarios about what could have been different, if only . . .

After several months, Gus decided that a new home was not change enough. He needed to leave Tillamook and everything that was familiar, too. His closest friend, Jay Nicholls, offered him the use of a rustic A-frame house in the Elkhorn Valley in the Cascade mountain range, about an hour's drive from Portland.

GUS: It helped tremendously to move away from where we had lived together. The year Audrey and I spent living in the mountains was very healing for me. We lived close to nature.

Our days took on a certain routine. We ate, napped, walked, fed the raccoons, watched coyotes, played with radio-controlled cars, watched Mr. Rogers; we had fun.

One thing that helped my healing process was taking up golf. I was surprised to find a golf course nearby in the middle of the Cascades. I didn't play golf, but I decided I could learn. I got an old set of clubs, and most days Audrey and I would pack up snacks and head for the course. The practice of learning a new skill helped me because it gave my mind something else to focus on besides Vicki's murder. There are a lot of things you have to think about when you are golfing, especially when you are first starting out. Issues like where to place the drive, which club to use, how to get out of the sand traps, how flat does the green lie—all these questions consumed mental energy that would have otherwise been spent obsessing about the crime.

It also helped that I saw a former psychology professor, Frank Miles. Once a week, I drove into Monmouth, Oregon, near Salem, for a session with him. The main issue I needed help with was the incessant nightmares that continued to plague me. Frank offered me a sympathetic ear and some useful suggestions on coping with grief.

As it turned out, my outward journey on the golf course matched my inner journey of therapy. As my game improved, so did my mental health.

The biggest issue I had to work on, and am still working on, is the profound feeling of abandonment I had when Vicki died. I knew it was completely irrational, but I was very angry with her for dying and leaving me. I grew up in a very stable loving family. Vicki's death was my first real experience of being abandoned. I have come a long way in my healing, but I still struggle with that issue today.

•　　•　　•　　•

While Gus and Audrey spent the year living in the Cascades, Randy Reeves faced two counts of felony murder in Nebraska. Vicki's family followed the criminal case and attended the various court proceedings. Gus did not pay much attention to it.

GUS: I knew the case was going on. I'm sure I was curious about it, but I don't remember talking to anybody about it. At that point I couldn't do anything about it. The outcome was going to be pretty negligible on me, considering what I was dealing with. I had just become a single parent under really awful circumstances. I couldn't afford to think about the trial. My brain was already chock-full of stuff I didn't want to think about. I really didn't care about Randy. I didn't care what happened to him. I couldn't care. I didn't have the energy to invest in caring.

Of course, part of the reason I didn't worry about the outcome is that I knew it was going to be an open-and-shut case. Randy had been identified by Janet and found covered with blood shortly after. His wallet was at the crime scene. I knew he would be found guilty, so I didn't need to worry about that.

After that year, Gus's grief had subsided enough for him to leave the mountains and return to civilization. As he predicted, the jury found Randy guilty of the two murders, and a three-judge panel sentenced him to death by electrocution. Gus did not pay much attention to the verdict or the sentence, although he thought it unlikely that Randy would actually be executed.

GUS: Nobody from the prosecutor's office ever called me to ask how I wanted the case to be resolved. The only time I heard from anyone "official" in connection with the case was in September of 1981 after Randy was convicted but before he was sentenced. I got a phone call from someone who identified himself as a "presentence investigator." He asked me whether I thought Randy should get the death penalty. My first thought was that no person should have the power to decide who lives and who dies, so I said something like, "I'd hate to be the person who had to make that decision." But to make sure he understood that I did not support it, I told him that both Vicki and I opposed the death penalty. He asked me how Audrey and I were. I told him that Audrey was okay. I said that I still had nightmares a lot of the time but that I would be okay, too.

• • • •

Gus spent the next eighteen years raising his daughter. Early in her education, a teacher told Gus that Audrey was very bright and recommended that he move to a school district that had a program for gifted children. Gus followed the teacher's advice and did everything possible to help his daughter get a good education. By age twelve, she had taken the college entrance examination. Gus went back to school himself and got his bachelor's degree.

When he wasn't working, Gus played his guitar and spent as much time outdoors as possible. He even invented a sport called riverboarding, using a board he designed, similar to a boogie board, to ride whitewater waves. The circumstances were not what he would have chosen, but he did the best he could with what he had.

GUS: I kept in touch with the Zessins. I wanted Audrey to have a relationship with her maternal grandparents, but it was difficult to spend time with them. They were consumed by bitterness and anger over Vicki's murder. It was especially hard for us to be around Mr. Zessin. He referred to Randy as "Geronimo" and complained about "the niggers" taking over the jobs at Goodyear. Even at a young age, these remarks bothered Audrey. When she was little it was easier, but as she matured she developed her own opinions. Audrey was very much like her mother, and not surprisingly over time she began to clash with her grandparents, just as her mother had. Over the years the visits became less frequent.

One of the last times we visited the Zessins, my parents came with Audrey and me. After the visit my mom took me aside and said, "All they think about is the murder." She was right; it consumed them to the core. It was like watching a disease spread through the family. There was so much anger and hatred. Vicki's brother and sister were infected with this disease of hate, and their children were infected, too. They spoke longingly about how happy they would be to see him executed, as if once Randy was dead everything would be okay.

In November 1998, Gus sat alone in his living room playing the song "Making Whoopee" on his acoustic guitar when the phone rang. He considered ignoring it, but its persistent ringing interrupted his flow. He finally answered it and heard, "Hello, Gus. It's Nancy." Gus paused, trying to put the name together with the voice. It was Nancy Mesner, Janet's cousin. Nancy was Vicki's lifelong best friend. Gus and Nancy had spoken a few times over the years, but she was not in the habit of calling him socially. She asked after Audrey, then got straight to the point: "Gus, I didn't really call to socialize. I called to tell you that they have set an execution date for Randy Reeves—January 14. I don't know what you want to do, but I thought you would want to know. Randy's lawyer is Paula Hutchinson, and if you want more information you can call her."

GUS: When I hung up from Nancy, I remember feeling a little confused. I was crying. I couldn't figure out why this was happening now. I guess I never thought that Randy would actually be executed. I figured there must be some reason why this was happening now—somebody must be pushing for his execution.

The idea of the state putting to death this man nineteen years after the murder seemed absurd, and I knew right away that I opposed the execution. But I had some concerns about what would happen if I called Paula. I knew that if I came out against the death penalty it was probably going to cause interfamilial problems with the Zessins, and my relationship with them wasn't great already. Neither Audrey nor I had spoken with them in a couple of years. At first we had tried to maintain a relationship, but our values were so different and the distance was so great that it was easy to let the relationship slide. I suspect it was hard for them to see Audrey because it must have reminded them of Vicki.

My mind raced back and forth over the pros and cons of the situation. I knew I would have to go back and deal with a lot of stuff again, and I knew that I would no doubt be in line for some more tears, since I was already crying. But I had spent a lot of time processing my grief, and I felt pretty good about my emotional health. I thought I could handle returning to Nebraska. Then I thought about Audrey. I wondered what it would be like for her if I, or we, went to Nebraska. I hoped that the trip would be a chance for Audrey to meet people who knew her mother—people who could provide a different perspective on Vicki's life. Audrey had left home and was living on her own. She had not gone to college, and she was unsure of what to do with her life. I wondered if going to Nebraska might help her focus.

I also thought a lot about Randy's parents. I knew their names, Don and Barbara. I knew they were good people, and I knew that if Randy was executed they would go through the same hell that I did when Vicki died. I couldn't see the point in it. The whole idea of planning Randy's execution seemed like a surreal nightmare. I didn't want to be a part of that nightmare. I wanted to be a force for good. I had this visceral feeling that trying to save Randy's life was the right thing to do. I did not want to live with myself knowing that I had not tried to.

I debated all these things with myself in the space of twenty minutes. Then I called Paula. It was late in the evening, but I couldn't wait until the next day. When she answered I said, "My name is Gus Lamm. Vicki Zessin was my wife. I don't know if there is anything I can do, but I oppose the death penalty and want to help save Randy's life." I heard Paula crying on the other end of the phone. We discussed what to do. She suggested that I come to Nebraska and work to save Randy's life. I agreed.

As soon as I hung up the phone I called Audrey, and she completely agreed with me that we had to go to Nebraska. I had just started a job as a therapist at Sisters of Providence Saint Vincent Hospital. I told my supervisor about the situation, and she told me to take as much time as I needed. We bought plane tickets to leave the next week.

· · · ·

At age forty-five, five feet, two inches tall with dark hair, Paula Hutchinson exuded energy and confidence. Her friends described her as intense but hum-

*Gus and Audrey Lamm. Photograph provided with permission of the family.*

ble. Paula worked as a defense attorney and had been associated in some way with most of the recent capital cases in Nebraska. She had witnessed the execution of her client Harold Otey, the first person the State of Nebraska killed after reinstating the death penalty in 1976. Although Harold was killed in 1994, Paula still kept his name and address in her Rolodex.

If you ask Paula about the night of September 4, 1994, she'll tell you about what it was like to watch her client's body jolted full of electricity. She'll describe how his body twitched uncontrollably until all movement ceased. She still remembers the odor of burning flesh, which she could smell even though the room she was in was separated from the execution chamber by thick glass. It took the state four applications of electricity to kill Harold. A reporter later observed that Harold was still breathing after the second round.

As disturbing as watching the state electrocute her client, Paula remembers, was watching the crowds of people who gathered outside the prison the night of the execution, as excited as if they were attending a championship football game. She was appalled as they shouted, "Go Big Red" and "Fry the nigger."

Paula knew about Gus and Audrey. She had hired a private investigator, Bill Roundy, who located them in Oregon. From what she knew of Gus, she suspected he would oppose the death penalty. However, as much as Paula wanted to pursue every possible avenue to save Randy's life, she could not bring herself to contact them. She had not wanted to intrude on their privacy and remind them of their tragedy.

She discussed her dilemma with Nancy Mesner, Janet's cousin, who, along with Janet's parents, Kenneth and Mildred, opposed the death penalty and had consistently spoken against Randy's execution from the very beginning. Janet's Grandmother Mesner had placed two roses at the front of the Friends meeting on the Sunday after Janet was killed—one for Janet and one for Randy. At Janet's memorial service, her parents told Don and Barbara Reeves that they hoped the state would not execute Randy, because it would not bring Janet back and would only add another senseless death.

The Mesners never wavered from this position. Kenneth and Mildred were both called as defense witnesses during Randy's trial. Kenneth testified in support of a bill to abolish the death penalty during the trial and at successive hearings in each session of the Nebraska legislature during the 1980s and most of the 1990s. Janet's brother, Kurt, and sister, Marilyn, also spoke out against the death penalty and against Randy's execution.

Paula was grateful when Nancy offered to call Gus to broach the subject of Randy's execution, and she rejoiced when Gus called her and said he wanted to help save Randy's life.

In preparation for their trip to Nebraska, Gus showed Audrey photographs of her mother and talked to her about her mother's life. One of the photographs, a three-by-five black-and-white, yellow with age, depicted Gus and Vicki holding Audrey between them. Bob Nelson, a family friend, took the picture for Gus to use in a photo album he made for his parents as a Christmas gift. Gus had never imagined that that Christmas would be their last as a family.

In late November 1998, Gus and Audrey made their first pilgrimage to Nebraska to try to save Randy Reeves's life. Paula Hutchinson met them at the Omaha airport and took them right away to a local television station for their first interview.

GUS: They made us do what is called a "walk and talk" where the camera-person followed us as we told a bit about our story. I was nervous, but it was just a short segment and we didn't say all that much.

The next day in Lincoln, we had a much longer interview. This one was more difficult for me because I was not the kind of guy that went around making public disclosures about my private life. Many of my close friends didn't even know that my wife had been murdered, and now I was going to tell the whole world.

Thankfully, the reporter was very nice and not at all intimidating. After the television interview in Lincoln, we held our first press conference with print media. Already, I felt myself losing my reticence about speaking publicly. Talking about my life made me feel empowered—more in control than I had felt since the murder.

Gus did not do all the talking. As it turned out, Audrey was a natural spokesperson who quickly learned how to speak in short, cohesive sound bites, which reporters love. Gus's natural style was to expound and elaborate, so it made more sense to put Audrey in front of the television cameras. Gus also preferred that reporters photograph Audrey; tall and willowy with pale blonde hair, she was, Gus believed, more photogenic.

In the ensuing days, Gus and Audrey made countless public appearances at churches and schools, spoke to community groups, and gave dozens of press interviews. They spoke to anyone who would listen; no crowd was too small and no location too humble. They were on a crusade to save Randy's life. For Gus, the speaking tour was the opportunity to share his years of ruminating.

GUS: For the past nineteen years I had never really talked about these issues that I had thought about so often. Now people wanted to know what I thought. It was good to get it out. It was restorative.

The case was so dark—two women stabbed to death in a Quaker church. I thought that speaking out shone some light on the situation. I wanted people to know that the tragedy did not need to continue, that human suffering could be curtailed. I wanted Randy and Don and Barbara Reeves to know that Audrey and I were okay.

As I grew to know the Reeveses, my desire to help their son increased. Don and Barbara Reeves are such wonderful people. Don is so humble. You would never know that he recently served as the general secretary for the American Friends Service Committee, a very prestigious position within the Quaker community. Barbara looks like the archetypal grandmother. She laughs easily. I love to make her laugh. They are very genuine, unassuming people.

They have had to live with the pain and shame of Randy's murder and will continue to live with it for the rest of their lives. I do not want them to have to live with the pain of Randy's execution. It would devastate them. They do not deserve that.

•   •   •   •

One of the issues raised by the case was the fact that Nebraska's death row, like most in the country, was disproportionately populated by people of color. The Omaha tribe had taken up Randy's case. They and others organized a rally at the Lincoln Indian Center in mid-December 1998, a month before Randy's execution date. About eighty people attended, including the families of the victims. Randy's birth mother, Grace Blackbird, sat with the Reeveses. They were joined by SueZann Bosler, who had traveled from Florida to share her experience of spending more than a decade saving the life of the man who had killed her father and nearly killed her. (See chapter 6.)

Former governor Frank Morrison told the crowd that society had made the death penalty a cure-all for its inability to handle certain problems. "The state's motto," he said, "is 'equality before the law'—what a hypocrisy." He suggested that the death penalty in Nebraska was not fairly administered, being used primarily against poor people and people of color. Tribal leaders, Gus and Audrey, and the Mesner family also spoke at the rally.

The Mesners had been speaking against Randy's execution since their daughter's murder. Because of their unusual stance, reporters had contacted them almost every time Randy's case was in the news following each appeal or decision—at least two dozen times over the intervening nineteen years. The Lincoln Friends Meeting, in whose place of worship Janet and Vicki were killed, also opposed Randy's execution from the beginning and spoke out from time to time.

Some reporters and some public officials discounted the feelings of both the Mesners and the Lincoln Friends because they were Quakers, who are famous for their views on nonviolence and therefore not to be taken too seriously. The same could not be said for Gus and Audrey Lamm, who spoke out at this critical moment.

GUS: One thing that all the reporters wanted to know was if I was a Quaker. Everybody asked me that. I said I was familiar with the Society of Friends and their doctrine of nonviolence and I thought that the Quakers' opposition to the death penalty was dismissed because of this belief.

I saw people wanting to be able to pigeonhole me or dismiss my opposition to the death penalty. I didn't want to let them do that. When asked my religion, I first said I was a heathen, but then I told the truth, I was a Taoist, which sent them all to their dictionaries looking up the word in the *D* section. I recited a quote that seemed appropriate for the occasion. It was a quote from Lao Tzu, from the *Dao Te Ching.* "Man is not the executioner. Nature is the executioner. And when man attempts to usurp nature it is as though the apprentice has taken the master's cleaver, at which point he stands a better chance of harming himself than of completing the task."

Reporters also wanted to know why we were not asking for retribution. I kept talking about how electrocuting Randy would hurt not only Randy but lots of other people. I said that execution was the antithesis of what my wife would have wanted. I had looked at the situation from every angle a human being could look at it. I knew how miserable, how absolutely miserable it was to lose someone to murder. The feelings hover always near the surface, ready to choke you in pain at the least trigger of memory. I knew that that was how the Reeves would feel after the State of Nebraska killed their son. I did not want them to feel what I had felt. I knew they had suffered enough already. The execution was going to generate a whole new round of misery and do nothing to restore Audrey or me, or the Mesners or the Reeves. It was just another loss to deal with.

Through Paula, Gus learned more about Randy's case. He was surprised to learn that the jury foreman had told Paula that he would have preferred it if Randy had not been sentenced to death. However, under Nebraska law, once a person is convicted of first-degree murder, sentencing is done by the court—in this case by a three-judge panel—in a separate hearing. The sentencing decision was out of the jury's hands.

Gus learned that the judges relied on a report prepared by a presentencing investigator, in which Gus had been misquoted. The investigator who had called Gus back in 1989 wrote in his report that Gus had said that he had "washed his hands" of it when asked if he wanted Randy to receive the death penalty. Gus had actually said that he wouldn't want to have to make that decision. The investigator failed to mention that both Gus and Vicki opposed the death penalty. The report also inaccurately stated that Audrey had nightmares and had been in therapy since age two.

The investigator had also inaccurately represented statements made by Janet's parents, Ken and Mildred Mesner. The investigator wrote that Mildred claimed not to desire Randy's death, but it was his opinion that she did not really mean that. He added that Mildred had said that Randy was "an angry person," which she never said. Gus and the Mesners were understandably upset that their words had been misconstrued and relied upon by the judges to decide to sentence Randy to death.

•　•　•　•

The Nebraska constitution establishes both a Parole Board and a Board of Pardons. The Board of Pardons is composed of three elected officials: the governor, the secretary of state, and the attorney general. The Parole Board has the authority to make nonbinding recommendations in clemency cases to the Pardons Board, which has the authority to make the final decision.

The Parole Board had a reputation of being tough-minded. It was nicknamed the "Patrol Board" because a number of its members were retired police officers. An exception to that norm was Bob Boozer, a well-known retired professional basketball player.

Paula wanted the Lamms and Mesners to have an opportunity to state their opposition to Randy's execution in an official forum. She arranged for the families to appear before the Parole Board in December 1998. All seven members of the board agreed to meet with the two families.

Accompanied by Paula, the Mesners and the Lamms sat across the table from the panel and asked the members to commute Randy's sentence from death to life in prison.

GUS: I said that the situation was an interfamilial tragedy. The people involved had already been traumatized. I said it would serve me no purpose at all to have Randy executed and it was a disservice to my wife's memory. Audrey talked about her experience of traveling around the state and meeting people that had known her mother. She told the Parole Board members, "Everywhere I have gone I have spoken to people who knew my mother. She was a very compassionate person. She would not want to see the Reeveses suffer from Randy's execution."

When we finished, the chairwoman, Jean Lovell, reached over to me, took my hand, and said, "Your daughter glows." Bob Boozer remarked, "Those two people are worth a thousand of those that come in looking for a pound of flesh." We felt good about the hearing, but we didn't know what to expect.

The next step was for the Parole Board to make a recommendation to the Pardons Board, which the Pardons Board could either accept or deny. The Pardons Board would consider Randy's case sometime before the execution date, but it was not required to meet formally; it could make its decision based on a written record. At this point, all we could do was wait.

During their stay in Nebraska, Gus and Audrey lived in an apartment in the same complex where Paula and her family lived. Audrey and Gus got to know Paula's husband, Jim, and their two children, nine-year-old Max and seven-year-old Paige. When Gus and Audrey were not on the road talking about Randy's case, the two families spent time together. By the end of their month-long visit, Gus and Audrey felt like part of the Hutchinson family. Just before Christmas, Gus and Audrey went home to Oregon, planning to return to Nebraska for the Pardons Board meeting.

GUS: After returning to Oregon, we celebrated Christmas. It's hard to describe what that time was like. On the one hand, we were facing this horrible specter of Randy's pending execution. On the other hand, the experience of telling my story had been very cathartic for me. It was a time of epiphanies. I felt so empowered. I felt so changed. My life was transformed.

During the last twenty years I had learned to make peace with my demons by focusing on the fact that my daughter had miraculously survived with no memory of the night. Instead of concentrating on my wife's murder, I accepted my fate, realizing that my arms were "too short to box with God." I didn't want Audrey to be traumatized by having a basket case for a father. But it wasn't until the trip to Nebraska, when I started speaking out, that I felt like I gained back control of my life. Instead of living with my demons, I felt like I had slain them.

In January 1999, Audrey and Gus returned to Nebraska. Randy's execution was still scheduled for January 14. Audrey left at the beginning of January, a week before Gus, in order to have more time to travel around the state talking about Randy's case. Their strategy was to try to raise its profile in hopes of generating political pressure on the Pardons Board to grant Randy clemency.

Audrey was sick with a bad case of flu when she arrived in Nebraska. Despite her ill health, she stuck to her schedule of speaking events and press conferences.

Audrey's experience in Nebraska differed from her dad's. While Gus experienced a catharsis, working out his grief and putting demons to rest, the trip stirred up feelings of grief for Audrey. During her travels she frequently met people who had known Vicki, and they often shared stories about her with Audrey. The constant reminders of her mother highlighted the acuteness of her loss.

Audrey's decision to publicly oppose Randy's execution further alienated her from her mother's family and caused her stress. Audrey was not close to her mother's father, Al Zessin, but she wanted to be. As a child, Audrey had visited her grandparents Al and Dorothy at least once a year for a few weeks. Her maternal uncle Greg and aunt Brenda lived near the Zessins so she also visited with them and their families.

AUDREY: My mother's parents were lifelines for me. Along with my mother's brother, Greg, they were the only blood connection to my mother. I visited them fairly regularly when I was a child, but the visits stopped when my grandmother died when I was fourteen. My grandmother had been the one to arrange the visits—to figure out the time and buy the plane tickets. After she died, my grandfather never took over making those arrangements, so visits became less frequent. I hadn't seen him in many years, although we kept in touch by phone.

Over the years I asked my grandparents a lot of questions about my mother, but they didn't like to talk about her. I think it was very painful for them to remember her. They didn't talk that much about Randy Reeves, but whenever they did their comments were always extremely negative.

I had hoped that spending time in Nebraska would help me reestablish a relationship with my grandfather. Midway through the week, I was speaking in a town near where he lived. I was nervous about calling him, but I did it anyway. He picked up the phone, and when he realized it was me he grew distant. I told him that I was nearby and asked if he'd like some company. He said, "I'm not inclined to see you. You know we are on opposite sides of this issue." I said that we didn't have to talk about the case, that we could talk about other things. He mumbled something like, "Well, if you want to come by," but I knew he didn't want to see me.

I felt so sad and hurt but I wanted him to know that I loved him even though we disagreed about the death penalty. Before I hung up the phone I said, "I love you, Grandpa." He said, "I like you, too."

That conversation really broke my heart. I felt sad, but also frustrated because I didn't understand why our differences had to get in the way of us having a relationship. Fortunately, I met many other people that week who told me wonderful stories about my mother and made me feel very welcome. That helped to make up for the disappointment with my grandfather.

At the end of the week, Gus joined Audrey in Lincoln, in time for the Pardons Board meeting. On January 11, Audrey and Gus, along with Paula Hutchinson and a group of about sixty supporters, crammed into a small room in the capitol. The Pardons Board was not legally required to hold a formal hearing, but all present hoped that it would. The Parole Board had not yet announced its recommendation in the Reeves case, but Paula assumed that at the very least it would recommend holding a formal hearing.

Before the meeting, Paula gave Audrey three pink roses—in memory of Vicki, Janet, and Randy. Audrey sat next to Paula in the front row along with Frank LaMere, a Native American activist. Vicki's brother, Greg Zessin, and Janet's parents, Mildred and Ken Mesner, were also in the room. Because the room was so crowded, Gus and some others listened to the proceedings over speakers set up in the hallway.

At that time, the members of the Pardons Board were three white men: Governor Michael Johanns, Secretary of State Scott Moore, and Attorney General Donald B. Stenberg. Governor Johanns presided over the meeting. He had just been sworn in as governor two days earlier and was undoubtedly disturbed to be facing such a controversial situation so early in his tenure.

The first order of business was to decide whether to hold an official hearing. The Parole Board had voted five to zero in favor of granting a clemency hearing, its first unanimous recommendation in memory. Governor Johanns called for a vote on the motion to hold a hearing, which failed by two to one. Scott Moore cast the vote in favor.

The board then briefly discussed whether to hear any witnesses before making its decision on Randy Reeves's clemency petition. The three men decided not to hear from the victims' families.

When the crowd realized that the Pardons Board was about to deny Randy's clemency request without giving any of the victims' families an opportunity to speak, people began booing. Scott Moore asked for and was granted a fifteen-minute recess. Attorney General Stenberg left the room, but Governor Johanns and Secretary of State Moore stayed behind.

AUDREY: I couldn't believe what was going on. I was sure that we were going to be given an opportunity to speak on behalf of my mother. I was still sick and I felt so tired, but I could not just sit silent. I stood up and said to the governor, "Don't do this to my mother." The governor said, "You're out of order. Sit down."

I was crying, and the television reporters all turned their cameras on me. My dad came into the room to comfort me. Uncle Greg who seemed embarrassed by what I had done, said to me, "We're in recess," meaning that I should not speak out of turn. My dad said, "Oh good, I always liked recess." Then my dad said to Greg, "You know your sister would not approve of this." "But she's not here, is she?" Uncle Greg said. Dad asked angrily, "Are you happy now?" Greg didn't reply. I felt bad for Greg, so later on I made a point to reach out to him and tell him that I loved him. I did not want the situation to bring so much tension to my family, but I felt like my dad and I were doing what my mom would have wanted.

Audrey's remarks inspired others to speak out, too. Mildred Mesner, Don Reeves, and several others addressed brief comments to the governor. Frank LaMere said, "One hundred years from now our children's children will speak of this day." However, none of these expressions of opposition to Randy's execution became part of the meeting record.

After the recess, the board reconvened. Attorney General Stenberg read a letter from Vicki's sister, Brenda Cheever, on behalf of the Zessin family urging the board to deny Randy's petition for clemency and to go forward with the execution. Immediately afterward, the board voted to deny Randy's clemency petition and adjourned. Stunned, Audrey sought the three men out.

AUDREY: I decided to give the members of the board the three flowers in honor of my mom, Janet, and Randy. I handed a flower to both Secretary of State Moore and Attorney General Stenberg, but when I tried to give the flower to the governor, he pushed my arm away.

My dad saw the governor push my arm and got very angry. He said to the governor, "Why can't we speak?" The governor did not answer. My dad said, "My wife was a woman of peace, a woman who loved life and dedicated her life to helping others. She would not want someone executed on her behalf." The governor would not answer our questions or even look at us. Paula Hutchinson was there and she said, "Governor, at least have the decency to look at Mr. Lamm when he is addressing you."

People were very upset by the way the governor treated us. A group of Randy's supporters decided that we would give the governor a rose whether he wanted one or not. Moira Ferguson, a long-time supporter of victims' rights in Nebraska, made some phone calls and arranged to buy hundreds of pink flowers, which we planned to deliver to the governor in the morning.

That night we went back to the Hutchinsons' place. My dad and I were very upset. We felt like we had failed, that if only we had found the right words we could have saved Randy.

The next morning, Gus, Audrey, and a few supporters hand-delivered two thousand pink flowers to the governor. They meticulously laid out each one, creating a huge bouquet at the entrance to the governor's mansion. Within a few minutes reporters arrived, and once again Audrey made the evening news.

While Gus and Audrey delivered the flowers, Paula delivered one last appeal to the state supreme court. The appeal had been prepared for a while, but Paula had hoped that the Pardons Board would commute Randy's sentence and make it unnecessary. The supreme court is very near the governor's mansion, and if the judges had looked out of their windows that day, they would have seen the flowers with a large banner that read FROM AUDREY.

The appeal raised two legal issues. The main issue challenged Randy's sentence under a newly passed provision of the Nebraska constitution. The previous November, Nebraska voters had passed an "equal protection" amendment, which had taken effect on January 1, only eleven days earlier. In the appeal, Paula alleged that Nebraska's system of capital punishment violated the equal protection clause because it was applied unequally depending on a person's race. While Native Americans and blacks comprised approximately 4 percent of the state's total population, they were 30 percent of the people sentenced to death during the previous two decades.

Randy's appeal also included an argument that the Nebraska Supreme Court had exceeded its constitutional mandate by resentencing Randy in 1994, after a federal court had set aside his original death sentence.

Paula met up with Gus and Audrey outside the courthouse. Gus and her son, Max, were doing handstands while Audrey was sitting in the Ford Explorer trying to stay warm. As soon as she saw them Paula screamed, "We got a stay!" The court had accepted the equal protection appeal and granted an indefinite stay in order to consider the claim. Randy would live beyond the fourteenth. Paula, Audrey, and Gus hollered with delight and relief. The work of the past two months had paid off.

GUS: I felt so relieved. I felt vindicated. Well, maybe validated is a better word. I felt a huge sense of relief. We were within a day of him being killed. And I just looked at all the people that were around me that had been working so hard. I felt a tremendous sense of gratitude. So many people had done so much for Audrey and me. Only after the stay had been granted did I realize how much pressure we had been under. Randy was forty-eight hours from death. He had already been placed on death watch at the prison.

The next day's front-page headline read "Reeves Granted Reprieve."[1] A half-page photograph of Gus and Audrey delivering the flowers to the governor's mansion dominated the page. Exhausted but thrilled, Gus and Audrey felt that their mission was complete, at least for the time being.

The Zessins did not have the same reaction to the decision. "I just want that man out of sight," Al told a reporter. "It's been eighteen years that my family has had to suffer from Randolph Reeves. I'd been looking forward to Thursday, January 14, 10 A.M. for a while. I thought he was finally going to be gone."[2]

Having devoted the last two months to saving Randy's life, Gus felt that he and Audrey needed to meet him. Gus wanted Randy to know that he and Audrey were okay, that in spite of the murder they were leading happy and productive lives. Gus told Audrey, "Randy needs to see you to know that you are all right." Trusting her dad's instincts, Audrey agreed.

Arranging a meeting with Randy on Nebraska's death row was not an easy task. Prison officials at first did not know how to respond to the unusual request. They decided to allow the visit but required a mediator to be present in case Gus or Audrey "freaked out."

Gus, Audrey, and Randy all objected to the idea of a mediator. They wanted to speak openly without a stranger present, but since they had to have someone, the ideal person would be a trained mediator who was willing to attend the meeting but not act as a mediator. Paula called several mediation firms, but none could understand why someone would hire a mediator to sit in a room and do nothing. When he heard what Paula was trying to arrange, Dick Hargeshiemer, a family friend and trained mediator, contacted her to offer his services. Paula and Dick thought that the prison officials might balk at the idea of Dick serving as the mediator because he was a death penalty abolitionist and regularly visited men on death row. But the warden approved Dick's certification without trouble.

•    •    •    •

Unbeknownst to Gus and Audrey, Randy Reeves had written a letter to them when he believed that he might be executed; he had given the letter to Paula and asked her to give it to Gus and Audrey after he was dead. Paula decided that it would help Gus and Audrey now, so before the visit she gave it to them.

Hello,

In so many ways, I always hoped this day would never come. But it has, and I feel the full impact of this day, in ways that I will never be able to explain, or confess to you or anyone. The fullness of my crime has never been complete. Not until now. Your presence, your words, your actions, has brought your wife, your mother, alive to me in a way that has not existed for me before.

My words can only be so empty, so meaningless. And I am not an elegant person, when it comes to these kinds of words. To merely tell you of my sorrow over what happened, would never serve either you, or her memory.

I never knew Vicky. Never to my knowledge saw her before. Never heard her speak, or walk, or anything that would of given me an idea of who she was, or might have been. Your presence and the things you have done have brought Vicky's presence to me in a way that I have not known until now. All these years, I have only carried one person with each and everyday. A single person, whom I mourned, and missed, and felt a deep pain for that has never left me.

I have never been able to heal the pain inside me over my actions. Friends have told me that I must forgive myself. That is something that is not possible. I cannot imagine the loneliness and pain in raising a child all alone, under such circumstances.

And I have another kind of sorrow, horror that will stay inside me forever. Which is something that will eat away at me forever, and I would have it no other way. The only comfort I have on this, is that an angel must of held you close, and talked with you, keeping away the fear, in those long horrible moments.

I never had the right to ask anything of either of you. And your actions on my behalf leave me stunned and shaken. And my thanks can only rightfully be for the comfort, in what you have given to my family, my friends. And those who still, despite it all, still care for me. That you have been willing to give them a feeling of faith, of hope. And a sense of grace, is something I cannot fully understand.

And perhaps, it is something, I am not meant to understand. But I thank you for the gift you have given my family, and others. Your actions and words, have brought so much to so many. And for that, I will never be able to thank you enough.

If I could tell you why this happened, I would. Because I owe it to you. Not because of your actions on my behalf. If you felt the other way, I would still deeply feel this way. That was something that was missing in my life. And while this brings me new misery as well, it is in its way, a sense of completion I did not have before.

I have no right to ask you for anything. But now I do. And that is, that I never thought I was capable of such an act. Yet it happened, and I was the sole cause of all this. And that you believe that this was never anything that I wanted to happen. I am so ashamed, and my sorrow for both of you over what I did, is something, that is a living part of me.

I would not ask for your forgiveness, let alone your pity. I do not have that right, nor the courage to ask for it. All I can do is tell you of my sorrow.

Thank you so much for what you have done.

Randy Reeves.[3]

GUS: Paula gave us the letter from Randy a couple of hours before we went to the prison. I didn't even know he had written one. I'm not sure why Paula gave it to us. I suspect that she wanted us to have something to ponder before we went to see him. After reading the letter I felt, oh, I just cried—I don't think I made it through the first paragraph, I was so moved. I mean, I probably read that letter twenty or thirty times. I still read it. Whenever I am feeling overwhelmed and unsure if I can continue on with this work, I'll take it out and read it and say to myself, "Here is an individual who is damned by what he knows and damned by what he doesn't know. Here's somebody who has also had a long time to think about this and obviously understands the impact of what has happened and has some very genuine feelings of remorse and loathing at what he has done."

· · · ·

Neither Gus nor Audrey had ever been to a prison, let alone visited death row. Upon entering the prison they passed through a metal detector. The guards ordered them to take off their shoes, which were inspected for hidden weapons. They were not allowed to take any personal belongings inside the prison, although Gus was permitted to take in thirty-five cents so that he could buy Randy a Dr. Pepper.

After they went through security, a guard escorted Gus, Audrey, and Dick through a maze of dark, cold corridors. A series of automatic steel doors opened noisily and closed quickly behind them. Gus thought of the proverb "When one door closes, another door opens."

Gus and Audrey had decided that they would each visit Randy individually and that Gus would go first. The guards led Gus and Dick to the visiting room, leaving Audrey behind in a small waiting room. Dick settled himself into the farthest corner to read a book in an effort to be as unobtrusive as possible. Then the guards escorted Randy into an adjacent room separated by a thick glass partition. Each room had a telephone that visitors used to speak with the prisoners.

As soon as Randy entered the room, Gus walked to the partition and placed his hand up against the glass. Randy did the same. Each picked up his phone. Randy said, "Gus," and Gus said, "Randy."

GUS: I went to death row and met a very contemplative and self-effacing man who was anything but a monster. Randy was very subdued and very soft-spoken. We talked for forty-five minutes about philosophy, religion, and growing up. We didn't talk about the crime, really. The only time I mentioned it was to tell him that I would not have picked the circumstances under which I became a single parent but that I was grateful for the experience. I told him to "rest easy." From the letter and the visit I sensed that Randy lived with constant remorse for what he had done.

At one point during our visit I looked at Randy's hand. I watched his pulse, saw the blood course through his veins. I thought to myself, "If the governor had had his way, Randy would not be sitting here with me." Seeing that pulse made me feel that all the pain and frustration had been worth it because Randy was still alive.

I noticed that when Randy spoke to me, he looked me in the eyes, something Governor Johanns had not done. I thought it strange that I enjoyed spending time with my wife's murderer more than with the governor. It reminded me of a David Mamet movie with good bad guys and bad good guys. In spite of the crime he committed, Randy was very genuine and accessible.

Audrey's visit with Randy was enlightening as well. They also talked for about forty-five minutes. He asked her about all kinds of things—books, her childhood, and what she wanted to do with her life. As we were leaving the prison I remarked to Audrey that Randy didn't seem like a murderer. Audrey said, "Well, you know, Dad, he was only a murderer for one night of his life."

•    •    •    •

Soon after the visit, Gus returned to Oregon, but Audrey decided to stay on in Nebraska. Paula offered her a job as a tutor, nanny, and legal assistant, which she accepted.

Besides representing Randy, Paula took on Gus and Audrey as clients. She brought suit on their behalf alleging that the state had violated their rights as victims. The Nebraska constitution accords victims of crime the right to be heard during criminal cases, and Paula believed that the Pardons Board's decision not to hold a formal hearing denied Gus and Audrey that right. The board's action was particularly troubling given that it had considered the opinion of the Zessins, who had supported Randy's execution.

In April, Gus returned to Nebraska, this time for a photo shoot for *Elle* magazine, which was running a feature story. The photographer arranged to take a picture of Gus and Audrey in front of the Quaker meetinghouse where Vicki was murdered.

GUS: I don't like having my picture taken anyway, and I especially dreaded going to the meetinghouse, but I decided I'd go anywhere if it would help save Randy's life.

As we stood near the entrance to the building, I thought about how we don't get to choose when we die. When a person dies I think they want to have friends and people they love around them. Vicki and Janet loved each other, so it brought me some comfort to know they were together when they died. I believed that Vicki died trying to protect her friend. There is nothing more honorable a person can do than to give their life for another.

Before we left, we walked around the building. We saw the kitchen window where Randy had entered the house. It was strange because on the one hand the building had such significance, and on the other hand it was just a building. I was thinking about time, how strange it is. Sometimes Vicki's murder seems so long ago, like it was another lifetime; at other times, like that day, it felt so recent that I still cried at the smallest reminder of her.

I had very mixed feelings that day. I was very proud of Audrey. I loved her so much and felt that Vicki would have been pleased by my efforts as a parent. If I were the type to believe in angels, I would have said that Vicki was there with us at the place of her death, smiling at us. But while these thoughts comforted me, I also felt sad. I couldn't help wondering what it would have been like to raise Audrey with Vicki.

After the photo shoot, we visited Vicki's grave.

After getting involved in Randy's case, I had begun to wonder if I should have gotten involved at the very beginning. Perhaps it would have made a difference if I had spoken out earlier. But I look at Vicki's family and see how being intimately involved in the case affected them. Vicki's mother died years ago, and both Al and Greg blame her premature death on the stress of Vicki's murder.

Although I disagree with them about the death penalty, I empathize with them, too. It must have been horrendous for them to attend the trial—to relive the death of their pregnant daughter and sister. There were unresolved issues between Vicki and her father, which only complicated the situation and made it more painful for him. I am sure that supporting the death penalty is his way of being loyal to his daughter. I think what they are all looking for is "closure." But this is not a matter of closure. It will never be over. There will never be a winner, just survivors.

·  ·  ·  ·

In May 2000, the Nebraska Supreme Court rendered its decision in Randy's case. It denied Randy's equal protection claim but reversed his sentence, acknowledging that it had erred in resentencing Randy to death in 1994. The court ordered a new sentencing hearing in the original Lancaster County Court. This brought the case back to the jurisdiction of prosecutor Gary Lacey, who had been the assistant prosecutor in the original trial nearly twenty years earlier. Everyone wondered if he would seek the death penalty again or agree to settle for a life sentence.

•   •   •   •

It was twenty degrees and snowing in Omaha on December 8, 2000, when Gus and Audrey returned to Nebraska, this time in connection with their own case. The Lancaster County District Court had ruled that their constitutional rights as victims had not been violated. The court held that it did not consider the Lamms "victims" under Nebraska's Victims Bill of Rights because, in its judgment, they were acting on Reeves's behalf, not of their own accord. The court reasoned that because Gus and Audrey were not victims, they were not entitled to the same rights as other victims. Paula had appealed this ruling, and the Nebraska Supreme Court was going to hear oral argument on the issue.

During argument, Paula pointed out that the Zessins had been given the opportunity to give their opinion in support of the death penalty. "Is this law saying that if victims support the prosecution then the law supports you?" she asked.

Don and Barbara Reeves attended the hearing to support Gus and Audrey.

At Paula's request, prosecutor Gary Lacey had arranged for a meeting after the court hearing between Paula, Greg Zessin, and the Mesners; because of the animosity between Greg and Gus, Gus was not invited. Both attorneys hoped that there might be a way to resolve Randy's case without another death penalty sentencing hearing: if the Zessins approved, Gary would not seek a death sentence in exchange for Randy agreeing to a life sentence. Gus and Audrey, the Mesners, and Don and Barbara Reeves all hoped for that outcome. Unfortunately, at the last minute, Greg refused to attend.

After court, Don and Barbara drove Gus and Audrey back to Paula's house, where they were spending the weekend before flying back to Oregon. Although it weighed heavily on everyone's mind, they did not discuss the case.

Soon after the December hearing, the Nebraska Supreme Court ruled on the Lamms' claim. The court disagreed with the lower court's finding that the Lamms were not victims. It held that the Nebraska constitution had established rights for victims but that the rights were meaningless because the legislature had failed to pass enacting legislation to protect them. Although the decision did not help Audrey and Gus, it did highlight a flaw in the law. In February, Senator Kermit Brashear of Omaha introduced legislation to give effect to the amendment. Gus was philosophical about the decision.

> **GUS:** We were disappointed by the court's decision, but more importantly we were concerned with Randy's fate. We kept hoping that Prosecutor Lacey would agree to a life sentence, but he would not. The court scheduled another sentencing trial for September. I did not look forward to yet another trip to Nebraska.

Paula continued preparing for the sentencing trial, which was scheduled to begin on September 21 and last for nine days. The fact that Randy had been sentenced two decades earlier made it hard to review the case. Exhibits and evidence from the first hearing were missing, and the pathologist who had conducted the autopsies on the bodies and the detective who had interviewed Randy were both dead.

Meanwhile, in August, the Baldus study on Nebraska's use of the death penalty was released. Although it found no real disparity in the application of the death penalty based on race, it did note that widely differing prosecutorial actions had the effect of discrimination against minorities.

Gus arranged to take time off from work to attend the sentencing hearing. But on Thursday, September 6, Paula called to tell him that the prosecutor had decided not to pursue the death penalty after all. At a press conference on Friday afternoon, an emotionally distraught Gary Lacey told reporters that he had been working on the case for twenty-one years and it was time to put an end to it. He said that he had weighed a number of factors, most of them emotional, and that the prospect of exposing the families to even more stress weighed heavily on his decision.[4]

As expected, the Lamms and Mesners were happy with the decision, whereas the Zessins were not. Gus told reporters from the *Nebraska Star Journal* that Gary's decision was courageous and compassionate: "I think he looked at all the facts in the case and looked at what was the greater good. The greater good was not another death."[5]

Greg Zessin denounced the decision, telling *Star* reporter Butch Mabin, "The system doesn't care about the rights of victims' families." He added, "I hope you never have to go to the morgue and see your sister bled to death." He agreed with Gary Lacey that the case had put tremendous stress on the families, but he disagreed that the decision not to seek the death penalty would alleviate that stress. "How is this going to alleviate any stress for me? I told him that I want Randy out of my life." He said that the decision left him disappointed and bitter, and he questioned whether he had done enough to advocate his position to the prosecutor. "I didn't go to his office every day. I feel like I let my family down."6

Two weeks later, Gus and Audrey headed for Nebraska again to attend the September 21 hearing. The Mesners, the Lamms, the Reeveses, and Greg Zessin were all present in the courtroom. Gary Lacey made a brief statement asserting that the case had taken too long and it was time to end it. He reiterated his concern for the victims' families. He pointed to Al Zessin's poor health as a factor in his decision and noted that the stress of the case had created a rift between Audrey and her grandfather. Paula praised her adversary's decision, saying that it showed he had not played politics with the case. She agreed that the case had taken a long time but said that all the appeals had been brought in good faith and had not been a waste of time. Randy, who was in attendance wearing leg irons and handcuffs, publicly spoke for the first time in twenty-one years. He stood up and said simply, "I'd like to thank the Lamms and Mesners for all the support they gave my family." The three-judge panel sentenced Randy to two life sentences. (The next day's paper misquoted Randy, saying that he had thanked the Lamms and Mesners for all the support they had given to him. Paula called and asked the reporter to set the record straight, and the paper printed a correction the next day.)

Both the Mesners and the Lamms said the outcome was what Janet and Vicki would have wanted. Gus said that he was greatly relieved: "We've all been held captive for twenty-one years. It's like being able to breathe again." On the other hand, Greg Zessin told reporters for the Associated Press, "I guess my family has just been sentenced to life in prison."7

•    •    •    •

Now, although he is glad to have the nearly two-year-long struggle to save Randy's life behind him, Gus does not regret his decision to get involved in the case.

> GUS: I know my decision to become involved in Randy's case disrupted Audrey's life immeasurably. But I never had the sense that if I didn't go

to Nebraska it would be better. I knew that what I had to say had the ability to impact people if I could just get it out there. I also thought that Audrey would be able to influence people. She is extremely perceptive. She has a world-class mind. Her message was going to be different from my message. A different audience would be drawn to her for different reasons.

As I had hoped, the experience helped Audrey get to know her mother a little better. It helped her fill in some blanks. Growing up, Audrey didn't feel like she could ask people about her mom because she didn't want people to have to deal with that sadness all over again.

I wish things were different with the Zessins. We didn't even speak to Greg at the September sentencing hearing. I think if I had spoken to him he might have punched me. I would like Audrey to have a relationship with Vicki's family, but they are angry, bitter people. I think they honestly thought that seeing Randy executed would relieve their pain.

I see them as being a tragic example of what happens when people really clamor for the death penalty. Vicki's brother, Greg, is aged beyond his years. He is forty-four but looks sixty. I can't help but think that he is a most reluctant participant in this process. His mom and dad became invested in the trial and the outcome, and as they got older, he took over representing their interests. At this point, he is stuck in a situation where he can't please anyone. He does not like being put in the position of advocating for the death penalty, but if he does not, he feels that he is betraying his family. I feel really sorry for him. Al Zessin has been bitter and angry for a long time. He won't even see his granddaughter—the closest link he has to his daughter.

Twenty-one years later they are reaping the seeds they sowed. They get to keep all of the hate they fostered over the years. That is what they invested in. I think the answer to surviving something like the murder of someone you love is to ask yourself how you want to invest your time and energy. It is one thing to be disturbed or angry or look at a social ill and have it bother you. It is another thing to decide to do something about it, to try to address it, alleviate it.

Instead of hatred towards Randy Reeves, I invested my time in my daughter. The requirements of parenting are easy —give them basic care and feeding, unconditional love, and then stay out of their way. I was really into being a parent. I was present at Audrey's delivery and spent as much time with her as possible. I would have breast-fed her had I been able to. The first word she said was "Dad." I knew I was only going to get one chance to do this right with Audrey. I could not afford to mess up.

When you have kids you want them to grow up to be integrated and compassionate, and you do that by modeling it for them. I had to come to grips with the fact that I was not the first individual on this planet that had had tragedy visited upon him. Whole tribes have been decimated. It was simply my turn, and I made choices, and those choices have gotten me to where I am today. And quite frankly I feel okay. My kid is okay, and I guess that is what really matters most of all.

# RESTORATIVE JUSTICE

Restorative justice (RJ) is a problem-solving approach to crime that involves the entire community—the offender, the victim, the victim's family, and sometimes the offender's family. It is based on two assumptions: that crime originates in social conditions and relationships in the community and that effective crime prevention depends on communities taking some responsibility for remedying the conditions that cause crime. Restorative justice accomplishes these goals by helping the offender take responsibility for his crime and making the victims whole. As we have seen, the traditional retribution-based model of criminal justice often fails to restore the victim or help the offender reintegrate into the larger community. It thus keeps intact the conditions that helped cause the crime and increases the likelihood of recidivism.

The RJ movement began in this country in the 1970s when some practitioners experimented with using mediation and other dispute resolution practices to encourage reconciliation between victims and offenders. Historically, many traditional justice systems have used similar techniques to address criminal behavior and help restore harmony within the community. Although the term "restorative justice" can refer to any number of alternative dispute resolution techniques, most encounters involve a meeting between the victim and the offender, often with a third party present, which results in a commitment by the offender to make some type of amends to restore the victim. These amends, or reparations, as they are often called, can take such forms as financial restitution, working for the victim or for a community cause selected by the victim, or undertaking a specific task such as attending counseling.

As a result of the direct interaction between the victim and the offender, both parties are likely to have more favorable attitudes toward the justice system. A 1994 study by Dr. Mark Umbreit of RJ programs in Albuquerque, New Mexico, Austin, Texas, Oakland, California, and Minneapolis, Minnesota found:

- A total of 3,142 cases were referred to the four programs during a two-year period, with 95 percent of the mediation sessions resulting in a successfully negotiated restitution agreement to restore the victim's losses.
- Victims of crime who met the offender to discuss the impact of the crime on their lives were far more likely to be satisfied (79 percent) with the justice system than similar victims who simply went through the normal court process (57 percent).
- After meeting the offender, victims were significantly less fearful of being revictimized.
- Considerably fewer and less serious crimes were committed by offenders who participated in the victim offender mediation (18 percent) than by similar offenders who did not meet with their victim (27 percent).[1]

All but two of the people whose stories are featured in this book have met the person who killed their loved one. The two who have not met the killer, Jennifer Bishop and SueZann Bosler, would like to do so. However, Linda White (chapter 9) and Azim Khamisa (chapter 10) have gone further: they are both actively involved in advocating for the use of restorative justice.

Cathy Daniel's mother, Linda White, and daughter, Ami, took part in a formal victim/offender mediation program sponsored by the Texas Department of Corrections. Linda is herself a victim/offender mediation counselor, working with individual victims and offenders as well as victim/offender encounter groups.

Although not as part of a formal program, Azim Khamisa met and established a relationship with the young man who

killed his son. Azim is convinced that a criminal justice system based on reconciliation is much more effective than one
based on retribution. Azim believes so strongly in the power
of reconciliation that he and the father of the boy who killed
his son established a foundation together to prevent youth
violence.

CHAPTER 9

# Beyond Retribution

Late at night on November 17, 1986, Cathy O'Daniel pulled her cream-colored early 1976 Pontiac Grand Prix into a service station in northeast Houston. Outgoing and vivacious, Cathy was a person who went out of her way to help people in need. Her slender figure did not yet reveal her eight-week pregnancy.

Fifteen-year-old Gary Phillip Brown and Marion Douglas Berry were on the run from a juvenile detention facility in Houston. Since their escape a few days earlier, they had stolen a .22-caliber gun and a station wagon. They, too, had pulled up to this Houston service station. The station wagon wasn't running properly, and they needed another vehicle, or at least a ride to their next destination. They asked Cathy if she would give them a lift. Despite the lateness of the hour, Cathy took pity on the boys, who looked young and scared, and agreed.

The boys instructed Cathy to drive to an isolated area four miles south of Alvin in Brazoria County on Texas Route 35. Their original plan had been to get her to a secluded location, steal her car, and leave her behind, but at some point they changed their minds. Unexpectedly, perhaps even to themselves, they decided to rape Cathy. Each boy took his turn assaulting her while the other held a gun to her head. When they finished, Marion shot her in the leg so she could not go for help. Hearing the shot brought home to them the gravity of what they had done, so the boys decided to kill her. Knowing their intention, Cathy said to them, "I forgive you, and God will, too." She put down her head and waited for the shots that killed her.

Unsure what to do with the body, the boys tried to make her unidentifiable by burning her face and hair, but it was too damp outside. Instead they covered her in a layer of debris.

At eight A.M. on November 18, Cathy's five-year-old daughter, Ami O'Daniel, woke to an empty house. Ami resembled her mother, with the same

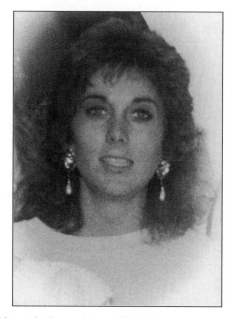

*Cathy O'Daniel. Photograph provided with permission of the family.*

light brown hair, slender figure, and aqua-blue eyes. She looked in her mom's room but found it empty, and the bed looked like no one had slept in it.

Ami walked down the freestanding staircase, gingerly stepping on each carpet-wrapped step. She looked behind the stairs in the master bedroom where her Uncle Steve slept, but he was not there, either. She entered the kitchen next to the bedroom and looked through the dining room and then the living room. She peeked out the window of the patio door. Seeing no cars in the driveway, she realized with a little fear that no one else was home.

Ami climbed the stairs and got the hall telephone with the long cord and took it into her room. She shut the door behind her and turned on the television. Ami did not feel really scared, but she wanted the TV on for company. She called "Nana," Cathy's mother, Linda White, who lived in Magnolia. She dialed the number from memory, something Grandfather John had taught her to do when she was three years old. Twenty miles away, the phone rang in Linda White's bedroom.

LINDA: I was in bed when the phone rang. It was a little late for me to still be in bed, but I was planning on spending the day with my mother. It was her seventieth birthday, and she wanted me to visit and play her favorite game, rummy cube. When the phone rang, I assumed it was my mother calling to confirm our plans.

I was very surprised to hear Ami. I asked her how she was and she said, "Nana, nobody is here. I'm all by myself." I tried not to sound too alarmed, so I asked her, "Are you sure nobody else is home, honey?" She told me that she had looked everywhere. I told her to hang up the phone and I'd call her right back.

My first reaction was to be annoyed with Cathy and Steve. I assumed Cathy had fallen asleep while visiting her fiancé, Willis. I was also annoyed at my son, Steve, that he didn't realize Ami was at home alone. I dialed Willis's number and asked if Cathy was there. He said that he hadn't seen Cathy since Sunday when the two had been at our house for dinner. Willis was a busy emergency room doctor working twelve-hour shifts and studying for his medical boards, so it was not unusual for the two of them to go a few days without seeing each other. At this point, I started worrying.

I called Ami back and told her I'd be right over to get her. I kept talking to her and only put the phone down when I had to, like when I pulled my shirt over my head. I asked Ami if she was scared. She said she was okay, so I told her to stay in her room and watch TV until I got there.

Driving to Cathy's place, I was trying to stifle my growing anxiety. I tried to cheer myself up by thinking about our family get-together the previous Sunday. Cathy brought Willis home to meet us. Both my husband, John, and I liked him very much. She told us that she was pregnant and that she and Willis were engaged.

After Cathy and Willis left, John and I were chatting while getting ready for bed when we realized a funny coincidence. Willis had grown up in Cortez, Colorado, and we had lived there for a year when Cathy was a baby. Willis had told us that his father had been a doctor and John and I realized that Dr. Parmley, Willis's father, had been our family doctor and had taken care of Cathy from the ages of four months to sixteen months.

I had wanted to tell Cathy about our realization right away, so I called her at Willis's place. Willis told me that Cathy had already gone home, but I told him the story and we had a good laugh. I called Cathy at her house, and we chatted for a while. I told her how much her dad and I liked Willis and how happy we were for her. I hadn't spoken with her since.

It took me about half an hour to get to Ami. I dressed her and took her to prekindergarten. Then I went to spend the day with my mother as planned. I called Steve, and he said that he had been in an early morning fog and hadn't noticed that Cathy's car wasn't there. He agreed to help me make some calls to try to find Cathy.

After work, Steve picked up Ami and took her back to their house. As soon as he got home, the phone rang. A boy on the other end told Steve that he was calling on behalf of Cathy. He said that Cathy had asked him to call and let him know that she was okay. She was having personal problems and needed some time to get away and think.

We thought it was strange that Cathy would go away without telling anyone, but we wanted very much to believe that that was what had happened. The story was not completely out of the question. Cathy had just learned that she was pregnant, and it seemed plausible that she might need time to mull over her options. Cathy and Willis had seemed very happy on Sunday but we thought it might be possible that she had been masking other feelings.

On the morning of Thursday, November 20, three days after Cathy's murder, a police officer in Greenville, about thirty miles east of Dallas, pulled over the Grand Prix. The officer checked the registration, which indicated that the car belonged to John and Linda White. He called the Magnolia police department and asked an officer there to find out if the boys had permission to drive the Whites' car. Two officers from Magnolia drove to the Whites' house; when no one came to the door they left their business card. Neither Linda nor John saw the card, however, because the officers had left it on the front door, which the family did not use regularly. The Greenville officer eventually reached the Whites by phone and asked if Marion Berry and Gary Brown had permission to drive their car. The Whites said no.

The dread that Linda had fought to contain since Tuesday seeped into her pores. She called Willis, who came over right away to wait for further word from the police.

LINDA: It was extremely helpful to me that Willis was so compassionate and caring. We didn't hear anything that night, and we didn't hear anything the following day. Friday night John and I discussed for the first time the very real possibility that something horrible had happened to Cathy. We talked about Ami and both agreed that we wanted to raise her if that was necessary. We also talked for the first time about consulting a child psychologist for guidance on breaking any bad news to her.

During that time of uncertainty, I tried to keep busy. I made an effort to keep Ami occupied. Ami kept asking me, "Where is my mommy?" On Saturday afternoon I went with some friends from my aerobics class to a shopping mall to attend an opera publicity event. The butterflies in my stomach never went away.

Back at the Whites' home, Harris County Police Officer Diaz knocked. John answered the door, and as soon as he saw the officer he said, "Oh no." Officer Diaz said, "Yes, I'm afraid so." He confirmed that Cathy was dead and said they needed someone to identify the body. John did not think he was up to the task of identifying his daughter. He thought that he would call Willis and ask him to go along for moral support, but Officer Diaz suggested that John give him a recent photograph of Cathy instead. John did so, and Officer Diaz offered to make the formal identification.

LINDA: I got home about five with Ami. We live at the back of five acres filled with trees, so you can't see the house from the street even with the leaves gone from the deciduous trees. I got halfway up the drive and could see cars everywhere, and then I knew that Cathy was dead. Driving up the rest of that driveway was one of the hardest things I have ever done.

Ami saw all the cars and thought we were having a party. I opened the door and let her go inside, knowing that people would realize I was home and somebody would come out and tell me. I couldn't go in and hear the news in front of all those people. I just couldn't do it. My husband and older son came out and told me. They said, "The worst that you can possibly imagine is what happened."

John knew that I would be worried about Ami. After Cathy and Phil, Ami's dad, divorced, Phil had not been a regular presence in Ami's life. I was worried about what would happen to Ami if she had to leave us and go live with a person who was not as familiar to her as we were. Reading my mind, John said, "Don't worry about Ami. We'll take care of Ami. Ami will always be all right. If it is too much work, we'll get a nanny." After several minutes, I finally summoned the courage to go inside.

Harris County prosecutors arrested Gary and Marion, and both confessed to the murder and rape, although they denied kidnapping Cathy. The boys claimed that she had voluntarily driven them to Brazoria County. The authorities did not believe the story but, since the boys had confessed to the rape and murder, decided to charge them with only those crimes. Because the rape and murder occurred in Brazoria County, Harris County prosecutors transferred the case there.

LINDA: The prosecutors in both counties were very kind and very supportive. You hear a lot of horror stories about the way people are treated, but that wasn't our experience. The officers were extremely compassionate. We especially appreciated the officer who agreed to identify Cathy to spare us the pain of having to do it. For the most part the police kept in touch with us about the progress of the case. There was only one detail that they did not tell us—that the boys had tried to burn Cathy's face and hair to make her unidentifiable. I think it was an oversight that they didn't tell us. When I eventually learned months later I was horrified, but then I thought, *What difference does it make?* She was beyond hurt anyway.

At the time all this was happening, I really never thought very much about Gary and Marion. I believed the system would take care of them. We had much bigger worries. We had a small child to care for. We consulted a child psychologist for advice. He told us that Ami needed stability, safety, and security. He recommended that we minimize other changes in her life. He advised us to share our feelings with her and to model for her what grief looked like. He said that she would have a lot of strange feelings she would not understand, so she needed to learn how to handle grief by watching the adults in her life.

However, even though we got advice from a psychologist, telling Ami that her mother was gone was the hardest thing we've ever had to do. John and I and both of our sons did it together. We told her in her room. She looked at us like what we were saying was impossible and said, "But my mommy's pegnant." When she said that, I totally lost it. Then she ran out of the room saying, "No no no no no," and ran into the kitchen and hid in the pantry. I never thought about it before, but that was kind of like me when I stayed outside.

The next hardest thing I had to do was to attend my daughter's funeral. The funeral was huge. There were a lot of people there. It was very emotional. The minister, an Episcopalian priest named Father Nick, didn't really know Cathy, but he knew me through an organization that I had been active in and kindly agreed to perform the service.

Not all of the emotions were negative. It was very positive that so many people showed up and there was such an outpouring of love. A particularly emotional part of the service came when Father Nick read a note that my sons had found in Cathy's Bible—a Bible that she obviously intended to give to Ami someday. In the note, Cathy wrote to Ami about the importance of her relationship with God and how she hoped that Ami would experience the same thing someday. She finished expressing her love for Ami and ended by writing, "Never forget that you are a blessing to me and you are a child of God." We liked that phrase so much that we put it on Cathy's headstone, "A blessing and a child of God."

It was kind of eerie that Cathy wrote this beautiful note to her daughter soon before she was killed. It seemed like she might have had a premonition of her own death.

·　·　·　·

Linda and John assumed they would care for Ami after Cathy's death. Ami's father, Phil O'Daniel, had not provided financial or emotional support since the divorce. A single mother without a college degree, Cathy had worked several jobs to make ends meet. At the time of her death she was waiting tables, working at a car rental agency, and doing some freelance work for her fiancé's brother. She was also taking computer courses at a technical school, hoping that the training would lead to a better job opportunity.

Cathy did not have any health insurance, so she relied heavily on her parents for financial assistance with medical expenses. They also helped with childcare while she worked. For all intents and purposes, Ami had three parents: Cathy, John, and Linda.

LINDA: It did not occur to us that Phil would want custody of Ami. In fact, we didn't even call him to tell him that Cathy had been killed. He learned about Cathy's death because his family saw a report on TV. Of course I should have called him, but he was so estranged from us that I didn't think of him as family any longer.

I had been disappointed in him as an absentee father. He hadn't been supportive financially or in ways that I thought he should—which had surprised me, because I knew he had loved Ami when she was a baby.

At the funeral Phil told us that he thought Ami should stay with us in the short term, but in the long term she should live with him. All of my daughter's friends had told us that the last thing in the world Cathy would have wanted was for Phil to have custody. We asked him to relinquish his parental rights. He didn't like the idea, but he wasn't too pushy about it. Meanwhile we filed for custody in early December.

A couple of days before Christmas, Phil's parents called and asked if Ami could spend the weekend with them. We wanted to show Phil and his family that we were sincere about keeping the O'Daniels in her life. As it turned out, Phil took Ami out of state without telling us where he was going. He sent a message to us through his parents that he had Ami and would not be returning. He told them to thank us for filling in for him all those years.

I couldn't believe that he did that to us, one month after Cathy's murder! I couldn't believe that he could be that cruel. For the next five weeks we had no contact from Ami. I was absolutely furious with Phil for what he had done. Those five weeks were the longest five weeks of my life. It was, without question, unmitigated hell. I remember sitting in front of an electric space heater, it was so hard to get warm emotionally and physically.

A child psychologist swore out an affidavit that it was very important for Ami's well-being to be in a familiar place with people she knew and trusted. Our attorney went to court and got an order for Phil to return Ami to our custody. Since we did not know where Phil had taken Ami, the court issued a subpoena to obtain the telephone records of Phil's parents, which helped us locate where Phil was living.

John accompanied the police when they went to get Ami. Ami seemed extremely glad to be home. She had lost weight. It had not been good for her to be taken away from the most secure environment she had known. They lived a pretty lean existence during that time since Phil was in hiding trying to keep their whereabouts unknown.

The last thing I wanted was to be a part of a custody battle. It conjured up images of Solomon and his knife splitting the child in half. I hated what it was doing to our families, but at that point in his life Phil would not have been able to care for Ami, and his mother would have ended up raising her. I thought if Ami was going to be raised by a grandmother it should be me. Phil's mother had fourteen or fifteen grandchildren already. We had more time for Ami, and we had already been surrogate parents to her. It made sense that she live with us. The court agreed and in February of 1987 ordered that Ami remain with us pending a decision on permanent custody.

The court ordered that both of our families submit to psychological testing. As part of the testing, the psychologist used a "Rotter" instrument. This test required the person being tested to complete certain phrases like, "I'm frequently afraid that . . ." There were about fifty of them. The idea was to say the first thing that came to your mind. The last phrase was something like, "My secret desire has always been." By that point I had gotten on a roll and I wrote: "to be a psychologist."

When I saw what I had written, I realized it was true. I had always wanted to be a psychologist, but people discouraged me—even my husband. He said that, due to the current job market, psychologists were a dime a dozen and I probably wouldn't be able to get a job. In the past, I had allowed myself to be discouraged. This time I thought to myself, "I am going to do it." All the reading I had done about grief had been cathartic and informative. I thought that I could study death and dying and be an educator. I could help people learn how to grieve. The more I thought about it, the more I became convinced that that was what I needed to do. There were very few things in my life I was so sure of.

•    •    •    •

The custody battle over Ami moved on a parallel track to the criminal case. A month after the court awarded temporary custody to Linda and John, the criminal cases of Gary and Marion began. Although they were both charged with "capital" homicide, neither boy was eligible for the death penalty because they were only fifteen years old. In fact, the state could not automatically prosecute the boys in adult court; it had to first petition a judge to transfer their cases from juvenile to adult court.

The petition hearing against Marion was temporarily delayed when Judge Jim Blackstone ordered him to undergo psychological testing at a state mental hospital to determine whether he was competent to stand trial. Ultimately, Marion was found to be competent, and by the end of March both cases were transferred to adult court. Marion was held in jail without bond, and Gary was held on a one hundred thousand dollar bond.

Several months later, on October 5, 1987, the court granted permanent custody of Ami to Linda and John. Eleven days after that, Marion Berry's trial began. On the day jury selection started, Marion pled guilty before District Judge Ogden Bass in Angleton. Because both boys had confessed to the murder at the time of their arrest, neither had a very strong case to take to trial. In exchange for Marion's plea, the state agreed to a fifty-five-year sentence. Gary held out for a "better deal," but three months later, he pleaded guilty, too, agreeing to a fifty-four-year prison term. One of the terms of both plea bargains required that the boys admit they had used a deadly weapon, which meant they would be required to serve at least one-third of their sentence before becoming eligible for parole. The state dispatched both boys to adult prisons.

•   •   •   •

Having decided to pursue her psychology degree, Linda wasted no time. In the fall of 1987, at age forty-six, she enrolled at Sam Houston University.

LINDA: My studies and my career choice were motivated by my own need to grieve and to "fill the hole" left by Cathy's murder. I had lots of experience with grieving, and I wanted to share those experiences with others. Grief is such a strange thing. Sometimes I'd be in public places and I'd feel the grief washing all over me and couldn't stop crying, but then I'd get home all by myself and be dry.

I grieved a lot in my car. You do a lot of driving when you live an hour outside of Houston, Texas. I used to hear this song, "You and Me Against the World," that was always a trigger for me. One of the lines, "Someday when one of us is gone and one of us is left to carry on," always broke me up because it was supposed to be the young person who got left behind.

I benefited tremendously from the advice I received from various psychologists, which probably contributed to my desire to be one. The most beneficial piece of advice I got was from the first psychologist we consulted, who told us not to hide our feelings. He said, "Don't try to protect Ami from your feelings, because that is not real protection."

Besides professional help, people were very kind to me. A total stranger from my aerobics class gave me a book called *When Going to Pieces Helps Put You Together*. That book helped me to understand that things like panic attacks were normal.

Linda completed her undergraduate degree in psychology and philosophy in 1990 and immediately started on her master's. In the five years since Cathy's murder, life had become somewhat "normal" for the Whites. One day in the fall of 1992, John was out of town on a business trip and Linda and Ami were driving home from dinner at Ami's favorite restaurant. Ami, then eleven, asked Linda if she could be adopted.

LINDA: When Ami asked if we would adopt her, I asked her if she really wanted to do that. She said, "I'd like to have my name be the same as yours."

John and I had talked off and on about legally adopting Ami but were also anxious about it because we thought if we went back to court we might be stirring up a hornet's nest. The last custody battle had been very costly, both financially and emotionally. It's not as though the idea of adopting Ami had never crossed our minds, but we already considered ourselves a family, and we thought it might be better to let sleeping dogs lie.

But we set the legal wheels in motion, and thankfully Phil agreed to relinquish custody. We were very grateful to him, and still are to this day.

On the morning of March 29, 1993, the three of us went to court. The hearing did not take long. Ami wanted to say something, so she decided to read a Mother's Day essay that she had written about me when she was in the second grade, three years after Cathy's death, called "My Special Mom":

"My Mom has green eyes and blond curly hair. She is very special to me. Her smile brightens up my life. Her touch is warm and her laugh brings me joy. Her life makes me happy. When I am around her, she makes me feel safe. I think of her all of the time. My mother's love is enough for infinity. She's the best person in the whole wide world. No one can ever change my mind. I have a wonderful mother. I love her very much."

The essay made everyone in the courtroom cry, and the guardian ad litem [who represents the child's interests in court cases involving minors] suggested that Ami give the essay to the judge so that it would become part of the official court record. Needless to say, it was a very emotional day for everyone involved.

By the time of Ami's adoption, we had rich, full lives and she was doing really well. She had been going to counseling for a couple of years and had begun to come out of herself. She was in the fifth grade and doing well in school. Ami had a very talented school counselor named Marie Romain, who was wonderful with her. Marie doted on her, and when other kids had hard times she sent them to Ami for support. It helped Ami a lot to be able to help the other kids.

Ami had gradually accepted her mother's death. It is surprising how well children between the ages of five and seven can come to understand death. They know that death is biological, universal, and final. Almost from the beginning, she understood that Cathy wasn't coming back. It helped that she was able to talk about how much she missed her mommy.

·　·　·　·

In January 1992, Linda's career path took another detour. While in graduate school, she had the opportunity to work as a teaching assistant.

LINDA: On January 16, 1992, I taught my first class. It was such an exhilarating experience. I felt like I was doing what I should have been doing my whole life. I had about sixty or seventy students in my class. They were attentive and asked good questions. I had gone in, of course, with a bit of trepidation. I had never taught anything but little bitty kids in Sunday school. But I knew my subject well, and it just felt right. My supervisor told me afterwards, "You like having a captive audience," and I said, "Yeah, I guess I do." Sometimes you just know this is what you were meant to do. I knew that teaching was what I should be doing.

I taught three semesters of Introductory Psychology, then three semesters of Death and Dying. Normally a graduate assistant did not teach the upper-level Death and Dying class, but one semester the department had an unexpected vacancy and needed someone to teach the class. I was recruited to fill the vacancy. During my last semester at Sam Houston, I also taught Death and Dying at a local community college.

The more I taught Death and Dying, the more I got into the issues involved, one of which is violence. I found myself thinking about violence more and more. I was teaching a class the day after Susan Smith in North Carolina was arrested for killing her children. Susan Smith attracted national attention when she put her three sons in a car and drove it into a lake, drowning them. Smith initially claimed a black man had abducted her children. The fact that a mother killed her children generated a lot of controversy.

We started talking about the case in class, and one of my students asked me what I thought about it. I said it was sad, and they proceeded to tell me how awful Smith was and how she should be punished. About eight or ten of them competed to come up with the worst punishment to make her suffer. One young man, who was normally very kind and a good student, told us in very deliberate terms how he would tie her in a car and drive it into the water and watch her die the same way she killed her own sons. The expression on his face spoke volumes. I stood there in horror at the display of raw violence I was witnessing and realized that few if any of them would ever associate their behavior with violence.

The episode in the classroom was the catalyst that made me open to thinking about violence in a whole new light. A short time later, I attended a meeting of the Houston Presbytery—a gathering of over one hundred Presbyterian churches in the Houston area. At the meeting I saw a book called *Restorative Justice—Towards Non-Violence*. The title intrigued me, and I picked it up. The book described a whole new paradigm of justice. It spoke about how our criminal justice system is violent. We are, in effect, trying to fight violence with violence.

Restorative justice doesn't focus on the crime and who did it so much as focusing on the harm that was done and what needs to be done to make it right. The greatest strength of restorative justice for me is the desire not to add to the harm that has already been done.

From that day on I read everything I could on the subject of restorative justice. I read a book by Gerald Austin McHugh, called *Christian Faith and Criminal Justice: Toward a Christian Response to Crime and Punishment*. The book explored how our professions of Christian faith do not match very well with our ideas about crime or criminals. One statement of McHugh's hit me especially hard: "Christianity was originally preached by its founder and his disciples as a religion for the social outcasts, for the weak, the poor, the hated, the forgotten—the prisoner. The unique power of Christianity was its concern for the unwanted as individual human beings, and its unconcern with social status and the preservation of the status quo."

McHugh wrote about the dehumanization process going on in every prison in the United States. One chapter made the point that if you really want to make a difference you need to volunteer at a prison, which is one way of helping to restore relationships between the prisoners and the community. Another suggestion was to teach. When I read that, the words leaped off the page at me. I knew that Sam Houston offered classes in three of Texas's prison units. Soon after that, I asked the department secretary, Bess Davis, if they needed more people to teach at the prison, and one week later I was on the schedule to teach Death and Dying the following semester. I thought that the way it all came together was an indication that teaching in prison was something I was supposed to do.

On a Tuesday night in mid-January 1997, Linda entered the Huntsville Unit of the Texas Department of Corrections to teach her first class. The Huntsville prison is known as the "Walls Unit." It is where the State of Texas carries out its executions.

LINDA: I walked up the big stairs in front and was struck by the beautiful brass side rails. I entered through one set of doors, the first "picket," then showed my ID, and they let me into the "bullpen," a small waiting area totally surrounded by more of these beautiful brass bars. I had mixed feelings—I mean, the bars were beautiful, but at the same time there is not a lot nice you can say about bars. I walked through a total of three sets of locked doors—one solid and the other two with bars. As the last set of doors closed behind me I thought to myself, *What is a nice girl like me doing in a place like this?*

My classroom was in the library, which required me to walk across the prison yard—a big open space in the middle of the prison with exercise equipment, benches, a basketball court, and even a volleyball court. The Walls Unit is an old, old prison, at least 150 years old. The yard is where the prisoners do most of their congregating, and there were prisoners all around me. I was nervous, but there were many guards around, and I knew that I was safe.

In my first class I had about twenty-five students. They had been told to expect a "Mr." White, so when they saw me everybody laughed, which helped break the ice. What struck me was how dedicated and appreciative the students were. They were a joy to teach because they were motivated to learn and grow and develop. Generally, I find them more open as a group than the kids on a college campus. And, because these guys don't have the freedom to go to bars or worry about their dates, they seem to really focus on what they are doing.

That first class, I didn't tell my students right away that I was the mother of a murder victim. I let them get to know me gradually, so by the time they learned about Cathy's murder, they really knew me. They acted shocked and surprised that I would be teaching in a prison. They were shocked that anybody would do that to me, and they were very protective of me. Now, on the advice of a restorative justice colleague, I no longer wait but tell my students about the murder on the first day of class.

I started teaching in prison during the spring of 1997, and five years later I am still there. As much as I love teaching, I love teaching at the prisons even more. It has been an eye-opener for me. It has really filled up the hole left by Cathy's death, as much as anything could. I like my students a lot, and I hear through the prison grapevine that most of them like me. They appreciate me because I treat them as human beings. I don't ask them why they are there; if they tell me, I accept them. I just treat them the same way no matter what they have done. The experience has made an impact both ways. I think the fact that I can put a human face on crime victims for them makes them take a different look at some of the things they have done.

Teaching at the prisons also opened my eyes to the reality of prison life. For the first time in years I found myself thinking about Gary Brown and Marion Berry. I had tried so hard to push them out of my mind that I actually got to the point where I couldn't remember their names. I started carrying around a newspaper clip about Cathy's murder so that I would remember them.

Getting to know my students made Gary and Marion more real to me. Prisoners are not all alike. They are multi-dimensional, like other people. Over time, I found myself caring about what happened to them. I understood a little bit better how things like murder happen and I knew what they went through being in an adult prison at age fifteen.

•   •   •   •   •

In the fall of 1997, Linda entered a doctoral program in psychology at Texas A&M. She continued teaching at the prisons, and in the spring of 1998 one of her prison students told her about a victim/offender mediation program recently established by the Victims' Services Division of the Texas Department of Criminal Justice. At the time, Linda was considering different topics for her dissertation. She mentioned the idea to a former professor and his wife who encouraged her to pursue the topic.

The Texas Victim/Offender Mediation Program was created in large part because victims expressed their desire to have one. It was developed under the direction of Raven Kazen, the director of Victims' Services, who hired David Doerfler to be its first coordinator.

It also found a great deal of support from a dynamic woman named Ellen Halbert, who had been brutally raped by an intruder in her home and left for dead. As she healed from her experience, Ellen became interested in working with other victims. In 1991, the Texas legislature passed a law requiring that one of the slots on the board of the Texas Department of Criminal Justice be filled by a victims' representative. Governor Ann Richards appointed Ellen to serve as the first victim member.

While serving on the board, Ellen helped establish the mediation program, which became a model for programs around the country. Most programs worked only on cases involving property crimes, but Texas's also served victims and offenders in cases of violent crime. In 1999, Linda signed up to be a volunteer mediator.

LINDA: When I signed up to be a volunteer mediator, I was not thinking of participating in mediation myself. I thought it was a great program, but I didn't really think I needed it. Luci Kelly, the volunteer coordinator, asked me if I would be interested and I said, "I've done all the healing I need already." Then she asked me if I would be against the idea and I said, "No, you can put me down as a person who might be interested someday."

As part of our training, we needed to learn to be sensitive to the needs of both victims and offenders we would serve. We had an "offender sensitivity" training where we spent the day at Huntsville. We viewed the death chamber where people are legally murdered, and we spent several hours in one of the units. We had a face-to-face meeting with eight offenders and had a chance to ask each one questions.

One of the men told the story of his crime. It was extremely powerful for me. At the beginning, this man was scared of us. He started talking about his family and became very upset. He was crying the whole time he told his story. The facts of his case were almost identical to Cathy's—abduction, sexual assault, and murder. After he spoke I told him a little of my story, and he started crying all over again. I told him that it was beneficial for me to hear his remorse. That was the beginning of my realization that mediation could be really beneficial for me. I talked to Ami about it, and she said that she was also interested in doing a mediation session. Ami was nineteen years old now, and pregnant. I thought the process might help her sort some things out before she became a mother. In the spring of 2000, I called Luci and told her that Ami and I wanted to do a mediation session.

The first step in victim/offender mediation is determining whether the offender is an appropriate candidate; mediation is more successful if the person is remorseful and open to a genuine reconciliation with the victim. To assess this, someone from the program goes to visit the prisoner unannounced, the idea being that if the offender does not know that he is meeting someone from the mediation program, his response to whether he'd like to participate in the program will be genuine instead of rehearsed. Besides visiting the offender, the staff person reviews the inmate's prison records and talks to the warden and guards and asks their opinion about the offender's readiness for mediation.

From their preliminary investigation, the staff believed that Gary would be a more appropriate candidate for mediation than Marion, who had serious mental health problems that decreased the chance of a successful session. Luci visited Gary unannounced and asked him if he would be interested. When Gary heard that Linda and Ami wanted to meet with him, he started to cry. He told Luci that he had been praying for a chance to meet them.

The staff decided that Gary was an appropriate candidate for the program. However, months of preparation were needed before the meeting would take place. At Linda's request, Ellen agreed to be the mediator. She met with Ami and Linda and then separately with Gary. She assigned all of them "homework," written assignments designed to help them reflect upon their experiences and imagine how the other people feel. Sometimes people in mediation write to each other before they actually meet; Gary sent Linda and Ami a Christmas card with a letter and a poem called "Brighter Days." In the letter, Gary apologized for killing Cathy.

The things I am going to say, I don't expect you to believe how sorry I am. I will understand if you never believe what I say. Why cause its my fault and it always will be my fault. I cause yall to feel that way to towards me. I have no-one to blame but myself. All I can do is deal with what I have done. [He finished with a P.S.] Yes, I know this letter doesn't make anything right. I'm just trying to start somewhere. But no matter what I do, I can't make it right or change that. There is a part of me I will always hate myself for what I have done.

LINDA: At the time that I decided that I wanted to meet Gary, I felt like I had already forgiven him. What that meant to me was that I had let go of whatever negative power he had in my life. I stopped focusing on anger or bitterness. Forgiveness is not easy when you are talking about murder. It is one thing to say you forgive someone who hurts your feelings or misses a lunch date. In those cases, it is easy to say, "That's okay." But it's not so easy to overlook murder.

For me forgiveness was a process. It was largely unconscious. When Luci told me Gary's reaction—how remorseful he was—I felt compassion for him. That helped me realize how much I had forgiven him. I liked hearing that he was remorseful, but I still wanted to hear it from him.

If Gary had been completely without remorse, he would have been considered inappropriate for the program, and I would have had to deal with that. There are a lot of offenders who never get to meet with their victims and vice versa. A lot of times you have to do it in a surrogate relationship.

I felt that the work I had done as a volunteer in the mediation program had helped me get to the point where I was ready to meet Gary. Ami had been doing some growing up as well. When she became pregnant in the fall of 1999, it seemed like déjà vu. As with Cathy, the father was a young man who was not ready to be a father. Like Cathy, Ami needed to depend on us for assistance.

Her pregnancy had brought out the best in what we had together, at the same time that it brought out what we lacked—Cathy. Ami found herself wanting to know more about Cathy than ever before, and from people other than us. She sought out her biological father, Phil, and asked him to describe Cathy from his perspective.

We began to talk about Cathy more and more, realizing that this missing link between us needed expression as never before. For medical reasons, Ami had to go on complete bed rest for the last few weeks of her pregnancy, and we spent a lot of time together then. It was wonderful—we worked on our homework for the mediation together, sharing our thoughts and feelings as we went. We spent many hours writing the answers to all the premediation homework. It was very healing. It made me appreciate that the preparation time was just as important as the actual meeting.

On June 6, 2000, Ami gave birth to a boy she named Chase.

.   .   .   .

After months of anticipation and many attempts at coordinating everyone's schedules, Ellen set a date for the mediation—Saturday, April 28, 2001. An independent television producer learned about the mediation and asked Linda, Ami, and Gary if they would be willing to be in a documentary about restorative justice and the mediation process. They agreed.

LINDA: Ami and I flew to Wichita Falls on Friday the twenty-seventh at around ten o'clock in the morning. Because of the documentary, a cameraperson spent the last twenty-four hours before the mediation with Ami and me, and another cameraperson spent the time with Gary.

When we arrived in Wichita, we drove out to the prison. We met Warden Robert Treon. Warden Treon is a stocky man. Not too tall. Well spoken. He has very much the philosophical leanings that one would expect from a warden of a prison, but he was very professional. I wouldn't say he is part of the good-old-boy network, although I believe he shares some of their beliefs. Even so he was very warm; very welcoming and kind.

Ellen had joined us from Austin. She first went and spent about an hour or so with Gary. That evening all of us went to dinner—Ami, Ellen, the three people making the documentary, and me. We ate Mexican food and were really very jovial. It felt good that all of the work we had done for a long time was culminating the next day.

Although Ami and I felt a little apprehensive, we were really looking forward to it. We went back to our hotel room and watched a movie. We are not usually in hotel rooms together, so it was kind of like having a slumber party. It was a very emotional time for us. The whole process had brought us closer together and really bonded us.

The next morning we met the warden again. Although he did not understand why anyone would want to do mediation, he supported our right to do it. He basically said that the only reason he would want to do mediation would be to try to hide a weapon and go in to take care of the offender personally. His particular philosophical bent would be like most Americans'. The idea of turning the other cheek just didn't really exist for him. He wouldn't entertain the notion of even sitting in the room with a person who had killed his family member except perhaps to watch him suffer. The concept that this type of program could be beneficial to offenders eluded him completely, which was really unfortunate. Our system is only about punishment and not really about accountability. In actuality, there is no higher accountability for the offender than having to sit down and look into the eyes of the mother whose daughter you killed.

When we got to the prison, it took longer than they expected to set up the cameras, so we didn't really get started until around 10:30. The prison officials set up the session to take place in the chapel. They had set out water and pads of paper for us. The guards planned to watch from the chaplain's office so that we could have some privacy.

Ami and I got to the room first. We sat on Ellen's left, and Gary was going to be on her right. All three of the people from the documentary were working cameras. When Gary came in the room he was already crying. That was a total surprise. He talks really fast, especially when he's answering questions. I know that he takes medication for a disorder. It was apparent to me that he is bipolar.

He looked like a lost little boy to me, even at thirty. He just doesn't look like a tough kid. I could see him pretending to be tough but what I saw was a lost, forlorn little boy.

Because of his emotional state it was very hard for him to talk, so I thought it made sense to start out talking about something besides the crime. I asked him to tell us about the family of an older inmate who had befriended him.

Gary told us that when this man first reached out to him, he assumed the man wanted to take advantage of him. It was hard for Gary to accept that the man didn't want anything from him, except to be his friend. The man told Gary to put his family down on his visitor's list and they would visit him. Eventually Gary did. This family took an interest in him. It was really the first time Gary ever got any love or acceptance from anybody.

Gary had had a very difficult childhood, and it was very hard for him to trust other people. He had been sexually abused by his dad. He lived mostly with his mother and stepfather, but he was also in foster care for a while. He spent the first few years of his life in an orphanage. He doesn't know his real last name—apparently his mother didn't tell him. He doesn't have a birth certificate. When he started school, he took the last name of his stepfather at the time.

His life was just a train wreck.

Gary has attempted suicide ten times—the first time when he was eight years old. He took pills, lots of Tylenol. He wasn't old enough or sophisticated enough to know how to kill himself.

I had questions I wanted to ask—missing details about the case. There were some things I had not wanted to know at first, but as he told the story in progression I was able to listen to them.

We had always believed that Cathy had stopped at the gas station looking for water because her car radiator was having problems. It turned out that she had stopped for gas. She saw the two of them jumping up and down on the fender trying to shake up the gas tank. The station wagon they had stolen wasn't working because they had put in the wrong type of gas.

They gave Cathy this sad story about having car problems and how they needed to get to Alvin. Gary said she offered to give them a ride. I never had believed that before, but when I saw Gary and saw how young and vulnerable he looks now, I can only imagine what he looked like at fifteen. It was conceivable to me that she could have given them a ride. I also believed Gary because he told everything in such a straightforward manner and didn't really have any reason to lie. Nothing that he said made him look any better.

They had always intended to steal Cathy's car, but at some point they decided to turn it into something else. They could have stolen her car without raping her. I'm not real sure that I know how they decided to do that. As far as I know, neither of them had ever done anything like that before. I don't know if it was the fact that they had a gun and the power that represented, or the fact that they had been drinking Mogen David "Mad Dog 20-20" and doing other drugs. They were not exactly in their right minds.

He told me how they took turns holding the gun while the other one raped her. At this point he was crying a lot. He said that they shot her in the leg and that they only intended to disable her. Somehow the resonance of the shot brought them back to the magnitude of what they had done.

He said one thing he remembered over the years and could never forget was her last words. Ellen had already told us that he had something to tell us that we would want to hear. He said that after they raped Cathy they were talking to each other trying to decide what to do. Cathy told them to take the car. She said she wouldn't do anything, but she knew they were going to kill her. Apparently it was Marion that shot her. One interesting thing is that Gary referred to Marion as "Marvin." It made me think that the two did not know each other very well.

Gary said that "Marvin" pointed the gun and Cathy looked up and said, "I forgive you, and God will forgive you, too." Then she put her head down to look away.

By this point, both Ami and I were bawling. That was the hardest part of the mediation, but it was also without question the best part. If she could say those words to them, then she had to have transcended whatever was going on in some way. I had always thought that Cathy's last moments were filled with terror, but the fact that she said that made me think otherwise. She had already achieved a level of peace that put her beyond fear. That piece of information alone was a total validation of the mediation process.

We took a break for lunch. Then Ami and I had some tough things we wanted to tell him. We showed him pictures of all of us—old pictures of Cathy and new pictures of Ami's baby. Ami talked about the fact that her son was growing up without knowing his grandmother. She talked about some of the fears that she had had growing up and problems based on not having her original mom. I talked about how both of my sons had had a lot of problems being able to grieve and dealing with other issues in their lives.

We shared a lot of our lives with one another during those hours. We were at the prison until 5:30. At the end we wanted to take a picture with him. It just seemed like a natural progression from the day. Ami and I were sitting down, and Gary stood a ways behind us. I said, "Gary, you can get closer than that." So we stood up and went over next to him. Eventually, with a little prodding, he put his arms around us, and at that point it was a friendly picture.

Some people will have problems with that. They will not understand how we could forgive him and get to the point where we could sit across from him and have our picture taken with him. It is hard for people to

Left to right: *Ami Lyn White, Gary Brown, and Linda White. Photograph by Ellen Halbert.*

understand. If you forgive someone, then you must really do it, I believe. No halfway measures will do.

•    •    •    •

After the mediation in April 2001, Linda finished her dissertation. In the fall of that year she became Dr. Linda White, and she is an adjunct professor of psychology at Sam Houston University. The hole left by Cathy's death is still there, but from that loss she has found meaning and direction. Cathy's death spurred her decision to become a psychologist. All of her experiences— teaching Death and Dying, going to work in the prisons, her interest in restorative justice, becoming a volunteer mediator, and finally meeting the young man who killed her daughter—have both helped her heal and helped her to use her tragedy to help others. The documentary about the mediation, *Meeting with a Killer: One Family's Journey,* aired on Court TV on September 19, 2001.

Linda, Ami, and Ron Carlson (see chapter 3) are forming a fledgling chapter of Murder Victims' Families for Reconciliation in Texas. Linda also serves on the national board of directors. In her work with MVFR, Linda speaks frequently about her experiences and her opposition to the death penalty. She is an ardent supporter of victim/offender mediation and encourages victims to make a connection with the person who killed their loved one.

**LINDA:** Before the mediation I read a book called *Beyond Retribution* written by a man named Christopher Marshall. Marshall says that whenever there is a crime, a relationship is established between the victim and the offender, or in this case the victim's family. You have a choice about what you do with that relationship. You can ignore it, you can make it be nothing more than an ugly relationship, or you can use the relationship to help you heal. A lot of healing can happen if people allow themselves to need one another. The mediation process helped me use the relationship to heal.

When I was working on my dissertation, I observed that one of the things victims need to hear is remorse from the person who harmed them. Some of us say things like, "It doesn't matter what he says. It won't bring the person back." That is true, but even so, you can still honor the fact that the person was willing to say it.

I knew that Gary was remorseful, but I wanted to hear him say it. It was also important for me to tell Gary that we wished him well. We told him that one thing he could do for us was to change his life in a positive direction. I told him I would appreciate that. Change is meaningful.

I had never been totally clear about why I wanted to do the mediation, but after I did it I realized that part of why I wanted to do it was to prove to myself that I could. I knew that I was comfortable working with offenders. I knew I could envision all the forgiveness and reconciliation stuff, but I wondered if I could really put my money where my mouth was. The mediation was a reality check for me.

Taking part in the mediation was one of the most liberating things I have ever done. It helped me to restore a relationship and thus to restore part of myself. There have been people in my life who have helped me heal the last fifteen years, and I have to admit that Gary was one of them. No one else could have brought to me what he did, because no one else was there. No one else saw her.

The mediation helped Ami, too. The time we spent together preparing for the mediation brought Cathy's presence back into our lives as it hadn't been for many years; and as it did, I realized how much like her mother Ami was—her first mother, I mean. I guess in reality, she's much like both of us, yet totally her own person. I am very proud of her compassion, her willingness to see the best in others. She has grown into a beautiful young woman, and I know that Cathy would be very proud of her, and me, too.

Ami is very independent even though she has to depend on us for assistance, which she's had to do since Chase was born. His father has been no help at all with anything. I keep feeling I've lived this life before.

Ami has a new relationship with a great guy I really like. He is good with Chase, and his family really likes Ami and Chase both, which is wonderful. He has a good job, is going to college part-time, and has a nice family. I admit I have great hopes!

Restorative justice is an entirely different paradigm from retributive justice. When Gary murdered Cathy, he didn't just break a law—he harmed Linda and Ami and John and all the members of our family and extended family and friends. It was a tremendous disruption of relationships in our community.

When you look back at Gary's life and see all the missing pieces, society has to take some responsibility for what he did. Gary has to take responsibility, but so does the larger community. There is a shared responsibility. How much good can be done just through punishment if there is no intentional rehabilitation or efforts to restore relationships? Punishment with no other purpose has immense negative consequences. Sometimes incarceration is necessary, but there has to be more to prison than just demonizing the offenders. How meaningful is that? What is the point of it?

# CHAPTER 10

# Healing the Soul

It was near closing time at DeMille's Italian Restaurant in San Diego, California, on Saturday night, January 21, 1995. Nineteen-year-old Tariq Khamisa was looking forward to ending his shift and spending the rest of the evening at home with his fiancée, Jennifer. Tariq worked weekends and evenings delivering pizzas to support his studies at San Diego State University, where he was majoring in art with a specific focus on photography. Jennifer was also an artist. They had been talking about moving to New York together to pursue their careers. Tariq did not like Southern California, finding it plastic and hedonistic.

Short of stature, but not of character, Tariq had a handsome face with a lovely smile and warm eyes. His friends and family described him as "wise" and as having an "old soul." People frequently sought his advice, and he was always happy to listen. He was well liked by his co-workers and schoolmates.

Just as Tariq was ending his shift, a girl called in a phone order for two large pizzas. Tariq reluctantly agreed to make one last delivery. On his way, he stopped by his apartment to deliver a soda to Jennifer. He told her that he had one more delivery to make but wanted to see her first. He kissed her good-bye and promised he'd be home soon.

Tariq drove to the delivery address, a large housing project on Louisiana Street in San Diego's working-class North Park neighborhood. He searched in vain for Unit D. After knocking on several doors, he realized there was no Unit D; the order had been a hoax. As he walked back to his Volkswagen a boy pointed a gun at him and said, "Pizza man, give me those pizzas." Tariq ignored him and kept walking back to his car. He tossed the pizzas inside and started to drive away. The boy fired. The nine-millimeter slug shattered the car window, then ripped through Tariq's arms and chest, killing him instantly.

When Tariq did not return home as expected, Jennifer called the restaurant. She asked owner Sal Gaicalone what had happened to Tariq. San Diego police had just informed him that Tariq had been shot dead while making the delivery, but because they were not sure of all the facts, the police asked Sal not to tell Jennifer. Sal told Jennifer that he didn't know where Tariq was but he'd have him call her as soon as he got in. Jennifer continued to call the restaurant throughout the night, but Sal just let the phone ring without answering it. Finally, at four A.M. a homicide detective called to tell Jennifer that Tariq was dead.

While Tariq made his last delivery, his father, Azim Khamisa, was landing at the San Diego airport, returning from a trip to Mexico. As an international investment banker, Azim traveled constantly, but this night he was particularly grateful that his best friend, Dan Pearson, and Dan's wife, Kit Goldman, met him at the airport. Besides feeling tired from his travels, Azim was preoccupied by a number of worries. He had just ended a romantic relationship, and his father had recently undergone open heart surgery and was recovering in a hospital in Vancouver. Azim's friends, not wanting him to spend the evening alone, took him to a party. By the time he returned to his condominium just past midnight, his spirits were lifted, and he fell into a deep sleep.

**AZIM:** I woke up Sunday morning feeling refreshed. My housekeeper arrived at around 8:30 and handed me a business card that she discovered tucked in the screen door. I called the name on the card—Sergeant Lampert—and a woman answered the line, saying that the sergeant was not in. When I told her my name she said, "I'm sorry. Tariq Khamisa was shot last night."

The fatal phone call is etched deeply and forever on my mind and heart. When I got the news, I simply could not accept the reality. However, after speaking with Tariq's fiancée, Jennifer, and the coroner's office, the truth began to sink in. It felt like a nuclear bomb had detonated inside of me and blown me into millions of pieces that could never all be found or put back together. Life drained out of me, and I was enveloped by total helplessness. I called Tariq's mother, Almas, who lives in Seattle, and she collapsed to the floor with a loud, piercing shriek, which I can still hear in my inner ear. My next call, to my daughter, Tasreen, was enormously difficult. I was the father. Aren't fathers supposed to make everything all right—to make the world safe and secure for their children? I had failed. Her only brother was dead. Although Tariq was younger, he always protected his sister like an elder brother. Again, I was overcome with helplessness.

I was simply not prepared to deal with my son's death. The fact is I had never doubted that Tariq would lead a happy life. He was healthy, smart, good-hearted, handsome, happy, and engaged to a wonderful girl. He was in college, eagerly studying for a career in the arts. During break he worked hard to earn his own money—delivering pizzas all over San Diego. Being the victim of murder was not supposed to happen to my son.

When Tariq was eighteen, he had written an essay about his philosophy of life. He based it on six aphorisms he lived by: live by giving; use your time wisely; hang in there when the odds are against you; a winner can never allow himself to be discouraged; treat others the way you want to be treated; and give life your best effort. Tariq was a young man a father could be proud of. So while Tariq lived his life I went about with my own busy life, working eighty to a hundred hours a week, certain that Tariq was fine—and so was I. That phone call ended my certainty.

Azim grew up in Africa and studied in England. After finishing his education, he returned to Uganda, where he and Almas had their first child, Tasreen. In the early 1970s, with their parents, they fled their country because of ethnic persecution by the Idi Amin regime. Almas was pregnant with Tariq at the time. They immigrated to Vancouver, where Tariq was born on March 6, 1974. Eventually, the four moved to Seattle, but both Azim's and Almas's parents stayed in Vancouver. Azim left Seattle in the early eighties, after he and Almas divorced, and settled in San Diego. Tariq had moved there to attend college and live near his father.

As a result of all his travels, Azim had family and friends on several continents who needed to be informed of Tariq's passing. Azim's town house was a buzz of activity with phone calls coming in from around the world and friends arriving with gifts of food. Almas and Tasreen flew in from Seattle.

The press also called with questions. Azim asked a friend, Ward Leber, chief executive officer of the Child Safety Network Trust, to act as the spokesperson for the family. Ward made a public plea through the media for any information about the murder and gave the phone number of the organization's hot line.

The following Tuesday, Tariq's family and friends gathered for a memorial service in San Diego. Jennifer wrote a moving eulogy but was too grief-stricken to speak. A family friend delivered the eulogy, which included an entry from a journal that Tariq had recently begun keeping, where he wrote: "Today I took control of my life. I can no longer blame others for my mistakes. I am responsible for my actions. No one is perfect—I don't want to be perfect. I know that I don't know. That's all I need to know."

.   .   .   .   .

While the family attended to the memorial service and burial, the San Diego police department worked the case. The first lead came from a teenage girl who called the Child Safety Network Trust hot line the Monday after the murder. Melody Argentine from the trust got the message and immediately called the girl back. The girl told Melody that she had called in the pizza order. She agreed to meet with police the next morning. But before the meeting she changed her mind, saying she was too afraid of Q-Tip, the gang leader who had organized the pizza-jacking. After much persuasion, the girl finally agreed to meet with the police. She gave the names of four boys, all members of the Black Mob gang: Q-Tip, Solo, Hook, and the boy who pulled the trigger, Tony Hicks.

The police easily located Tony Hicks, who was already in California Youth Authority custody for stealing a shotgun from Ples Felix, his grandfather. Tony lived with Ples, who had raised him as his son. Ples had reported the gun and Tony missing to the police when he returned home on January 21 to find a note from Tony that said, "Daddy, I love you. But I've run away. Tony."

Tony did not realize the kind of trouble he was facing. Less than a month before Tariq's murder, on January 1, 1995, the State of California had enacted one of the harshest laws in the country to punish youthful offenders. Before January 1, children under the age of sixteen could not be prosecuted as adults in California; however, after January 1, children as young as fourteen—Tony's age—could be. Had Tony killed Tariq a month earlier, his case would have been handled in the juvenile system and the maximum punishment would have been detention by the California Youth Authority until age twenty-five. Under the new law, Tony faced a possible life sentence for his crime.

The police convinced Tony that they already had enough evidence to prove he had committed the murder. Tony confessed to Detective Ron Larmour.[1]

> I was mad at Daddy. We got into a fight on Friday night about a pink slip
> I got for skippin' school on Thursday. Hakeem and I spent the day

kickin' it and smokin' bud [marijuana]. Daddy didn't know about the bud but was trippin' on the pink slip. It was Saturday, he was gone when I got up, but he left me a bunch of chores to do. I didn't care about the usual stuff, but this list was crazy, gonna keep me goin' all day and Daddy and me were arguing a lot. He was strict. I had to be in every night by dark, but none of my friends had to come home until curfew kicked in at ten o'clock. My homeboys were startin' to tease me about it. Daddy wanted me to be the perfect little boy. I didn't want to be perfect and I wasn't little. I left the note where Daddy would find it. I went to Hakeem's. Then we got Solomon and went to another dude's to smoke some bud. Then we went to Alabama Street to see what was goin' on.

I told them I was goin' to L.A. and I needed money. I knew where Daddy kept a gauge [shotgun] so we went back to the house to get it; thought I could sell it and get enough to get me to L.A. I gave Solo my key and he went in. Hook and I kept a lookout. I knew I was in deep now; there was no way Daddy was gonna forget about this.

Solo broke a window to make it look like a burglary. Solo was always thinkin'. He stuffed the gauge down his pants and we started back to Alabama. Solo went down the alley limpin' like a fool. Hakeem said if we saw any cops we'd have to shoot them.

Q-Tip thought the gauge was cool and wanted to keep it. They stuck it in Pa-Ru's closet. [Pa-Ru was a nickname for Paul, the younger brother of the girl who rented the apartment.] I was thinkin', *What about my money?*

We smoked some more weed. 'Cause they took my damn gauge, we had to go back to my house to get some money. I wanted my Sega, too. I was thinkin', *Man, Daddy's gonna kill me already so I might as well really get him mad.*

Went back to Alabama [Street] and kicked it for the rest of the day. Homies came and went. We smoked bud, played vids [video games] and I think some of them were drinkin' 40s [40-ounce bottles] of malt liquor.

Nothin' happened the rest of the day until later when I got hungry.

Around 8:30 that evening, the gang got hungry, but having no money they decided to do a "pizza-jack." They asked a sixteen-year-old girl to call in the order, agreeing to "pay" her with two pieces of pizza. She first called San Diego Pizza, but they refused the order because they had already stopped delivering for the night. Next, the girl called DeMille's, and Tariq was dispatched to deliver the order. The gang headed outside to wait for the delivery, bringing with them a nine-millimeter pistol. Tony described to the police what happened when the boys went outside to wait for the pizza.

Q-Tip told Solo to give me the strap [gun]. He didn't think I would do nothin' with it. Solo had a bad temper and Hook was crazy so Q-Tip figured I was the best one to hold it. He didn't know how mad I was at everyone and everything.

Q-Tip wasn't gonna hold it 'cause he was eighteen and could get in a lot more trouble than us kids if we got caught.

Pizza man went into the apartment building. We heard him poundin' on doors, askin' people if they ordered a pizza. It was pretty funny. He came back to the street and he was trippin'. Pizza man was real mad by now.

I took out the nine and crossed the street. Q-Tip was behind me. When pizza man turns around, he's starin' at the nine and me. I said, "Give me the pizzas." Pizza man just looks at me, goes to get in the car like he don't care I'm pointin' a gun at him.

He gets in the car. I'm really mad now. What's this world comin' to? He starts the car, rolls up the window and starts to back up. I go 'longside the car, pointin' the gun at him, not knowin' what to do. I pull the slide back and jack a bullet into the nine.

Q-Tip starts shoutin' at me, "Bust him, Bone, bust him!" So I did. I pulled the trigger. The nine kicks hard, the window broke, and pizza man yelled. Blood was comin' out of him. I knew he was hurt bad. Pizza man was stupid; he should have give up the pizzas.

• • • •

The family decided to bury Tariq in Vancouver because of the strong family and religious ties they had to the area. Both sets of grandparents were active in the large Ismaili Muslim community there. Azim's mother had the responsibility of opening the mosque early every morning.

Another reason to hold the funeral in Vancouver was so that Azim's father, Noordin, could attend. On the advice of doctors, the family had not yet told Noordin about Tariq's murder fearing that the shock of such stressful news so soon after heart surgery might interfere with his recovery and possibly even kill him. However, as more time passed, Azim felt increasingly uncomfortable hiding the truth. Noordin had already missed his grandson's memorial service. Azim felt that it was unfair to deny his father the right to attend the funeral. The family decided to tell Noordin, who insisted on coming.

The day after the memorial service, the family left for Vancouver to bury Tariq. They flew to Seattle, where Almas and Tasreen picked up some things, and drove from there, accompanied by Dan and Kit, to Vancouver. During the drive, Ward Leber called Azim on his cell phone to say that the San Diego police had arrested four boys in connection with Tariq's murder—three fourteen-year-olds and one eighteen-year-old. Too consumed with grief and funeral preparations, Azim could not fully process the reality that children had killed his son.

Thursday, January 26, was a cold, gray day in Vancouver. Fourteen hundred people crowded the mosque to pay their respects to Tariq. He lay on the ground wrapped in a white shroud. There was no formal seating in the mosque, so the family sat on the floor surrounding Tariq's body—women on one side, men on the other—except Noordin, who sat in his wheelchair at Azim's side.

The *mukhi* and the *kamadia*, elders who served as lay leaders for the mosque, offered prayers from the Koran. For two and a half hours the crowd chanted the Salwat, a prayer for the salvation of Tariq's soul meant to help him to pass into the afterlife.

AZIM: It is such an unnatural experience to bury your child. By this time I was physically exhausted and emotionally spent. I carried the body all the way to the hearse, but as I passed through the two lines of men, each helped carry the load with me. I got my strength from the chanting.

I felt tremendous love from my community. Probably 70 percent of the Ismaili community attended Tariq's service. Because my mother opens the mosque every morning, she is very well known. The whole community made a special effort to offer their support because Tariq was so young and had died under such painful circumstances.

After the chanting, every person passed by Tariq to pay his respects, and the *mukhi* nodded to each. Almas, Tasreen, Jennifer, and I each kissed him good-bye. Then a dozen men placed Tariq's body on a litter while five hundred men formed two lines facing each other. The lines stretched from the mosque to the hearse waiting outside. I took my place at the front of the litter, and the pallbearers placed it on my shoulders.

I walked down the long line of men, and as I passed, each one helped carry the load of Tariq's body to the hearse. Then we drove to the cemetery.

In the Muslim faith, only men attend the burial. We do not use coffins but instead dig a large hole in the ground supported by a wooden frame. As is the custom, I jumped into the cold, wet pit to accept Tariq's body. Standing in the hole, I was tempted to just stay inside and let the others bury me with Tariq. I really wondered how I would find the strength to keep living. I looked up and saw my friend Dan, and because we are so close I knew he could read my thoughts. When I saw his deep look of concern, I gave him a look to reassure him. He reached over and helped pull me out of the grave.

In the Ismaili faith, we say prayers for the departed soul at regular intervals—first at the funeral, then after ten days, forty days, three months, six months, a year, and every year thereafter. I stayed in Vancouver through the ten-day prayers.

It is the custom during the early period of mourning to go to the mosque every day. People bring food they have prepared, especially the favorite foods of the departed person. The food is auctioned off at a very low price for people who are not so financially able to get good food. I went to the mosque nearly every day, and of course my mother went every day.

My thoughts and emotions began to return the day after we buried Tariq. One of the first emotions I felt was anger. However, it was not directed at Tariq's assailants. The entire society was the object of my rage. I wondered how it was that in our great country children too young to have a driver's license are not too young to carry a gun. Why do we spend billions on wars on foreign soil or conquering space when every day, in our own backyard, our defenseless children are wiped out in a frenzy of bizarre violence? Why couldn't our intelligent nation, the world's only superpower, get its priorities right? How many more children would have to be sacrificed? When did we start accepting these killings? And why did we allow them to continue?

•   •   •   •

As Azim struggled internally to process the complicated emotions of Tariq's murder, a similar struggle was taking place in the larger society. What should be done with a fourteen-year-old killer?

A heated public debate sprang up as to whether fourteen-year-olds should be prosecuted as adults. Passions flared on both sides. One camp vociferously opposed prosecuting a fourteen-year-old as an adult, while the other believed that "if you do an adult crime, you do adult time." The second camp circulated a petition and got fourteen hundred signatures in favor of prosecuting Tony as an adult.

Azim stayed out of the debate. The newly elected district attorney of San Diego County, Paul Pfingst, had run on a "get tough on crime" platform. This case tested that commitment.

AZIM: I did not take part in the debate about whether to prosecute Tony Hicks as an adult. Even if I had wanted to, I don't think I could have done so. It was too difficult to do while I was dealing with such raw guilt. I felt like a failure as a father. After all, I had failed to protect my own son. I also felt guilt about all the hours I had spent working and all the time I missed with Tariq. If I had known his life would be so short, I would have made different choices.

I was more concerned about surviving my own grief than in determining how the boys should be punished. I trusted the prosecutor. I knew he was a nice man. He knew that I did not support trying children as adults, but I knew that he was getting a lot of public pressure to do so. I didn't want to take him on and challenge his decision.

However, from the very beginning of the case, the eye-for-an-eye philosophy didn't make much sense to me. I wondered why we weren't trying to figure out how to save these boys. Weren't they victims, too?

Around this time my work required me to travel to Bulgaria. I made the trip, but I could barely function. I attended the necessary meetings but functioned like a zombie, swathed in sorrow. It was very bad timing. I needed to be surrounded by love and support. It was too soon to travel so far from home.

As soon as the trip was over, I flew directly to Vancouver, returning for the next part of our grieving ritual—the forty-day prayers. I was not doing well. The trip to Bulgaria really wiped me out, and I desperately needed all the help and guidance anyone could offer. One evening after a prayer session, one of my spiritual teachers returned to my parents' home to eat a meal with us. He sensed the pain I was in and how much I needed hope and inspiration. After dinner he approached me and said, "After passing from this world, the soul remains in close proximity to the family and loved ones during the forty days of grieving. After forty days, the soul moves to a new level of consciousness. Grieving past this time impedes the soul's journey. It is human to grieve. But I recommend that you break the paralysis of grief, and find a good deed to do in Tariq's name. Compassionate acts undertaken in the name of the departed are spiritual currency, which will transfer to Tariq's soul and help speed his journey."

I told him I didn't understand why grief impeded Tariq's journey. He explained, "Life on earth is much more difficult than in the spiritual realm. The departed soul is quite happy on the other side. Your son has completed his assignment here. You are not grieving for his discomfort. You are feeling sorry for yourself. Instead, do something good in his name. It will be good for you. It will be good for the recipient of the deed. It will be good for Tariq's soul."

In the early spring of 1995, Azim went to the Sierra Nevadas to spend a few days in retreat at a friend's condominium at Mammoth Mountain.

AZIM: As I drove down I-5, I listened to an audiocassette of Deepak Chopra. The further I got from the city, the more my mind slowed. The flatlands morphed into mountains, and I felt awe looking at their majestic beauty.

I arrived at the cabin as the sun was setting, and after unpacking I went into town for a dinner of grilled Cajun fish and salad. I returned to the condo and made a fire. I gazed at the tongues of flame as they shape-shifted and danced. I willed my body to relax. My thoughts shifted like the flames—starting, stopping, and turning in unpredictable directions.

I should have spent more time with Tariq. I cursed myself for having been so busy. I remembered our last visit together. I had met Tariq for breakfast on January 9 at our favorite restaurant, the Hobnob, in the Hillcrest section of San Diego. That morning we tried something new and ordered corned beef hash to go with our usual steak and eggs.

We brought each other up-to-date on our lives. I told him about my business travels, and he told me about school and his relationship with Jennifer. He mentioned that they were thinking about moving to New York City to pursue their art careers. I was not too surprised to hear that, knowing that Tariq had never really liked Southern California.

The visit had been a wonderful interlude from our busy lives. It was impossible to believe that it had been three months ago; it seemed more like three lifetimes. It was impossible, too, to believe that I would never see him again, that I would never tousle his hair again. I remembered his thick hair and how I used to love to run my fingers through it. Sometimes I would do so in public and embarrass him horribly. These memories were too painful to bear.

During the next few days I reexamined my life and questioned my priorities. Each morning after a breakfast of fruit and tea, I skied. After lunch, I took long walks. My mind wandered. The fundamental question I kept asking myself was: how was I going to get through the rest of my life? How was I going to live with the agony of having been cheated out of sharing my son's life?

I thought about the advice from my spiritual advisor. Tariq was at peace; I was not. In order to find peace, I needed to find something I could do for him. I kept thinking of the phrases "spiritual currency" and "fuel for the journey of the soul." It was on a chilly night in April that I got my first inspiration about what I might do. What if I became a foe: not of the boy who killed my son, but of the forces that led him to kill my son? What if I reached out as far as I possibly could and devoted myself to fighting the plague of youth violence? I spent the rest of my time at Mammoth Mountain thinking about this idea. For the first time since Tariq's death, I felt the slightest return of my old energy. I saw the first glimmer of a reason why my own life should continue.

Returning from the mountains, Azim felt energized in a way he had not since Tariq's murder. A man of action, he poured his intelligence and stamina into his new idea. The answer to juvenile crime was not what to do with a fourteen-year-old who committed murder—it was preventing such murders in the first place. He would start a foundation in Tariq's name dedicated to ending youth violence. He would help reach young kids like Tony before they became killers.

Azim broached the idea for the project as he would any of his business dealings. He started with his best friends, Dan and Kit. Kit was a very creative person. She had experience in education and theater, everything from staging productions to making costumes. Dan had good business skills. Azim also approached Sal Gaicalone, the owner of DeMille's, and Peter Deddeh, the prosecuting attorney. He spent the summer reaching out to others. By the fall, he was ready to launch the new project—the Tariq Khamisa Foundation (TKF). On October 26, 1995, fifty people came to the first meeting.

**AZIM:** We defied the laws of space and managed to squeeze into my town house. After everyone had a chance to drink coffee and visit, Peter Deddeh gave an introductory speech, supporting our efforts. Several others spoke, and then Dan introduced me. Everyone there knew the facts of the case, so instead of talking about Tariq's murder, I talked about my inner feelings and the journey that had brought me to this point in time. I thanked them from my heart for their promise and commitment to work on behalf of our children. Mine were not the only tears shed that night.

I told the group of my desire to help children solve conflict nonviolently. I did not know exactly what the foundation would do to achieve that goal, but I imagined that we would make presentations to children at school. I saw already how powerful it was for people just to hear the story of Tariq's death. I hoped that by seeing firsthand the horrible aftermath of violence, some youngsters might be dissuaded from taking up gangs and guns.

During the meeting I knew that there was someone else who needed to be part of this project. An idea had been brewing inside for a while, and after that gathering, I knew the time was right to act on it. At the end of the meeting I took Peter aside and told him I wanted to meet Tony's grandfather, Ples Felix.

District Attorney Peter Deddeh had never dealt with a victim's family member like Azim Khamisa. From the very beginning, Azim's calm presence and peaceful demeanor impressed Peter. He dealt with crime victims all the time, but usually he saw rage and cries for vengeance and retribution.

Normally, Peter would have strongly discouraged the family members of victims from meeting with the family of the perpetrators, but when Azim told him about his desire to meet Ples, he thought it was a good idea. Like Azim, Ples was deeply spiritual. Peter thought the two might be able to support each other.

Peter agreed to Azim's request and arranged a meeting at the downtown office of Tony's attorney, Henry Coker. Azim invited Mike Reynolds, a writer and filmmaker who had been following the case closely, to accompany him.

On November 3, Azim picked up Mike and drove to Henry's office, expecting to discuss arrangements for meeting Ples. When he walked into the room, there stood Ples.

AZIM: My first reaction was simple shock, because I hadn't known Ples was going to be there. I think I actually took a step back before we shook hands. Then we all sat down. Ples's appearance was part Western and part African. He wore his hair in dreadlocks, covered by a large, colorful African-style cap, almost as large as a turban, with his suit and tie.

I told Ples that I did not have any feelings of revenge toward him or his family. We both felt the grief of having lost a young life. I told him about the work we were going to undertake through the Tariq Khamisa Foundation—to fight the plight of youth violence that had wounded us both so severely.

I told him that I just wanted to reach out and connect with him as part of my healing process. I had no idea what his reaction would be. I had no expectations.

Ples took my outstretched hand with no hesitation. He offered his condolences to my family and me with bedrock sincerity. He told me he wanted me to know that my family and I were in his prayers and meditations every day. This struck a deep, responsive chord in me because of the importance of meditation and spirituality in my own life. It created an instant, powerful bond. That bond was to stay with us and provide a mutual source of energy for the commitment we were to share. I felt from the beginning that he was a good man.

Ples said he would pledge to help in any way he could with the foundation's work. I was very moved by this—partly because I took an instant leap forward and realized what he might face. At every appearance or meeting, he could be seen by some as the man who had been the guardian of the killer, and therefore partially responsible for what had happened. I could not help but admire his courage.

Ples was as good as his word. The next week he attended the second meeting of the TKF, again held at my house. Ples agreed to speak to the group, which included Tariq's family: his grandparents; his mother, Almas; his aunt Neyleen; his sister, Tasreen; and his cousin Salim Nice. Ples looked all of us in the eye and pledged his commitment to the foundation and asked the others in the room to commit to the effort as well. When he finished speaking, everyone was crying.

Less than a year after Tariq's murder, Azim had formed a foundation in memory of his son. Now that he had the organizational structure in place, he needed to figure out the specifics of what to do. He continued to talk and share ideas as the program took root.

●　　●　　●　　●

During this time, the criminal case proceeded forward. Prosecutor Deddeh decided to start with the oldest, the one who acted as the ringleader, Antoine Pittman, or "Q-Tip" as his "homies" called him. Q-Tip faced two counts of murder—one for his part in Tariq's death and the other for the murder of a thirty-seven-year-old drifter named Lonnie Smithwick whom Q-Tip had killed after two girls complained that he refused to buy Thunderbird wine for them. Q-Tip stood trial for killing Lonnie in November and Tariq in December. He was convicted of both murders and was sentenced to life in prison without the possibility of parole.

On January 4, 1996, nearly a year after Tony killed Tariq, Judge Charles Patrick ordered him to stand trial as an adult for murder. Although Tony's case had been the first to be charged under the new law, the state had since prosecuted and convicted a fourteen-year-old Orange County boy as an adult. That case was on appeal to the state appeals court in San Diego.

Ples visited Tony at the San Diego juvenile hall as often as he could, trying to continue in his parenting role. Filmmaker Mike Reynolds often came along.

During the year that Tony had been detained at juvenile hall, he had begun to change. The reality of his crime haunted him. Ples told Tony about his relationship with Azim and the rest of Tariq's family and how they were not seeking vengeance. Remorse plagued him. Tony decided to plead guilty to the murder charge in order to spare everyone around him the pain of a trial. He did this even though the state offered him nothing in return for his plea. Tony's decision removed a huge burden from Azim, who had been dreading the prospect of a trial.

On April 11, 1996, Tony pleaded guilty to first-degree murder. Addressing the court on behalf of his client, Henry Coker told Judge Joan Weber that Tony was emotionally devastated by his crime, and exhausted by the legal process. He did not want to subject his family or the Khamisa family to the ordeal of a trial that would entail replaying the murder. Judge Weber set sentencing for June 18.

June 18, 1996, found Judge Weber's courtroom packed with spectators, many from the press. No one from the Khamisa family attended, but some supporters from the TKF appeared in their stead.

**AZIM:** I was still not ready to look at the face of the boy who killed my son. I had not attended any court proceedings and did not see the point in attending this one either.

The judge opened the hearing by saying, "I have been dreading this day. There is no pleasure in sentencing a boy to prison. I essentially see two lives destroyed by this."

Tony read a statement that his lawyer had helped him prepare:

Good Morning, Judge:

On January 21, 1995, I shot and killed Tariq Khamisa; a person I didn't even know and who didn't do anything wrong to me. On April 11, 1996, I pled guilty to first-degree murder because I am guilty. I wanted to save the Khamisa family and my family from further pain.

From my grandfather, I have learned about the Khamisa family and their only son Tariq. I have learned about the love they have for him. Through my grandfather and Mr. Reynolds, they have tried to explain to me the compassion the Khamisa family has for me.

I have had a lot of problems in my life. Over the last year, while I have been in Juvenile Hall, I have thought about my problems. I wish I didn't have the type of life I had. I wish I had a relationship with my father. I think about the warmth that my grandfather gave me. I wonder why I didn't listen and learn. Now, I wish I would have listened to my grandfather.

At night, when I'm alone, I cry and beg God to let me out of here. I promise Him that I will be a better person—I won't mess up. When I see my mom, I want to hold her as tight as I can, and beg her, "Take me out of jail!"

However, I don't want to use my problems as an excuse for my actions. I think I would have gone to jail sometime but I honestly don't think getting busted for a robbery or something like that would have changed me. I was too mad at everyone: my mom, my dad, and my grandfather. When I first came to the Hall I was mad at the D.A. and the people in the Hall for keeping me here. Now, I'm just scared and mad at myself.

I'm alone at Juvenile Hall. Even though the people at the Hall are pretty cool, I'm still alone. I often think about the night I shot Tariq, especially when I'm alone in my cell. When it's dark and quiet, I wonder what it's like to die. I wonder why I'm still alive. Sometimes when I roll over in bed and I lay next to the cold wall, I feel as far away from everything as possible. I wonder if that's what dying feels like.

I still don't know why I shot Tariq. I didn't really want to hurt him or anyone else. I'm sorry. I'm sorry for killing Tariq and hurting his family. I'm sorry for the pain that I caused for Tariq's father, Mr. Khamisa. I pray to God every day that Mr. Khamisa will forgive me for what I have done, and for as long as I live I will continue to pray to God to give him strength to deal with his loss.

My grandfather promised me that he will be Mr. Khamisa's friend and help him in any way he can for the rest of his life. I am very sorry for what I have done. Thank you for giving me the chance to speak.[2]

Judge Weber sentenced Tony to twenty-five years to life in prison. Tony would live at juvenile hall until he turned eighteen, at which time the state would transfer him to an adult prison. After the judge pronounced sentence, Tony and his mother, Loeta, hugged each other good-bye, both crying. An officer led Tony out of the courtroom.

Azim later saw a videotape of the sentencing hearing and marveled at Tony's transformation. He knew about the statement that Tony made after he killed Tariq, "Pizza man was stupid; he should have give up the pizzas." Now, eighteen months later, Tony had ceased blaming others and had taken responsibility for his crime. It gave Azim hope that Tony could be rehabilitated. The sentencing marked the end of the criminal proceeding, but for Azim, his work was only beginning.

AZIM: Sentencing Tony to prison did not make me feel whole. It did nothing to bring Tariq back. We need a justice system that is more holistic. We have to look at where violence comes from. Parents are not only responsible. All of society is responsible.

I was starting to think more about the concept of restorative justice, especially for juveniles. Our system is based on retributive justice, which punishes the offender and ends there. Restorative justice seeks to make both parties whole. We need to be realistic that if we do not change offenders, we as a society will continue to suffer.

Most criminals that are convicted and sentenced usually come out of jail. The average sentence is three years and eight months. There is an 85 percent rate of recidivism. Our criminal justice system actually trains them to be better criminals. When they reoffend, there are new victims, and society as a whole loses out.

I believe that everybody is born with something of value that only they can own. Even the most damaged criminals have something to offer. It's like mining precious minerals; you bring the diamonds up at the same time you bring up the dross. I am not comfortable closing the door on somebody forever because they made one bad mistake. They may have something to offer me that I won't be able to take advantage of if we give up on them.

But the most important reason to support restorative justice is that the victim needs to heal, too. When we are victimized it is natural to feel anger and revenge. Unabated anger directed at the perpetrator harms us, however, because anger is a very strong emotion and can become an all-consuming passion within us. It fills us with hatred and tension and blocks out love and joy. The only way to defuse that unabated anger is through forgiveness. The criminal needs the victim's forgiveness to heal. And in one of human nature's strange twists, full healing for the victim may require him or her to grant that forgiveness. There may be no other way to defuse the destructive anger one feels.

No one wants to feel used in such a process—no one wants to be duped by a slick operator. Forgiveness should not be casually handed out as if it were penny candy. The stage must be properly set. I knew that nothing was going to bring my son back, but I had to find some way to make his death more meaningful, and that is what restorative justice tries to accomplish.

Tony's conviction and sentencing made the front page of the local paper. Carol Roblauskas, a counselor at Alice Birney Elementary School, which Tony had attended, sensed confusion on the part of her students. Tony had seemed like a nice kid. Many remembered taking classes and playing sports with him. Some were even friends of his. Now Tony, who should be attending high school, was serving a sentence of twenty-five years to life for murder. The kids didn't know how to react.

Carol contacted TKF, which the article had mentioned, and asked if they would put on a program at the school to help the children process their conflicted emotions. Although the foundation had not yet created a program, all felt that they could not pass up the opportunity to address such a large number of students at such a crucial time. With less than two weeks, Azim, Dan, Kit, and Ples took out paper and pencil and brainstormed.

Fortunately, Kit had extensive experience designing programs and productions. As a writer, producer, and actress, Kit knew how to put on a show. They conceived a program called the Violence Impact Forum. The message was simple: violence is a choice; the impact of violence is terrible and irrevocable, and it always brings grim consequences. The program, too, would be simple and direct. Azim and Ples would tell the story of what happened to their sons and how it affected them. Acting as the hostess, Kit would use a talk-show format to engage the kids in dialogue.

AZIM: I was extremely nervous before the first program. I had never done much public speaking until then. An investment banker is always in the background, playing a support role. It was unusual for me to be in a leading role. But the passion for the cause came through. The kids really picked up on it. They felt my pain—they could see it in my face. If most of us knew how painful violence is, I don't think we would be violent.

Both Azim and Ples told their stories to the spellbound group of children. A former gang member named Kevin shared his experience and warned against becoming involved in a gang. Mike Reynolds spoke about visiting Tony in juvenile hall relaying to the kids what life behind steel bars and locked doors is like. He read a short letter that Tony had written for the group:

Hi. A lot of you kids may have seen or heard of me or know me. I went to this school from the fourth to the sixth grade. I'm in the ninth grade now, so I'm not much older than most of you. I'm a fifteen-year-old boy—serving a prison sentence of twenty-five to life.

I did a crime that I regret and that I'm ashamed of. When I first moved to San Diego from L.A., I needed friends. So I joined a gang. We didn't do much in the gang but hang out with our friends and have fun. I didn't stop to think of the people I was hurting while I was having fun. I just had fun.

I was arrested when I was fourteen for something I thought was going to be fun—until someone died. Now I see that what I was doing wasn't fun. I should have listened to the people who really cared about me—not the people I thought cared. You kids shouldn't need to have fun the way I did. It ain't worth hurtin' the ones you love. It just ain't worth it.

Thank you. I'm Tony Hicks.[3]

Mike then showed a videotape of Tony's sentencing statement. Many cried, including Kit.

After the tape, Kit refocused the forum by engaging the kids in dialogue. She asked them about the kinds of pressures they faced in their lives. Each time a child answered or asked a question, Kit echoed the theme of the presentation—you always have a choice, and violence is a bad choice to make. One of the last questions came from a girl who was about twelve or thirteen years old. "Why do people wait until somebody gets killed to make a foundation?" Kit answered, "Young woman, that's a very good question. You know what? We just didn't know. Life is a learning experience, and maybe the test is that once you know enough, can you change?"

The inaugural event exceeded everyone's expectations. Children wrote letters revealing how the program affected them. Requests poured in from other schools around San Diego.

The group kept the same basic format but refined the program to include a Garden of Life tree- and flower-planting ceremony at the end; all the children planted flowers in memory of someone they had lost. The group also incorporated a pre- and postforum questionnaire to assess whether students' attitudes about using violence changed as a result of the program.

Within months the program received national attention through a number of news stories and features, including an appearance by Azim and Ples on the *Today* show. In April 1997, Attorney General Janet Reno awarded Azim and Ples a Special Community Service Award, which included a hundred-thousand-dollar grant from the Department of Justice's Office for Victims of Crime.

The work of the TKF continued to grow. Between that and his work as an investment banker, Azim kept long hours and traveled constantly. However, as pleased as he was with the TKF, there remained one task to complete before full reconciliation would be possible. Azim needed to meet Tony.

Left to right: *Ples Felix, Tony Hicks, and Azim Khamisa. Photograph provided with permission of the family.*

In April 2000, five years and three months after the murder of his son, Azim made the long trip to New Folsom prison outside Sacramento. Azim had been ready to meet Tony about six months earlier, but Tony had not been ready. The time had finally arrived.

Azim drove with Ples to the large, imposing structure surrounded by four towers, each manned with a guard carrying a shotgun. With thirty-five hundred prisoners, New Folsom is one of the country's largest prisons. It takes nearly an hour to make it through all the security posts. The visiting room is a large windowless room with plastic tables and chairs. Visitors can take in small amounts of money to buy snacks from vending machines. Also, for three dollars, visitors can purchase in advance a Polaroid photograph to be taken inside with the inmate. Azim paid for three photographs—one each for himself, Ples, and Tony.

AZIM: The visit with Tony and his grandfather lasted about three hours. It obviously was a difficult meeting—to come eyeball to eyeball, face to face with my son's killer. There were gaps in the story that I needed to fill— I was ready. I met with Tony and Ples together, and after about thirty minutes Ples excused himself so Tony and I could speak privately. Then I left so that Ples and Tony could talk.

Tony asked for my forgiveness. I believed that if it were possible, Tony would have brought Tariq back. Tony had committed to living a better life. He had been in jail for more than five years and during that time had avoided getting involved with gangs or drugs. He had done everything possible to further his education. He wanted to complete his GED, but he hadn't been able to because there was a two-year wait to get into the program. He continued his education by reading about five books a month.

Tony wants to be a child psychologist. I supported him in that choice. I encouraged him to stay on the straight and narrow. He'll be in prison for twenty-two years before he is eligible for parole. I asked him to work with me at the foundation when he is released. He agreed to help. In the meantime, his grandfather is carrying half the load of the foundation.

What impressed me about Tony was that he did not have the attitude of a typical nineteen-year-old. He was very well mannered, gentle, kind, remorseful, and respectful. I could see that he had done a lot of work to improve himself.

It is difficult for him in prison. Not only is it difficult to be confined, it is difficult to stay out of trouble. He tries to keep a low profile. He has to be like a chameleon. He doesn't go into the yard, or if he does he disappears into the wall so he doesn't become a target. He tries to use his time productively. He has taught people how to read and play chess.

At the end of the visit we took three Polaroid pictures of the three of us. Tony wanted to keep two so that he could send one to his mother for Mother's Day. I told him to keep two and I'd make a copy for Ples. I made a commitment to Tony to visit him at least twice a year. It was an emotional day.

•   •   •   •

The Tariq Khamisa Foundation, which started with Azim and a handful of volunteers, now has an annual budget of five hundred thousand dollars and a paid staff of three, two full-time and one part-time. Tariq's sister, Tasreen, serves as executive director. It has received thirty-five awards and continues to be featured in the media.

In 2000, the TKF presented the Violence Impact Forum to seventy schools in the San Diego area reaching eighteen thousand fourth to sixth graders. The foundation decided to target middle-school children because most children of that age have not participated in any serious forms of violence. That is also the age when gang recruitment begins. The TKF has presented programs at over one hundred schools, and Azim and Ples have given nearly as many speeches to other groups. Still, the demand exceeds what the foundation can supply.

After programs, children often send letters to Azim, Tariq, and Tony. The TKF forwards Tony's letters to him, hoping that support from strangers will help keep him on the straight and narrow.

Azim has also served on the board of directors of Murder Victims' Families for Reconciliation. He spoke at the group's first national conference for survivors of murder victims, which took place in Boston the weekend before Timothy McVeigh's execution on June 11, 2001.

AZIM: I don't believe in the death penalty. I'm opposed to that type of solution to problems. It was not a good way to try to resolve what Timothy McVeigh did. I was disappointed that he never showed remorse. However, by executing him, we will create more Timothy McVeighs. He is very much against the establishment. His crime should serve as a wake-up call. We need to create a more peaceful society. I suggest we rename the Department of Defense the Department of Peace. We spend too much money on arms and weapons. We are not an exemplary role model. Instead of focusing on the death penalty, we need to put our resources up front into prevention so that we can prevent murder in the first place.

We need to focus more on forgiveness. I am working on my second book, which is going to be about forgiveness in action. I have a hypothesis. I believe if you are authentic in your forgiveness and you sincerely forgive the offender, that person will not reoffend, because you changed him at the soul level.

If we are able to save Tony, then Tony will save thousands and thousands of other children. If that happens, my son's death might impact more people than if he had lived. Tony's story is not over yet. If we succeed, we will send a very powerful message to the system that against all odds a fourteen-year-old in an adult prison with little going for him can still be saved.

*Tariq Khamisa. Photograph provided with permission of the family.*

I am learning in my journey that Western culture and society overemphasizes the mind and the body. I grew up with a healthy balance between the spiritual and the material. My mom opened the mosque every morning. My dad was an investment banker. I grew up with equal access to my spiritual and material needs.

I speak nationally and internationally. I live in Southern California, where we have a high standard of material wealth and place a lot of emphasis on our bodies. But we humans are mind, body, *and* soul. The soul is the only thing that is eternal; the other two are not, but we spend all our money on the mind and body. There is so much disconnection between our mind, body, and soul. The mind is a dangerous place to go alone. Our mind can justify anything, but it is in our soul where our high ideals live; ideals like love, compassion, unity, and forgiveness. When you are living in the soul, you can't be violent. It is an oxymoron.

We have increased our intellectual capacities and accomplished great things, but we don't do anything for the soul, things like prayer and meditation. Of course, there can also be too much focus on the spiritual and not the material, as in India, where you have healthy men meditating all day while their children go without food.

The soul is a divine spirit living within us. Humans need to be creative—we need to express our innermost selves. For example, I am a Sufi, and we love dancing. But as a society we are taking those things that nurture the spirit away from our children by cutting the arts out of our school budgets. This is very shortsighted.

Every day you have to do something to make yourself healthy, and that includes doing something for your soul. If we could all practice that and connect back with our souls, we would have a less violent society.

Kahlil Gibran says that when you are feeling joy, sorrow is sleeping on my bed; when you are feeling sorrow, joy is sleeping on my bed. Rumi says the cure for pain is in the pain. This is true even for a slight headache. If you do the work, you can heal.

You can't sweep a child's loss under the rug. It was very unnatural and painful to bury Tariq. I decided to address that pain, and in that pain I have been able to go to new levels in my heart. You just have to feel the pain.

It has been six years since my son died. When Tariq died, my grief was the size of Jupiter and my soul the size of a wine barrel. Every time I speak about him, I heal the wound caused by his death a little more. Today my grief is the size of planet Earth and my soul the size of the North American continent. I am looking forward to building more knowledge in this area. I'm in my sixth year, and I'm looking at gifts. I haven't laughed so much for a while, but now I am laughing and beginning to express some joy.

# Afterword

I wanted to end the book with Azim's story because it so powerfully demonstrates that the death penalty and long-term imprisonment are not solutions to violence. Incarcerating Tony Hicks for twenty-five years does nothing to restore Azim's life. What Azim wants from Tony is something much more. He wants Tony to use his time in prison to get an education, and improve himself, then get out of prison and help other young people to avoid lives of violence. No matter what Tony does, he cannot bring Tariq back, but if Tony helps make the world better, than Tariq's death is redeemed somewhat.

It is not enough to oppose the death penalty or abolish the death penalty. Our challenge as a society is to eliminate, or at least significantly reduce, violence. This is a tall order. The United States is one of the most violent democratic countries in the world. Interestingly, we are also the only Western democracy that uses the death penalty.

Now more than ever, in the wake of the September 11 attacks, our society is grappling with the appropriate response to violence. It is my hope that we can draw from the experiences of the people whose stories are told in this book and others like them. If there is one lesson from their experiences it is that forgiveness is the way to healing. In a letter to the *New York Times*, Orlando and Phyllis Rodriguez, whose son Greg died in the terrorist attacks on September 11, expressed their opposition to the death penalty:

> We can understand why victims' families would look to the death penalty as a justifiable punishment for convicted terrorists, but we feel that it is wrong to take a life. Nothing will erase the pain and loss that we must learn to live with, and causing others pain can only make it worse. ... If any good can come out of the disaster of Sept. 11, perhaps it will

include examination of how we can maintain our humanity in the face of terrorists' threats.[1]

I, for one, find it very difficult to practice forgiveness in my daily life. It is more common for me to feel resentment toward those I believe have harmed me. However, as a by-product of writing this book, I have been forced to consider forgiveness as an option in responding to the daily injustices of life. When I am disappointed or angry at someone I'll think about a murder victim's family member I know, like Marietta, and I'll say to myself, "If Marietta can forgive the man who kidnapped and killed her daughter, I can forgive this person." The times when I have truly forgiven have been extraordinarily liberating.

Forgiveness makes it possible to transform pain and loss into good. Each person in this book faced a situation of unbelievable grief, and all not only survived but used it to improve their lives or the lives of people around them. Gus Lamm says, "Evil is a temporary condition. Good can come from evil." He points out that we are already seeing good come in the wake of the September 11 attacks in acts of heroism and generosity from people across the country and around the world.

Perhaps the enduring lesson is that love and forgiveness are more powerful than any amount of hate and revenge.

# NOTES

## INTRODUCTION

1. U.S. Department of Justice Bureau of Justice Statistics, "Homicide Trends in the United States," 14 November 2001, www.ojp.usdoj.gov/bjs/.
2. Ken Armstrong and Steve Miller, "Ryan Suspends Death Penalty; Illinois First State to Impose Moratorium on Executions," *Chicago Tribune*, 31 January 2001.
3. Death Penalty Information Center, "100th Exoneration Imminent," www.deathpenaltyinfo.org/whatsnew.html#100DNA.
4. Harris poll, 20–25 July 2001, http://pollingreport.com/crime.htm#Death.
5. James S. Liebman, "A Broken System: Error Rates in Capital Cases," June 2000 (Columbia University School of Law).
6. "The Death Penalty in 2001: Year-End Report," Death Penalty Information Center, December 2001.
7. Amnesty International Report, "United States of America: Arbitrary, Discriminatory, and Cruel: An Aide-Memoire to 25 Years of Judicial Killing," 17 January 2002.
8. Death Penalty Information Center, "Financial Facts About the Death Penalty," www.deathpenaltyinfo.org/costs2.html.
9. Harris poll, http://pollingreport.com/crime.htm#Death; *Furman v. Georgia*, 408 U.S. 238 (1972).
10. *Gregg v. Georgia*, 428 U.S. 153 (1976); Harris poll, http://pollingreport.com/crime.htm#Death.
11. Craig Haney, "The Social Context of Capital Murder: Social Histories and the Logic of Mitigation," 35 *Santa Clara L. Rev.* 547, 548–59 (1995).
12. Ibid.

## CHAPTER 1: THE LOST CHILD

1. "Jaegers Tell of Faith in God," *Billings Gazette*, 29 September 1974.
2. Patrick Mullany, "To Forgive," copy of agency publication in author's possession.

## CHAPTER 3: THE LAST PARTY

1. Christy Drennan, "The Embodiment of Evil? Opinions Have Changed over Pickax Murderer Karla Faye Tucker," *Houston Chronicle*, 28 March 1986.
2. Ibid.
3. Ibid.
4. Kathy Walt, "Tucker Dies After Apologizing," *Houston Chronicle*, 3 February 1998.

## EXECUTING THE VULNERABLE

1. "Juvenile" is used to mean anyone under the age of eighteen at the time he or she committed the crime.
2. *Thompson v. Oklahoma*, 487 U.S. 815 (1988); *Stanford v. Kentucky*, 492 U.S. 361 (1989).
3. Victor L. Streib, "The Juvenile Death Penalty Today," www.law.onu.edu/faculty/streib/juvdeath.htm, updated by Death Penalty Information Center, www.deathpenaltyinfo.org.
4. "Beyond Reason: The Death Penalty and Offenders with Mental Retardation," report by Human Rights Watch, March 2001, vol. 13, no. 1 (G), www.hrw.org/reports/2001/ustat/ustat0301-07.htm#P846_147624.
5. Ibid., www.hrw.org/reports/2001/ustat/ustat0301-07.htm#P817_145472.
6. *Penry v. Lynaugh*, 492 U.S. 584 (1989).
7. *North Carolina v. McCarver*, 353 N.C. 366, 548 S.E.2d 522 (N.C. 2001); stay granted, *McCarver v. North Carolina*, 531 U.S. 1205,121 S.Ct. 1221, 149 L.Ed.2d 132, 69 USLW 3591 (2001); *certoriari* granted, *McCarver v. North Carolina*, 121 S.Ct. 1401, 149 L.Ed.2d 344, 69 USLW 3624 (2001).
8. *McCarver v. North Carolina*, 122 S.Ct. 22 (2001), *certiorari* dismissed as improvidently granted; *Atkins v. Virginia*, 534 S.E.2d 312 (Va. 2000), *certiorari* granted, 122 S.Ct. 24 (2001), order amended by *Atkins v. Virginia*, 122 S.Ct. 29 (2001).

## CHAPTER 4: THE ANSWER IS LOVE AND COMPASSION

1. Yvette Walker, "State Seeks Death Penalty for Girl Charged in Slaying," *Gary Post-Tribune*, 18 May 1985.
2. Staff reporter, "Case Unique Because Death Penalty Sought for Girls," *Gary Post-Tribune*, 21 July 1985.
3. Wes Smith and John O'Brien, "4 Unlikely Suspects in a Savage Slaying," *Gary Post-Tribune*, 17 June 1985.
4. Bill Dolan, "Girl Gets 35 Years in Death of Teacher," *Gary Post-Tribune*, 5 December 1985.
5. Star State Report, "Teen Gets 60-Year Prison Term in Slaying," *Indianapolis Star*, 31 May 1985.
6. Trial transcripts of Judge Kimbrough's sentencing remarks, *State v. Paula Cooper*, Exhibit C, pages A-11–A-20, pages 240–248. The judge's remarks were also reported (in summary form) in Bill Dolan, "Cooper Sentenced to Death," *Gary Post-Tribune*, 12 July 1986.
7. Lawrence Muhammed, "Kimbrough Still Ponders and Wonders," *Gary Post-Tribune*, 4 August 1986.

8. Lori Olszewski, "Should Cooper Die? Victim's Family Divided," *Gary Post-Tribune*, 12 May 1987.

9. "Protesters Can't Judge Sentence: Crawford," *Gary Post-Tribune*, 23 July 1986.

10. Mark Nichols, "Italian Friar Delivers Petitions for Clemency," *Indianapolis Star*, May 1988.

11. Associated Press, "Italians to Meet with Paula," *Vidette-Messenger*, 25 February 1989.

12. "Protesters Can't Judge Sentence."

13. Associated Press, "Pope, Reagan May Talk to Cooper," *Gary Post-Tribune*, 11 September 1987.

14. *Furman v. Georgia*, 408 U.S. 238 (1972); *Gregg v. Georgia*, 428 U.S. 153 (1976).

## CHAPTER 5: THE LAST WORD

1. George Papajohn and Jessica Seigal, "Reward Is Doubled in Winnetka Slayings," *Chicago Tribune*, 11 April 1990.

2. Jessica Seigal and George Papajohn, "Friends Mourn Winnetka Couple," *Chicago Tribune*, 12 April 1990.

3. Jessica Seigal and Joel Kaplan, "Winnetka Murder Case Shifts Gears," *Chicago Tribune*, 25 April 1990.

4. Joel Kaplan, "IRA Slaying Link Labeled a Smear; Police Seek Scapegoat, Activists Say," *Chicago Tribune*, 1 May 1990.

5. Joel Kaplan and George Papajohn, "Winnetka Killings Still a Puzzle," *Chicago Tribune*, 10 June 1990.

6. *Simon and Schuster, Inc. v. Members of the New York State Crime Victims' Board*, 502 U.S. 105 (1991).

7. Teresa Wiltz, "Murder-Torn Families Protest Death Penalty," *Chicago Tribune*, 13 June 1993.

## CHAPTER 6: KEEP HOPE ALIVE

1. Geoffrey Tomb, "Family of Murdered Pastor: Don't Give Killer the Chair," *Miami Herald*, 13 April 1988.

2. *Florida v. Campbell*, Findings of Fact and Sentence, Circuit Court of the 11th Judicial Circuit of Florida, Case No. 86-38693, 19 May 1988.

3. Christine Evans, "Spare Murderer, Relatives of Slain Pastor Implore," *Miami Herald*, 14 May 1988.

4. *Campbell v. Florida*, 571 So.2d 415, 419 (Fla. 1990).

5. Testimony of Nora Dickerson at Sentencing Hearing, Transcript 1189–1190.

6. *Campbell v. Florida*, 679 So.2d 720, 723-24 (Fla. 1996).

7. Ibid., 724.

8. Ibid., 724–25.

9. Letter dated 24 May 1997, Melodee A. Smith to Katherine F. Rundle.

## GRAVE INJUSTICES

1. Barry Scheck, Peter Neufeld, and Jim Dwyer, *Actual Innocence: Five Days to Execution and Other Dispatches from the Wrongly Convicted* (Garden City, N.Y.: Doubleday, 2000).

2. Errol Morris, *The Thin Blue Line* (Miramax, 1988).

3. Charles Lane, "O'Connor Expresses Death Penalty Doubt of Justice—Says Innocent May Be Killed," *Washington Post*, 4 July 2001.

4. Anna Quindlen, "The Best of the Supremes," *Newsweek*, 6 November 2000, 76.

5. U.S. General Accounting Office, "Death Penalty Sentencing: Research and Its Patterns of Racial Disparities," 1990.

6. Richard C. Dieter, Esq., "The Death Penalty in Black and White: Who Lives, Who Dies, Who Decides?" Death Penalty Information Center, June 1998.

7. "Fact Sheet No. 2," National Coalition to Abolish the Death Penalty, www.ncadp.org/html/fact2.html.

8. "Racial Disparities in Federal Death Penalty Prosecutions 1988–1994," Staff Report by the Subcommittee on Civil and Constitutional Rights, Committee of the Judiciary, 103rd Congress, 2d Session, March 1994.

9. *Gregg v. Georgia*, 428 U.S. 153 (1976).

10. *Peck v. Florida*, 488 So.2d 52, 56 (Fla. 1986).

11. Dieter, "The Death Penalty in Black and White."

12. Ken Hambleton, "Researcher: Limit Call for Executions," *Lincoln Journal Star*, 18 October 2001; David C. Baldus, George Woodworth, Gary L. Young, and Aaron M. Christ, "The Disposition of Nebraska Capital and Non-Capital Homicide Cases (1973–1999): A Legal and Empiral Analysis," 10 October 2001, www.state.ne.us/home/crimecom/homicide/finalreport2.pdf.

## CHAPTER 7: RUSH TO JUDGMENT

1. Charles Mount, "Lawyer Protests New Murder Trial," *Chicago Tribune*, 11 April 1996.

2. Tom Held, "Justice Gets 2nd Chance in Murder Case," *Milwaukee Journal Sentinel*, 12 June 1997.

3. Dave Daley, "Biker Gets Life Sentences in McHenry Slayings," *Chicago Tribune*, 13 October 2000. The judge's remarks here likely referred to the fact that Wisconsin does not have a death penalty. Nonetheless, because Randy Miller and James Schneider were prosecuted in the federal system, they could have faced a federal death penalty charge even in Wisconsin. However, it is common for U.S. attorneys in non–death penalty states to follow local practice when deciding whether to seek the death penalty. In this case, it appears that the U.S. attorneys in Wisconsin did not pursue the death penalty for Randy Miller.

4. Gretchen Schuldt, "Former Outlaw Sentenced to 45 Years," *Milwaukee Journal Sentinel*, 10 March 2001.

5. Charles Keeshan, "Gaugers' Real Killer Sentenced," *Chicago Daily Herald*, 10 March 2001.

## CHAPTER 8: MAKING CHOICES

1. Paul Hammel, "Latest Appeal Could Take Several Months," *Nebraska World Herald,* 13 January 1999.
2. Pam Bulluck, "Unusual Nebraska Case Being Watched by Death Penalty Experts," *Daily Nebraskan,* 20 February 1999.
3. A. R. Goldyn, "Fighting for Survival," *Omaha, Lincoln, and Council Bluffs Reader,* 15–21 August 2001.
4. Butch Mabin, "Families Remain Split on Reeves' Case," *Lincoln Star Journal,* 8 September 2001.
5. Margaret Reist, "Reeves Won't Face Death Penalty, Attorney Says," *Lincoln Star Journal,* 7 September 2001.
6. Mabin, "Families Remain Split."
7. Butch Mabin, "Reeves Gets Two Life Sentences," *Lincoln Star Journal,* 21 September 2001.

## RESTORATIVE JUSTICE

1. Office of Justice Programs, Department of Justice, "The Restorative Justice Fact Sheet," www.ojp.usdoj.gov/nij/rest-just/CH5/6_vofmed.htm.

## CHAPTER 10: HEALING THE SOUL

1. Tony's confession is taken from Azim's account of his experience. Azim Khamisa and Carl Goldman, *Azim's Bardo* (Los Altos: Rising Star Press, 1998), 29–35.
2. Ibid.
3. Ibid.

## AFTERWORD

1. Letter to the editor, Orlando and Phyllis Rodriguez, *New York Times,* 4 January 2002.

# RESOURCES

For additional information about the death penalty, please contact:

American Civil Liberties Union
Capital Punishment Project
1333 H St., N.W., 10<sup>th</sup> Floor
Washington, DC 20005
(202) 544-1631, www.aclu.org

National Coalition to Abolish the Death Penalty
920 Pennsylvania Ave., S.E.
Washington, DC 20003
(202) 543-9577, www.ncadp.org

Murder Victims' Families for Reconciliation
2161 Massachusetts Ave.
Cambridge, MA 02140
(617) 868-0007, www.mvfr.org

Journey of Hope . . . From Violence to Healing
P.O. Box 210390
Anchorage, AK 99521-0390
(877) 924-4483, www.journeyofhope.org

Tariq Khamisa Foundation
2550 Fifth Ave., Suite 65
San Diego, CA 92103
(619) 525-0062, (888) HELP-TKF

Abolitionist Action Committee
c/o CUADP
PMB 297
177 U.S. Hwy. #1
Tequesta, FL 33469
(800) 973-6548, www.abolition.org

Death Penalty Information Center
1320 Eighteenth St., N.W., 5th Floor
Washington, DC 20036
(202) 293-6970, www.deathpenaltyinfo.org

Equal Justice USA/Quixote Center
P.O. Box 5206
Hyattsville, MD 20782
(301) 699-0042, www.quixote.org/ej

## ABOUT THE AUTHOR

Rachel King is an attorney with the Washington National Office of the American Civil Liberties Union. She has been active in the death penalty abolitionist movement in many capacities, most notably as the founding director of Alaskans Against the Death Penalty and as a recent past board chair of the National Coalition to Abolish the Death Penalty. She lives in the Takoma Village Co-Housing Community in Washington, D.C. with her partner Richard McAlee.